Faith with Benefits

Faith with Benefits

*Hookup Culture on
Catholic Campuses*

JASON KING

OXFORD
UNIVERSITY PRESS

OXFORD
UNIVERSITY PRESS

Oxford University Press is a department of the University of Oxford. It furthers
the University's objective of excellence in research, scholarship, and education
by publishing worldwide. Oxford is a registered trade mark of Oxford University
Press in the UK and certain other countries.

Published in the United States of America by Oxford University Press
198 Madison Avenue, New York, NY 10016, United States of America.

Library of Congress Cataloging-in-Publication Data
Names: King, Jason E. (Jason Edward), 1971– author.
Title: Faith with benefits : hookup culture on Catholic campuses / Jason King.
Description: New York, NY, United States of America : Oxford University
Press, [2017] | Includes bibliographical references and index.
Identifiers: LCCN 2016028624 (print) | LCCN 2016039487 (ebook) |
ISBN 9780190244804 (cloth : alk. paper) | ISBN 9780190244811 (updf) |
ISBN 9780190244828 (epub)
Subjects: LCSH: Sex—Religious aspects—Catholic Church. |
Dating (Social customs)—Religious aspects—Catholic Church. |
Catholic universities and colleges—Social aspects.
Classification: LCC BX1795.S48 K54 2017 (print) | LCC BX1795.S48 (ebook) |
DDC 241/.6765—dc23
LC record available at https://lccn.loc.gov/2016028624

1 3 5 7 9 8 6 4 2

Printed by Sheridan Books, Inc., United States of America

For my students

Contents

Foreword

IN MANY WAYS, at the heart of this book and at the heart of all college students' struggles to navigate hookup culture is a question about vulnerability.

Jason King recounts a conversation he had during his interviews with a young woman named Riley, who worried that asking someone on a date to dinner was far too serious, but randomly hooking up with someone was far too unappealing. After reading about a concept called "parallel eating," Riley lightheartedly invited a friend in whom she had romantic interest to "parallel eat" with her in the cafeteria.

"Her approach navigated between 'not a date' and 'not saying anything' in order to communicate 'I'd like to get to know you better,'" King writes. It's what he explains next that gets to this question at the heart of students living within hookup culture. "It was a 'hanging out' or 'getting to know someone' script," King goes on, "and allowed *just the right amount of vulnerability* [my emphasis]."

Throughout *Faith with Benefits*, King draws on his findings from dozens of interviews and hundreds of surveys to discover the "frames" and the "scripts" Catholic college students use to navigate, participate in, dissent from, and flat-out reject hookup culture. That term is actually misleading, though, since as King demonstrates there are four distinct kinds of hookup culture on Catholic campuses, including a middle-way "relationship hookup culture" often found at what he calls Mostly Catholic schools. And even if hookup culture is only practiced by a tiny minority of students—as is the case at Very Catholic schools, according to King,—the pressure of hookup culture and having to find adequate "scripts" to thwart it is ever-present.

At the center of these "scripts," lies the question of what, exactly, is *just the right amount of vulnerability*? Riley's concern about walking this fine line in a culture that tugs her away from even the most basic of connections is echoed throughout all of King's interviews. Whether students attend Very, Mostly, or Somewhat Catholic schools, it's clear that both men and women yearn to love and be loved and to find a way into a romantic relationship of some sort, despite living in a culture which pushes them to avoid love and commitment altogether.

King's work on this subject is useful and unique. In my own research on campus hookup culture, Catholic colleges were difficult to distinguish from secular ones. By focusing only on Catholic colleges, King is able to add nuance and texture to this finding, to make fine distinctions between cultures at institutions of Catholic higher education and categorize them into types. No one else has done anything like this. He shows that student attitudes about sex and faith at Very Catholic campuses look remarkably similar to what I found at evangelical schools. King's research will open pathways for dialogue between evangelical and Very Catholic schools and the existence of what King calls an "anti-hookup culture" on their campuses. It will also create opportunities for dialogue among different kinds of Catholic schools about why and how certain campuses foster a Catholic peer culture that supports chastity and others do not.

Some readers will be alarmed at the restrictions found on Very Catholic campuses, like the policing of it in the residence halls ("If you want to have sex, they are saying just don't do it in the dorms," says Ethan), which push hookups and sexual intimacy off-campus, and likely problems like sexual assault off-campus with them. Add to this the near universal assumptions of heterosexuality in the structuring of residential life at these schools, which will give other readers pause. While there is a "freedom for Catholicism" on these campuses, which empowers students at Very Catholic institutions to live out their faith on all levels, this "freedom for" can be alienating to the small percentage of students who don't fit the norm.

King's research advances the conversation not only around college student religious identity, but also how that religious identity influences—or doesn't—sexual decision-making, attitudes, and the presence of hookup culture. There are many excellent books that explore young adult religiosity, and many exclusively dedicated to hookup culture, but very few that take up these two topics and their relationship to one another. In this way, *Faith with Benefits* rounds out the growing library of research on the attitudes and identities of the American college student and offers a unique and important voice to this conversation.

Administration, faculty, and student affairs professionals at Catholic institutions have long been eager to find ways to talk about hookup culture on their campuses, and *Faith with Benefits* is essential reading for them. King's chapters are lively—full of the voices of the college students he interviewed and surveyed in their own words—and better still, filled with King's incisive interpretation of his data. What's more, he points the way toward a practical response clearly drawn from his own background not only as a member of the faculty at a Catholic institution, but also his time working in student affairs.

Reflecting on student comments, King wonders, "Are [students] powerless? Helpless? Not really. Students on Mostly Catholic campuses utilize all kinds of scripts to find relationships. They use them to bend hookup culture toward relationships but also as alternative ways to meet people and get to know them.... Students want alternatives to hookup culture, and some students are devising them," he observes, before making a suggestion that pops up throughout *Faith with Benefits*. "Their schools need to encourage these alternatives," King says.

DONNA FREITAS

Acknowledgments

SO MANY PEOPLE helped me to bring this book to completion. My friend and colleague Christopher McMahon listened to my ideas and commented on them all while we were jogging, a practice we started in graduate school. Mark Rivardo, Antony Davies, and Andy Herr helped me with survey design and analysis.

Crucial to this project were the many site coordinators who provided support by doing the time-consuming work of getting approval for and deploying the survey on their campuses. I hope to thank each of you personally since I cannot name you here for fear of revealing the identity of your schools.

My friend Donna Freitas was essential to this project. Her own scholarship set the stage for this work, and her encouragement moved me to pursue this study. My conversations with her shaped the overall direction the project took. Also, Donna connected me with Theo Calderara, who was an indispensable contributor with a knack for asking exactly the right questions and offering the perfect comments that vastly improved the project at each stage of development.

Throughout the whole process, I had support from Saint Vincent College. Fr. Rene Kollar, the Dean of the School of Humanities and Fine Arts, was unrelenting in his support. The college also provided me with funding through the Faculty Development Grant Program and through a sabbatical. Both were essential to completing the project.

The Association of Catholic Colleges and Universities awarded me a small grant for some of the initial data analysis and published those results in the *Journal of Catholic Higher Education*.

Dr. Luke Briola provided invaluable feedback on drafts of these chapters. His theological sense and writing skills are superb and exactly what I needed.

The conversations I have had with my colleagues—especially Kari-Shane Davis Zimmerman, Charley Camosy, David Cloutier, Bill Mattison,

Dana Dillon, Julie Hanlon Rubio, Jim Caccamo, David McCarthy, Jana Bennett, Kent Lasnoski, and Mari Marrow—were essential to this work.

My kids have been patient with me throughout this project. They kept wondering why it took so long to write my book. Well, it is finally done. Now we can play.

My wife, Kelly King, helped me with every single aspect of this project. She provided encouragement and support in the beginning and, throughout, conversations about theology and relationships. She read an early draft of the manuscript for me because I knew she loved me enough to give me honest feedback. She reminded me that there are things more important than the book but also that I should get back to work on the book. In short, she loved me. I only hope I can love her just as well.

Finally, because my students have been so important to my thinking about and motivation for doing this work, this book is dedicated to them.

Faith with Benefits

Introduction

A FEW YEARS ago, I sat in my office talking to one of my best students, a theology major. He had excelled in every class, had a second major in politics, and was on his way to law school on a full scholarship. When I asked him what he would like to do for his senior research project, he said he wanted to write on "sexual ethics," perhaps focusing on John Paul II's theology of the body. "I just think it might help me with my relationships."

His comment, so honest and personal, should not have surprised me. I had been teaching classes on marriage and relationships at a small Catholic college for over a decade, and those classes were always full (and had waiting lists). Students were deeply engaged in the subject. I rarely got through the syllabus because they kept discussing, debating, and analyzing the material through the lenses of their own experiences, struggles, and hopes.

Spurred by my students' interest, I began to do research on relationships and college campuses. The picture that emerged was bleak. Hooking up dominated campuses. Relationships or dating or doing anything other than "hooking up" had practically disappeared.[1] Hooking up—whatever it entailed—was defined by the absence of commitment, and this seemed to trouble so many students. While there were some who enjoyed having "no strings attached," they seemed to be a small and select group of students.[2] Most regretted hookups that led nowhere, wanted sexual encounters to mean something, and held out hope for relationships.[3] Yet, to fit in to the prevailing culture, students had to hide these desires and pretend that they did not care. There seemed to be a huge divide between what students wanted and what was happening on campuses.

I thought Catholic colleges might be different, but none of the existing studies of hookup culture suggested that they were unique. In *Hooking*

Up, Kathleen Bogle found that students at Catholic schools were similar to students at large state schools when it came to sex.[4] Moreover, Bogle found that the students at the Catholic school she surveyed did not see religion as having any influence on their behavior. Donna Freitas surveyed Catholic schools as well as evangelical schools, large public universities, and smaller private colleges for her book, *Sex and the Soul*.[5] The only institutions that explicitly engaged in and debated hookup culture were evangelical schools. Like Bogle, Freitas found that hooking up on Catholic campuses was not discernibly different from doing so on public or private ones. Finally, in "Hooking Up at College: Does Religion Make a Difference?," Amy Burdette and her colleagues actually found that individuals who identified themselves as Catholic were *more* likely to hook up.[6]

Yet, in all of this research, something seemed incomplete. It was not that there were inaccuracies or mistakes but rather that only a portion of what was occurring on college campuses, especially Catholic ones was being discovered and documented. I had been teaching 200 students each year for a decade. They were not an abstinence-only kind of crowd, but neither were they enthusiastic about hooking up. The meaninglessness of the latter troubled them. They did not want to feel used or taken advantage of. They wanted kindness and fun, a connection with someone they cared about and who cared about them. They even hoped to be happily married someday.

In the conclusion of their research survey on hookup culture, Caroline Heldman and Lisa Wade noted that, "We still know very little about how hook-up culture varies from campus to campus."[7] Their point sent me back to the research on Catholic campuses. Bogle had included only one Catholic school; Freitas had included two. Amy Burdette studied only a small percentage of women at Catholic schools (approximately 55 out of 919). Moreover, these studies all seemed to come from one type of small Catholic liberal arts schools, and Melanie Morey and John Piderit argued that there were at least four different ways Catholic colleges and universities embodied religious identity.[8]

Finally, the research on Catholic colleges and universities seemed incomplete because it stood in such stark contrast to numerous studies indicating that religion affected sexual activity: the time of first intercourse, the number of partners, the connection between sex and affection for partners, and the chances of using contraception.[9] This was especially true for students who were attached to religious institutions, which hinder risky behavior and amplify the effects of students' own religious commitments.[10] In addition, because the typical college student lives independently from their parents, the religious and sexual practices of friends had almost as much impact as the students' own faith.[11]

My sense that the research was incomplete—and the persistent desire of my students for something more than meaningless hookups—led me to this study. I wanted to better understand what was happening on college campuses, particularly Catholic ones. I wanted to know if there was any benefit to faith and if these colleges and universities had any impact on hookup culture. My main hope was to find something that would help my students—not to tell them what to do or not to do but to help them pursue the kinds of relationships they desired.

The Study

Although this book was sparked by my experience in the classroom, it is grounded in empirical research. I began with a quantitative survey in the spring of 2013 at several Catholic colleges and universities. This survey had over 1,000 responses from students at twenty-six different Catholic institutions. This quantitative survey had three sections. The first section asked about students' personal information—primarily about their own religious beliefs and commitments. It also included questions about their friends' beliefs. The second section asked about the students' perceptions of the religious identity of their Catholic college or university: "Very Catholic," "Mostly Catholic," "Somewhat Catholic," or "Not Very Catholic." Following this classification, students were asked about the frequency of campus activities such as worship, community service, residential policies and programs, and religion classes. The final section asked about hookup culture—both students' perceptions of hookup culture and their own participation in it.

This set the context for the second part of the study. As less than 1% of the students categorized their school as "Not Very Catholic," I focused on gathering more data from representatives of the other three types of Catholic colleges and universities. I developed a qualitative survey, asking students to describe: (a) the Catholic culture on their campus, (b) hookup culture on their campus, and (c) relationships on their campus. The survey was deployed at six schools surveyed in the first study, two representing each type of Catholic culture.

At the end of the qualitative study, I gave students the option to enter an email address if they were willing to be contacted directly for follow-up questions, which would be the third part of the study. From those who agreed to a follow-up interview, I chose representatives from each of the different Catholic campuses and multiple schools within each type. These interviews allowed me to expand upon the answers given in the qualitative survey and to pursue a deeper understanding of students' perceptions, gathering more robust information on the three types of Catholic cultures.

Drawing on the data I collected, this book attempts to describe hookup culture at Catholic colleges and universities. Stereotypical hookup culture dominates campus life. It dominates even when most reject it, when most don't desire it, and when most are marginalized because of it. It is the unquestioned norm for college behavior that pushes all alternatives to the side. In the midst of this dominance though, students on Catholic campuses drew upon religious faith to generate alternatives to this culture—alternatives that provided better benefits.

There Is No Campus Hookup Culture; There Are Four

DANIEL, A JUNIOR, was the first student who made me question the typical depiction of hookup culture. He was very laid back. Nothing seemed to excite or worry him, not even questions about hooking up.

ME: How would you describe hookup culture on your campus?
DANIEL: Great. Very active. A lot of students are free spirited and open minded, open to exploration. Could be better with more attractive students.
ME: Why do you think people hook up?
DANIEL: Fun. Gratification. Curiosity. Party culture. Hormones.

Daniel was like this throughout the interview. Calm and almost disinterested, his answers came in single words and short phrases. What surprised me was that in my two years of surveying and interviewing students, Daniel was the first person to speak positively about hookup culture.

Daniel definitely was not alone in hooking up. In my two-year survey of over 1,000 students on twenty-six different campuses, I found that 47% of students had hooked up in the previous year, with 60% of these hookups including intercourse. Remarkably, these percentages were lower than almost every other study of the topic. The highest previous estimates had indicated that around 86% of students hooked up, with 50% of the men and 30% of the women having intercourse during the hookup.[1] Mark Regnerus and Jeremy Uecker provided the lowest estimate, arguing that about 64% of students hook up, with only 50% of these hookups including intercourse.[2] In *Hooking Up*, Kathleen Bogle estimated that 78% of students had hooked up at least once in the previous year and 38% of those that did had intercourse.[3] Of the two reviews of the research on hooking up, one indicated that the hookup rate was between 66% and 75%, with 38% of these including sexual intercourse and the other demonstrating that the rate was between 60% and 80%, with 70% of these including sex.[4] Together, these studies suggested that around 70% of students hooked up and that 40% to 50% of these hookups included sex.

If Daniel was not alone in hooking up, why was he the first to speak positively about it? While Daniel might embody the stereotype of college students who hook up, he was not the norm. In their article, "A New Perspective on Hooking Up Among College Students," Megan Manthos, Jesse Own, and Frank Finchman found that about 30% of students accounted for almost 75% of hookups.[5] In their overview of hookup literature, Caroline Heldman and Lisa Wade estimated that only around 20% of students hooked up ten times or more.[6] When I surveyed students about how often had they had hooked up in the past year, only 23% of students said they had hooked up more than five times, and only 12% said more than ten times.[7]

Student comments in my research followed this pattern. Out of 145 written descriptions of hookup culture, only four students used explicitly positive or enthusiastic language for it.

- "Students like partying, and that tends to lead to hookups."
- "It is pretty strong. There is parties on and off of campus and there is always drinking involved.... You start to have a good time and decide it is a good time to have even more fun and hook up with someone, or you find someone that becomes your significant other and you go from that perspective."
- "It's decent."
- "Very organized and engaging."

What emerged from the students' answers was not a voracious hookup culture that they enjoyed. Instead, a majority of students who hooked up did so rarely and almost always without enthusiasm. Daniel was as much a minority as a stereotype.

Relationship Hookup Culture

If Daniel was a minority, who was the majority? Chloe, an upbeat and talkative freshman, is a good example. She clearly seemed frustrated with hookup culture. "People know who is hooking up with who because this is a small campus. The people involved end up not even liking each other. They never become a couple." Her last phrase made me pause because she seemed to assume that people were hooking up to enter into a relationship. Typical descriptions of hooking up assume it to be a no-strings-attached affair, so I asked her why she thought people hooked up. She replied, "They think that since they aren't being watched by parents and siblings, they can do what they see in movies and what they hear about. It is typical college experiences that people feel they need to have. They think that since they are in college, it is understandable." She seemed to blame a lack of maturity or the culture for people wanting to hook up, but this did not explain her comment about relationships.

I continued. Were there relationships on campus? Chloe's tone turned from frustration to happiness. "There are many relationships. They are very strong, and couples are good to one another." I asked, "How do these relationships emerge in the midst of hookup culture?" After a moment, she said,

> It involves hooking up first, and then maybe trying to see if there is any connection with the other person after the deed is already done. In some cases, people are used as objects instead of loved as another human being. People become closed off and unable to trust in future relationships for fear of being hurt again. But, this doesn't speak for all hookups. There are relationships all around us as well.

Chloe's point was clear. Hooking up was typically not good, but even if it often did not work and people got hurt, occasionally relationships resulted from hooking up. And that was to the good.

Chloe's view captured what might be the most typical hookup culture, one in which relationships were still hoped for and pursued. In "Sexual Hookup Culture," Justin Garcia and his fellow authors surveyed research on hookup culture and found that "65% of women and 45% of men reported that they hoped their hookup encounter would become a committed relationship."[8] This was not just a private wish. Lots of people explicitly talked about it: 51% of women and 42% of men asked their partners about relationships *after* hooking up.[9] In fact, one of the main reasons often given for hooking up was the possibility of a relationship.[10]

The desire for relationships is found among both women and men. Lisa Wade and Caroline Heldman found that women wanted relationships, and so they avoided casual hookups in favor of hooking up with those whom they liked.[11] While studies show that men are more open to causal sex, most (75% according to one study) do not enjoy it.[12] Men want something more meaningful from their encounters. They definitely know what they, as men, are expected to want—sex without commitment—but they frequently do not act this way.[13] Instead, they manipulate or work around these social expectations so that they can seek out people with whom relationships might arise.

The pervasiveness of "relationship hookup culture" helps to explain why hooking up is rarely random or anonymous. Studies indicate that almost 70% of hookups are between people who know each other, are friends, or were formerly in a relationship.[14] It is why, in my own research, 49% of students believed that hookups between people who know each other happened "all the time" or "often."[15] It is why the phrase, "I hooked up with my girlfriend" exists. It is also why the term "friends-with-benefits" is a part of hookup culture. While both women and men find it difficult to maintain a friends-with-benefits relationship, the possibility exists because people are interested in hookups that, at the very least, mean something and might lead to a relationship. This seems to be why a series of hookups with the same person is more common than hooking up with someone only once—serial hookups more often lead to relationships (although this still does not happen often).[16]

What is most surprising about relationship hookup culture is that, although it is the statistical norm, it is not the dominant culture. Daniel's stereotypical hookup culture is considered "normal." What about Chloe? She, like the majority of students, is frustrated with the "normal." It is not what they want, even though they feel pressure to conform to it. Even so, Chloe and those like her work behind the scenes to find people they are interested in and people they know so that, then, when they hook up, they do so as a way into something more.

Anti-Hookup Culture

Some students are not happy with this workaround, though. They reject both stereotypical hookup culture and relationship hookup culture. Eleesha was one of these. An African American female in her senior year, Eleesha was exceptionally friendly but all business. She told me that, in addition to her five classes, she was working on her senior research project, planning a club event, and preparing her resume for jobs. When I asked her about hookup culture, her dislike was clear.

> A lot of times I hear comments from other people about hooking up. Most people, in my experience, seem to think that hooking up is all about sex. Hooking up doesn't mean falling in love—if you're a guy, you're not supposed to fall in love; if you're a girl, you're not supposed to fall too hard in love.

She explained that, because of hookup culture, sex dominated everything.

> It seems that if a couple, especially one in a long-term relationship, is not having sex, then something is wrong—then someone, if not both, is probably getting it elsewhere. People seem to have no concept of fidelity within a pre-marriage relationship.

Here, Eleesha became frustrated. While she acknowledged not participating in hookup culture, it still affected her personal relationship.

> Through my own experience, I have seen many shocked faces, heard many unbelieving comments, and even been belittled because of my choice to remain abstinent until marriage. Those who choose not to belittle me put me on a pedestal for being in a three-year relationship and still remaining true to my values. I get a lot of comments like, "I could never do that."

While Eleesha clearly disliked hookup culture and was comfortable not participating in it, she was not naïve enough to believe that there were no costs. From those who belittled her to those who, while seeming to support her, singled her out as unusual, she was socially on the fringe.[17]

Who would reject hooking up and risk social marginalization? They are people who see in hookup culture risks greater than social exclusion. In my study, women were significantly more likely to opt out of hookup culture than men. This is demonstrated in table 1.1.

Most other studies indicate that those who reject hookup culture tend to be minorities and from lower economic classes.[18] In both of these cases, students share an awareness that their missteps are more costly, safety nets less secure, and failure in college more destructive. In the schools

Table 1.1 Males compared to females in response
to the question: "How many times in the last year
have you hooked up?"

Number of times hooked up	Males (%)	Females (%)
0	49	57
1	8	10
2	4	8
3	3	5
4	5	3
≥ 5	13	8
≥ 10	18	9
Total	100	100

Men = 370; Women = 541; P-value = 0.00.

I surveyed, some women clearly faced greater costs in participating in hookup culture than in withdrawing from it. Men rarely faced this situation: it was almost always more costly for them to withdraw from hookup culture than to participate in it.[19] Whatever the case, it is clear that participating in hookup culture, in either its stereotypical form or as a way into relationship, was too costly for some. Social exclusion was less risky than damage to reputation, pregnancy, disease, anxiety, stress, or anything else that might jeopardize their success in school.[20]

While those who do not hook up are not a majority, they are a sizable minority. Most studies put them slightly below 30% of students. My study found the number closer to 53%. Even at Harvard University, 24% of students did not have sex during their college years, and 21% never had a relationship.[21] While not the norm, Eleesha is not unique either.

Still, there is a cost to not hooking up. Students like Eleesha risk being socially marginalized, if not outright ostracized, and so develop rationales to explain why they don't hook up. Eleesha valued love and relationships, was pursing professional goals, and had committed herself to abstaining from sex until marriage. From her perspective, the cost of going against her beliefs was too great.[22] In his study of men, Brian Sweeney noted that those who are privileged tend to think of college as "a time *before* adulthood" so that not caring and not committing were perfectly acceptable. Those who are not privileged understand college as "a time for assuming adult responsibilities and leaving childish things behind."[23] They tend to think of participation in hookup culture as immature and the people as "reckless, wild, and indiscriminate."[24] One student in Sweeney's study summed it up clearly by saying, "I'm not here to be stupid. I am here to be smart. I am here to learn."[25] This reevaluation of hooking up helped those rejecting it to have confidence in choosing to risk social penalties.

Even so, this devaluing of hooking up does not place these students outside of stereotypical hookup culture. Instead, what Eleesha and those like her are doing is staking out a counterculture, a culture defined against the dominant one. They have to account for their difference and to explain why they are not like everyone else. In other words, Eleesha cannot just have the kind of relationship she wants. Her kind of relationship stands out, so she has to have an explanation for it, one she must offer to others even if they belittle her for it. Eleesha must explain her rejection of hookup culture, while Daniel never has to think about or defend his participation in it.

Coercive Hookup Culture

As bad as social exclusion is, hookup culture can be worse. Gay men and women typically do not participate in campus hookup culture because it is not safe for them to do so.[26] If they are caught, they worry about being physically assaulted. Straight women often feel the same way. According to the Centers for Disease Control and Prevention, around 20% of dating relationships include nonsexual violence, and 20% of women in college experience rape or attempted rape.[27] Eighty-five percent of their assailants are known to them, usually boyfriends, ex-boyfriends, or classmates. Even though these sexual assault numbers have remained practically unchanged since 2007, only recently have colleges and universities started to address them, and then only after the Department of Education's began investigating several institutions of higher education for Title IX violations in early 2014.

Rarely did anyone in my research mention sexual assault. When they did, it was only in generalities. A sophomore male wrote, "People go to parties, get girls drunk, and then, inhumanly, take advantage of girls," while a female sophomore said, "I have yet to see any type of abusive or negative relationship between people. I'm sure it happens, but I have not been exposed to it."

In some ways, this silence should not be too surprising. When assaults occur, victims and perpetrators struggle to recognize it as such.[28] Even when they do, they rarely come forward, reporting it to police only 5% of the time.[29] Even when they do report it, they are often ignored or disparaged.[30]

Add to this the fact that hookup culture is saturated with alcohol that is often used to mask assaults. The result is that it becomes difficult to get a sense of how pervasive coercion is.

Sexual assault is an extension of stereotypical hookup culture, which exerts a subtle social coercion on everyone. Those pursuing relationships have to do so under the pretense that they are uninterested in relationships. Those who choose not to participate typically have to justify doing so and are still socially marginalized. Physically coercive hookup culture emerges from this social coercion.

Culture and the Four Hookup Cultures

Why are there four hookup cultures and not just one? How do they emerge? Are they all present on all campuses? Does stereotypical hookup culture always dominate campus cultures? Or are there places where relationship hookup culture and anti-hookup culture thrive—places where Chloe doesn't have to hide her desire for a relationship and Eleesha is not marginalized for eschewing hookups? Are there ways to thwart coercive hookup culture? To answer these questions, we must first understand how cultures work.

Frames and Scripts

Cultures are practical. They provide people with frames and scripts to help them navigate social life. Frames are mental structures people use to understand their experiences. Thus, students can look at a room full of chairs and quickly tell if it is a classroom, a cafeteria, or a lounge. Scripts are mental structures people use to guide their actions. Once students understand what the room full of chairs is, they employ a script to figure out what to do there. If it is a classroom, they find a desk and get ready to take notes. If it is a cafeteria, they get food and find people to eat with. If it is a lounge, they know they can relax there if they want to. Frames help people understand, and scripts help people act.[31]

In all the types of hookup cultures noted above, students know the frame. Eleesha, Chloe, and Daniel all knew that hooking up was a sexual act that does not imply commitment or attachment. They also knew the "hookup" script: to hook up, one goes to a party, drinks, finds someone, and has a physical encounter (which can range from kissing to sex). No matter how they felt about the frame or script and no matter whether they used them, Eleesha, Chloe, and Daniel knew them.

Why is there such agreement on the frames and scripts even if students have very different feelings about hooking up? Part of the answer is that students face similar problems. Most students are trying to figure out both their own perspectives and the social expectations around desires, sex, attractions, and relationships. These questions are common and pervasive, and frames and scripts have developed and exist to deal with them. They provide practical guidance about common issues and expectations for behavior.[32]

Repertoires

A culture is not just one frame and one script though. People pick up scripts from families, schools, work, friends, and the media, just to name some typical influences. Every person and every culture has repertoires of frames and scripts. These diverse sets of frames and scripts function like tools that can be used to go along with, alter, modify, or reject other frames and scripts.[33] As a result, dominant or common frames and scripts can never completely control or predict thinking and behavior. People can call forth different frames and use different scripts to figure out what to do.

Different hookup cultures emerge from such a process. Students draw upon other frames and scripts to interact with stereotypical hookup culture.[34] People who try to use hooking up for a relationship might draw on frames that link sexual acts with relationships, or love, or marriage.[35] They might utilize scripts that link sexual acts to degrees of intimacy or levels of a relationship. Like Chloe, students draw from widely available frames and scripts that suggest relationships are good and desirable and sex should be tied to care, concern, or love. They bring these frames and scripts into the stereotypical hookup culture and augment or modify what hooking up can mean. While students clearly know that this is difficult—only 6% of students believe their last hookup will lead to a relationship—they still attempt to work and rework a stereotypical hookup culture.[36]

Those rejecting hookup culture are also using other frames and scripts to guide their activities. Eleesha was trying to act in accordance with her beliefs and values. Others understood college as the time to mature or take on responsibilities, so they studied hard and pursued their careers. In other words, they use alternative frames and scripts to resist the dominant culture.

Coercive hookup culture adds to the mix of frames and scripts that legitimize the use of force. While there are several sources for this—including beliefs about alcohol, gender, and rape[37]—that are significant contributors to this reworking of hooking up, pornography is a clear example of one of them.[38] It is not simply the case that "pornography causes violence" but rather that there are scripts and frames in pornographic culture that rationalize sexual violence. Karen Lebacqz describes a basic one.

> Pornography would suggest that men are socialized to find both male power and female powerlessness sexually arousing. In pornography, domination of women by men is portrayed as sexy. It is the power of the man or men to make the woman do what she does not want to do—to make her do something humiliating, degrading, or antithetical to her character—that creates the sexual tension and excitement.... In pornography, women are raped tied up, beaten, humiliated—*and* are portrayed as initially resisting and ultimately enjoying their degradation.[39]

This description indicates how coercion can be legitimatized. The frame is that both women and men want and enjoy sex, and the use of coercion is exciting for both men and women. Men enjoy dominating, and women enjoy being dominated. The related script is men can force themselves on women because, even if they say no or resist or are incapacitated, they will enjoy it. Like all frames and scripts, these do not cause these acts but rather make them possibilities for thinking and acting. Given that 70% of 18- to 24-year-old males visit pornographic websites monthly, these frames and scripts are widely available and so can become part of college students' repertoire.[40] They can then draw upon these frames and scripts to alter stereotypical hookup culture into a coercive hookup culture.

While there are diverse frames and scripts, the variety in any one person's repertoire is limited. What one sees in these different configurations of hookup culture is a dominant frame and script for hooking up that is reworked, rejected, or augmented by frames and scripts drawn from other sources. Whatever repertoires emerge, their frames and scripts will only be adopted insofar as they work.

Socialized

Repertoires of frames and scripts are limited in other ways. People usually want to fit in, and to do so, they need to know how others typically think and act. Frames and scripts communicate this. Utilizing the most common frames and scripts indicates one's integration into the culture. Failing to do so usually means being ignored or rejected but sometimes can make you the target of others' hostility. At its worst, this socializing can generate a dominant ideology that marginalizes or victimizes anyone who doesn't conform. At its best, though, it helps people both to fit in and to deal effectively with recurring, practical problems.[41]

Socializing helps to explain why there is a stereotypical hookup culture in the first place. The hookup cultures noted above all exist because students respond to recurring questions about sex, attractions, and relationships. Stereotypical hookup culture provides a common and easily accessible frame and script for students to negotiate these questions, making it easy for new students to grasp the expectations guiding sexual behavior on their campus. Students may use, adjust, or reject these frames and scripts, but first they need to know them. Otherwise, they risk isolation. If they figure them out, they can find ways to work with them or, as in the case of Eleesha, choose to reject them while being fully aware of the consequences. Given these advantages, it is no wonder that even though most people did not practice stereotypical hookup culture, 88% of students in my survey still "agree" or "strongly agree" with the definition of "hooking up" as "sexual activity between two people without expectations of a relationship."[42]

Although this socializing eases integration, it also limits flexibility. Any variation from the dominant culture is seen within the context of that culture. Thus, Daniel has to offer no explanation for his acceptance of stereotypical hookup culture.[43] It is the norm, the default, the expectation. Chloe has to acknowledge that stereotypical hookup culture is the norm, and, if she wants a relationship, she has to work with it. Even though she opposed hooking up, Eleesha recognized that hooking up is the norm and accepted the social penalties for not participating. Even those in a coercive hookup culture have justifications for their violence by appealing to some frame or script beyond the stereotypical hookup ones. Whatever the justification, one has to do so, otherwise one's ability to navigate campus social life is difficult, if not impossible. One becomes misunderstood or excluded or feared for being too different.

Institutional Structures Support

Culture is sustained by more than people or groups of people. Institutional structures often emerge to support it. They can be material structures like buildings or immaterial structures like policies, but, in either case, they are stabilizing forces that allow for only slow or small changes. While this resistance to change can be problematic, it is also extremely helpful in at least three ways. First, institutional structures allow a culture to endure beyond individuals or even groups of individuals. Second, they sustain a culture's highly useful ways of thinking and behaving, its frames and scripts. Finally, these structures enable many people and, at times, generations of people to make use of them.[44]

This does not mean that institutional structures are independent determiners of a culture. They are also conditioned by it.[45] Yet, once institutional structures are established, they have their own momentum, exerting pressure on members of a community to think and behave in certain ways. So, institutional structures also set conditions on a culture, making it easy to operate in certain ways and difficult to operate in others. They neither completely control people nor leave them completely free.

On a college campus, many of these institutional structures are relatively easy to name.[46] Residence halls emerge to deal with the living situations of students. Curriculum requirements for majors and graduation develop to guide students in their selection of classes. Athletics and extracurricular activities arise in response to the various student interests. Just as much as these flow from students, they also sway students' actions. Restrictive visitation policies in the dorms can hinder hooking up, just as much as lax enforcement of these policies can make it easier. Religious clubs and required religion classes in the core can promote religious ways of thinking, while business clubs and a strong business school can promote business majors. Whatever these structures are, they will influence the shape of the culture.

A Definition of Culture

As described, a culture promotes particular behaviors through: (a) repertoires of frames and scripts that (b) foster certain ways of thinking and acting, (c) socialize people into these ways, and (d) often are supported and sustained by institutional structures.[47] People use frames and script to act, and they share them to help others. This sharing enables people to cooperate and socializes them. People develop institutional structures that enable their frames and scripts to be shared more broadly and consistently, and the process becomes self-reinforcing, perpetuating the culture, making it more difficult to dislodge. Even so, new frames and scripts can emerge, people can relate in new ways, institutional structures can be altered, and the culture can change.[48]

Understanding how hookup cultures arise and change requires further work, though. They do not emerge in a vacuum. Just as hooking up has its own cultures, so too do different campuses. The difficulty is discerning these campus cultures, especially since there are almost 5,000 colleges and universities in the United States, with different classifications and missions. This is one of the reasons my study focused on a distinctive subset of institutions, Catholic colleges and universities. What their cultures are like and why they are useful for understanding how campus cultures affect hookup culture is the subject of the next chapter.

2

There Is No Catholic Campus Culture; There are Three

WHEN I ASKED Brooklyn, a sophomore, to describe the Catholic culture of her campus, she seemed uninterested in the question. "There are lots of student here who are Catholic and lots of students here who are non-Catholic," she told me. "Personally, I am not Catholic. The culture is there if you want it, but is not in your face. There are things available if you seek them out." Mason, a sophomore from a different campus, was at the opposite extreme, saying, "The Catholic culture seems very strong here. People identify with it and are drawn to it. . . . The Catholicism resonates through all the campus." Finally, Gianna, a senior from a third university, had a slightly different take. "I feel like the Catholic culture is good. . . . I see it in the interactions with people. They are very nice. They say hello and open the door for you. Both professors and students. It is very hospitable." These three perspectives reflect three different kinds of culture on Catholic campuses.

Three Catholic Cultures

In the first phase of my survey, I asked students, "Which statement best describes the religious culture of your college or university?" Students could answer using one of four possible responses:

- "The culture is **not very Catholic**. Few faculty, staff, and students are Catholic. Catholicism is rarely a part of student life and academics."
- "The culture is **somewhat Catholic**. Some of the faculty, staff, and students are Catholic, and Catholicism is sometimes a part of student life and academics."

- "The culture is **mostly Catholic**. Many of the faculty, staff, and students are Catholic, and Catholicism is a large part of student life and academics."
- "The culture is **very Catholic**. Almost all of the faculty, staff, and students are Catholic, and Catholicism is a large part of the student life and academics."

Students overwhelmingly felt their campuses had a Catholic culture, with only a few students (1%) choosing "not very Catholic." The majority of students reported that their school was "mostly Catholic" (52%), followed by "very Catholic" (25%) and "somewhat Catholic" (22%).[1]

There was significant agreement among students on each campus, with a majority indicating that the campus was "very Catholic," "mostly Catholic," or "somewhat Catholic." For one school whose average indicated that it was "Mostly Catholic," 15% of its students considered it "very" Catholic, 64% "mostly" Catholic, 19% "somewhat" Catholic, and 1% "not very" Catholic. Similarly, in a school classified as "Very Catholic," 64% identified the school as such, while 33% said it was "mostly" Catholic, 2% "somewhat" Catholic, and no one thought it was "not very" Catholic. What distinguished these campuses from each other since each had a dominant culture? What gave them their distinctive Catholic culture?

Classes, Masses, and Dorms

When I spoke with Mason about why Catholicism "resonated throughout his campus," he provided a list of institutional structures:

> Campus ministry is very strong. They are out in the community doing service.... They have daily Mass twice daily and several times on the weekend. There is the church on campus and the priests. The residence halls seem Catholic too. They do a good job hiring staff who are Catholic and emphasizing Catholicism and its teachings during orientation week.... Everyone has to take three theology classes.

Mason could have been speaking for many students. While not all had active campus ministries or religion course requirements, for most students, institutional structures were the most important indicators of the religious culture of their campus. Of the 145 written comments responding to the question, "What aspects of life on your campus seem Catholic to you?," 44% said something like, "The opportunity to attend chapel on a regular basis" or "I would say having daily masses and 7 weekend masses." In other words, almost half the students noted the opportunities for worship—whether they attend or not—as indicators of the Catholic culture.

Close behind these comments were ones like, "We are required to take 3 theology classes" and "classes—a lot of our classes focus on the Catholic faith and even if they are not centered around faith, many times some aspect of religion comes up." Almost a third of students, 31%, felt that academics reflected the Catholic culture.

These qualitative comments were mainly adding color to what the quantitative survey revealed. There, students were asked to indicate how true the following statements were about their college or university:[2]

- Catholicism is talked about in the classroom.
- Catholicism is talked about among students.
- Students take classes on Catholicism.
- There are student religious groups.
- There are opportunities for volunteering.
- There are opportunities for prayer or worship.
- There are lectures about Catholicism.
- Visitation rules for guests of the opposite sex are enforced in the dormitories.
- Drug rules are enforced on campus.
- Alcohol rules are enforced on campus.
- There are programs in the dormitories about sexual behavior.
- There are programs in the dormitories about Catholicism.

Students responded to these statements by using a simple Likert scale:

1. Definitely True
2. Somewhat True
3 Somewhat False
4. Definitely False.

How did the perceptions of these features relate to students' categorization of the overall campus culture? (table 2.1) There was a clear connection between the overall classification and "there are opportunities for prayer and worship." Even so, the differences between Very, Mostly, and

Table 2.1 How true are the following statements about your college or university?

	Opportunities for prayer and worship	Catholicism talked about in classroom	Students take classes on Catholicism	Lectures about Catholicism	Visitation rules enforced
The culture is somewhat Catholic	1.15	1.86	1.51	1.67	2.54
The culture is mostly Catholic	1.09	1.50	1.32	1.53	2.11
The culture is very Catholic	1.04	1.18	1.09	1.16	1.46

1 = Definitely True, 2 = Somewhat True, 3 = Somewhat False, 4 = Definitely False.

P-Value = 0.00 for all correlations. N = 971–905 (students who responded "Don't Know" were removed from this count).

Somewhat Catholic schools were small, as all types averaged "definitely true" for opportunities for prayer or worship, and this seemed to indicate that no matter the type of campus, students were aware of these opportunities and connected them to the overall Catholic culture.

Academic life was similar. Just as students indicated that it was "definitely true" that they experienced opportunities for worship, they also indicated that it was "definitely true" that Catholicism was part of the academic curriculum. There were small variations between Very, Mostly, and Somewhat Catholic schools, with students' responses averaging between "definitely true" and "somewhat true" for whether Catholicism is talked about in the classroom, whether students take classes on Catholicism, and whether there are lectures about Catholicism. Overall, though, students believed Catholicism was well represented in academic life, and that informed their opinions about the Catholic culture of their colleges.

If schools are alike in academics and opportunities for worship, what factors lead to the formation of the three different Catholic cultures? The distinctions start to emerge with regard to residential life. While Mason thought his "residence halls seem Catholic too," he was one of the few who thought so. In student comments, only 4% mentioned residence halls in connection to the campus' Catholic culture. The quantitative survey provided the greatest clarity on this issue. Those students who said their campus was somewhat Catholic tended to say it was "somewhat false" that visitation rules were enforced. At Mostly Catholic campuses, students indicated that it was "somewhat true" that visitation policies were enforced. Finally, students at Very Catholic campuses said that it was "definitely true" that visitation policies were enforced. While Mason was typical in pointing to institutional structures as related to the Catholic culture, his experience of residential life indicated that he was on a Very Catholic campus.

Just Institutional Structures?

Were these institutional structures enough to explain students' diverse characterizations of their campuses? To answer this question, I gathered information about all of the schools at which students participated in the survey. I tallied:[3]

- · Whether the school had a religious (e.g., priest, sister, member of a religious congregation) president
- · The existence of an office of service learning
- · The number of required classes on Catholicism
- · The frequency of daily mass
- · The frequency of Sunday mass
- · The type of visitation rules in the dormitories
- · The enforcement of alcohol policies in the dormitories
- · The presence of coed or single-sex dorms

I gathered this data primarily through institutions' websites and bulletins. I coded each variable numerically in such a way that a higher number would mean "more Catholic" for the particular characteristic. This meant that if an institution had a religious president, it got "1" and if not, a "0." If it had an office of service learning, it received a "1"—otherwise a "0." An institution could receive a "0," "1," "2," or "3" depending on the number of required classes on Catholicism. It could receive "0" for no daily mass, "1" for occasional daily mass, and "2" for masses every day. The same numbering was used for Sunday masses. Visitation rules were numbered based on stringency. Institutions received a "3" if they were strict—for example, allowing students to visit only in common areas. They got a "2" for moderate rules, like limited visitation hours and no mixed-gender overnights and a "1" if they had less stringent rules, like fewer than five hours of nonvisitation time a day. Institutions could also receive a "0" for residential life if there were no stated visitation rules in the residence halls. Campuses earned a "2" for prohibiting alcohol on campus, a "1" for going beyond state laws, and a 0 for just following state law. Finally, colleges were given a "2" for having only single-sex dorms, "1" for some single-sex dorms, and "0" for having no single-sex dorms. I ran a linear regression to see if these variables affected students' perceptions of the overall religious culture.[4]

The result of this process was that four variables—coed dormitories, visitation policies, daily mass opportunities, and the number of required classes in Catholicism—explained just under 25% of students' perceptions of the overall culture (table 2.2).[5] Furthermore, the "more Catholic" these institutional structures were, the "more Catholic" students perceived the institution to be.

In others words, the institutional structures of a college or university affected students but did not define the whole culture. Students noted in their comments and perceptions that liturgy and academics were key aspects of their experience of Catholic culture. Masses and classes made their campuses seem more Catholic. Also, even though students commented less on residence halls and visitation policies, they still connected these to the Catholic culture. The "more Catholic" each of these institutional structures were, the "more Catholic" the place seemed to students. Yet, this does not explain everything about a campus' Catholic culture. Students clearly noted these structures, but they also did not seem to account for the majority of students' experiences of the Catholic culture. They seemed to account for less than 25% of their perceptions.

Table 2.2 **Results of linear regression with insignificant variables eliminated**

	Coefficients	t-Stat	P-Value
Intercept	1.641	10.332	0.000
Coed dorms	0.103	3.335	0.001
Visitation policy	0.239	3.730	0.000
Daily mass	0.232	3.095	0.002
Required Catholic courses	0.182	4.554	0.000

The Students' Role

When I spoke with Gianna about the Catholic culture at her school, she did not mention institutional structures. She talked about people. When she thought of her campus, she thought of "nice" people who "open the door for you" and are "very hospitable." Even when Gianna went on to speak about institutional structures, she was less concerned about their existence than about whether people utilized them. "At my high school, no one showed up to daily Mass. Here, like, thirty students show up to daily mass. My mom did not believe me, but I told her to come see it." For Gianna, it was not the mass so much as students showing up to mass. For her, it was the students who made the Catholic culture "good."

Of all the written comments describing the Catholic culture of a campus, more than a quarter of them—27%—mentioned how students acted or treated each other, making it as significant a factor in Catholic culture as academics. When asked what made their campus seem Catholic, students wrote, for example, "The way people treat each other" or "The number of groups devoted to faith, the friendliness of nearly everyone you pass, and the structure of the college are very Catholic."

Students' role in shaping the Catholic culture was clearly evident in the quantitative survey. First, there is the simple factor of the number of Catholic students on a campus. This number correlated with students' perception of the Catholic culture (see table 2.3). For Very Catholic campuses, 81% of the students identified as Catholic. For Mostly Catholic campuses, the number of students identifying as Catholic was 75%. For Somewhat Catholic campuses, 68% of the students indicated that they were Catholic.

Table 2.3 Institutional classification and students' religious affiliation

	Christian— Catholic (%)	Christian— Protestant, Other (%)	Jewish, Muslim, Buddhist, Hindu, Atheist, Agnostic, other (%)
The culture is somewhat Catholic	67.57	17.57	14.86
The culture is mostly Catholic	74.75	13.41	11.83
The culture is very Catholic	80.82	12.65	6.53

P-value = 0.01; somewhat Catholic N = 222; mostly Catholic N = 507; very Catholic N = 245.

While there are more dimensions to being a Catholic student than self-identifying as one, this correlation indicates that students' self-perception as Catholics affects the culture.[6]

Second, students help to shape a university's Catholic culture through their network of relationships. The more Catholic friends that Catholic students had, the more Catholic they perceived their campuses to be (see table 2.4). Many students who considered their campus Very Catholic indicated that "all" of their friends share their beliefs; at Mostly Catholic campuses, "most" of their friends share their beliefs; and at Somewhat Catholic campuses, "some" of their friends share their beliefs.[7]

A third way that students shape the Catholic culture of a campus is by discussing Catholicism (see table 2.5). Students who indicated that their school was Very Catholic stated that it was "definitely true" that students talked about Catholicism among themselves. Students indicating that their school was Mostly Catholic said it was "somewhat true," and for Somewhat Catholic campuses, students said it was somewhere between "somewhat true" and "somewhat false." This relationship held true even if Catholic and non-Catholic students were separated for purposes of the survey.[8] Basically, if a lot of students talked about Catholicism (and it does not matter who these students were), the campus seemed Catholic.

Finally, the mere existence of student religious groups on campus affected students' perceptions of the Catholic culture. On average, students stated that it was "definitely true" that there were religious groups for students on campus. While the students may not have participated

Table 2.4 Institutional classification and shared faith (Catholic)

	How many of your friends share your religious beliefs? (Catholic)				
	None (%)	Some (%)	Most (%)	All (%)	Mean
The culture is somewhat Catholic	1	57	40	2	2.43
The culture is mostly Catholic	1	39	57	3	2.63
The culture is very Catholic*	1	25	70	5	2.79

P-value = 0.00; somewhat Catholic N = 150; mostly Catholic N = 379; very Catholic N = 198.
* Percentages total 101% because of rounding.

Table 2.5 Catholicism is talked about among students

	Definitely true (%)	Somewhat true (%)	Somewhat false (%)	Definitely false (%)	Mean
The culture is somewhat Catholic	21	50	22	7	2.16
The culture is mostly Catholic	43	45	10	2	1.71
The culture is very Catholic	75	19	6	0	1.31

P-value = 0.00; somewhat Catholic N = 214; mostly Catholic N = 496; very Catholic N = 253. Students who responded "Don't Know" were removed from these counts.

Table 2.6 How true are the following statements about your college or university?—"There are student religious groups"

	Definitely true (%)	Somewhat true (%)	Somewhat false (%)	Definitely false (%)	Mean
The culture is somewhat Catholic	75	23	2	0	1.28
The culture is mostly Catholic*	87	11	1	0	1.14
The culture is very Catholic	94	5	1	0	1.08

P-value = 0.00; somewhat Catholic N = 219; mostly Catholic N = 497; very Catholic N = 240. Students who responded "Don't Know" were removed from these counts.

* Percentages total 99% because of rounding.

in these activities, they knew they existed, and the fact that they knew that other students were involved in these activities made the place seem Catholic to them. This was true for all three types of Catholic campuses. With only small variance, all types of schools averaged "definitely true" for student religious groups (see table 2.6). These religious groups were part of students' lives and part of their existence on Catholic campuses—just as conversation about Catholicism might be. Add Catholic students and their network of friends, and it is clear that it is the students themselves who significantly foster Catholic culture on college campuses.

Not One but Three Catholic Cultures

Brooklyn said that the Catholic culture of her campus was "there if you want it but is not in your face." It was a description that differed from Mason's, where the Catholicism "resonated" throughout the campus' institutional structures, and from Gianna's, where, in her opinion, students being "nice" captured the Catholicism. These comments indicate an aspect of culture in addition to institutional structures and student demographics. Campuses organize their liturgical schedules, their core classes, and their residence halls differently. Campuses have varying opportunities to go to mass, but just because these opportunities exist does not mean that students will, in fact, go to mass. They may, or they may not. Similarly, students on different campuses encounter different numbers of theology classes, lectures on Catholicism, and discussions about the faith in their other classes. As a result, various ways to understand the world through Catholic frames are being presented to students. Even so, students may or may not use this Catholicism in their lives. Finally, dormitory visitation policies range from strict to practically nonexistent, and students vary in the way they respond to these regulations. Student responses to masses, classes, and dorms depend on what their religion is, who their friends are, who they associate with, and how much they talk about Catholicism.

In this mixture of student relationships and institutions structures, the socializing aspect of the Catholic culture emerges. It is what is described as "there if you want it," "resonating," or "nice" expressions of Catholicism. To fully understand the various cultures of Catholic campuses, one needs to attend to not only the structure and the students but also the particular expression of Catholicism that emerges as a socializing force. To find these specifics requires looking more closely at the campuses students classified as being Very Catholic, Mostly Catholic, and Somewhat Catholic.

PART I

Very Catholic Campuses

3

Made to Love, Not to Hook Up

ANNA PERFECTLY DESCRIBED hookup culture on campuses designated in the research study as "Very Catholic." When I asked her what hooking up meant, this happy, thoughtful, and talkative sophomore said:

> It kind of depends on who you are talking to. If one of my friends said it, I would assume they made out. Otherwise, I would have to ask what they mean. When I think of it, I think of drinking involved. I don't think it is normal for people to hook up with people without drinking. They are not confident to do it without alcohol. Usually, people hook up at a party first and then, afterward, independently and alone. It is not like going to a state school because we don't have parties here.

Anna acknowledged that the term "hooking up" was ambiguous, even though she was clearly aware of the stereotypical hookup culture script of drinking alcohol, going to a party, and hooking up. Yet, she also noted that hooking up meant something different on her campus and among her friends. Stereotypical hookup culture did not really seem to be present at her school like it was at other schools. Her campus was "not like going to a state school." Her school did not have parties, and most of her friends did not hook up; or, if they did, it meant they just kissed someone they liked.

Who hooked up then? Anna initially said that on her campus, "it is mainly around athletes. It is athletes and the groupies of athletes. I think this is about a third of the campus, and they hook up. The rest of the campus, two-thirds of the campus, is here for the mission. They are non-athletes." Anna, though, quickly qualified her answer, seeming to reconsider. "Well, it's more complicated than that. Some teams are faith-based.

I am on the cross-country team, and it is faith-based. So is the tennis team. The basketball team is not faith-based. Football and baseball and basketball are not faith-based. For girls, basketball and softball are not faith-based. The soccer team is more secular than religious." The key, it turns out, was not whether students were athletes. The most important question was whether they were there "for the mission," and athletics was just a convenient example of why people would attend the college besides the mission.

Anna was astute. It turns out that the small group of students who hook up on Very Catholic campuses are ones who do not seem to be there "for the mission." Those who were there "for the mission" rarely, if ever, hooked up. Through these comments, Anna captured the particular hookup culture of Very Catholic campuses: most students reject hookup culture, but a small number of students perpetuates a stereotypical hookup culture.

Not Hooking Up Is and Is Not the Norm

As we saw with Eleesha earlier, rejecting hookup culture is a counter-cultural move, operating in opposition to stereotypical hookup culture. It assumes the dominance of the stereotypical hookup culture and then rejects it in favor of something else, such as one's beliefs, success in school, maturity, or safety. Students who reject hookup culture typically have to offer explanations as to why and are often excluded socially as a result of their actions. It is not surprising that they are usually small in number.

Things are quite different on Very Catholic campuses. At these colleges and universities, students who do not participate in hookup culture actually comprise the vast majority of the study body. Anna estimated that most students—around two-thirds—are not hooking up, but the statistics indicate that even her estimate was too low. On campuses where the majority of the students classified the culture as Very Catholic, 74% of the students did not hook up, leaving only 26% of students who did.[1] In fact, on Very Catholic campuses, the numbers are almost an exact reversal of the norm at colleges and universities as a whole where 70% of people are hooking up and 30% are not.

Given these percentages, it is no wonder that so many students' written comments echoed Anna's sense that only a small cohort of students were hooking up. On the qualitative survey, 58% of the students on Very

Catholic campuses described hookup culture as something in which only a few students participate.[2] They made comments such as the following:

- I know that it does occur in a minority of students, but I neither investigate it nor am I frequently confronted with it so I am unaware of details.
- There are still kids that party and find people to hook up with. It's not a large percent of the school's population, but it does happen.
- It is definitely a group. There are certain guys who are willing to use girls. There are certain girls who are willing to use guys. You can avoid it easily if you want to though.

Yet, despite the statistical dominance of those who rejected hookup culture, it still operated like a counterculture. The majority of students assumed that stereotypical hookup culture was the norm and that they were actively choosing to go against the tide. Students on Very Catholic campuses clearly knew the "hooking up" frame, with 88% indicating that they "agree" or "strongly agree" that "hooking up is sexual activity between two people without expectations of a relationship."[3] Moreover, students on these campuses also believed the "hookup" script was the norm. They thought hooking up without sex "often" occurred on their campuses and hooking up with sex "sometimes" happened (see table 3.1).

Most significantly, students on Very Catholic campuses also felt it was necessary to offer reasons for why they rejected hooking up, even though by not hooking up, they placed themselves firmly within the statistical majority. They felt compelled to explain themselves, to give reasons

Table 3.1 **For the following statements, estimate how often the particular behaviors occur on your campus**

	Never (%)	Rarely (%)	Sometimes (%)	Often (%)	All the time (%)	Average
Hooking up that does not involve sexual intercourse*	4	9	30	37	21	3.62
Hooking up involving sexual intercourse**	5	25	41	21	8	3.02

* N = 195. Percentages greater than 100% because of rounding. Those answering "Don't Know" were excluded.

** N = 186. Those answering "Don't Know" were excluded.

for being different—even though they were actually perfectly typical. Of course, as mentioned earlier, most who reject hooking up do so because they are vulnerable—socially, economically, or otherwise—and participation would be too risky. For instance, Eleesha's reason for not hooking up was her desire to be faithful to her values. The main distinction of students on Very Catholic campuses, however, was that their reasons for rejecting hooking up were religious. In fact, these students typically employed one of two theological frames to explain themselves.

Made to Love and Conversion

Although she was just a freshman when I interviewed her, Mia was composed, confident, and reflective. She clearly believed that rejecting hookup culture was the right thing to do, but she also felt pressure to conform. When I asked her about hookup culture on her campus, she said, "I would definitely say it is part of the culture, sadly. I feel like on our campus you choose to participate or not. There is a big group of people who do participate, and there is a big group of people who don't. So you can choose not to participate. My group does not." Even though Mia was in the 70% majority of students on her Very Catholic campus who did not hook up, she clearly felt that her "big group" was competing against a rival "big group" that hooked up. She felt pressured to choose. So I asked her how she and her friends were able to choose against hooking up.

> I am sort of innocent, so I distance myself from it. . . . All I know is what I have heard from my friends, which is not that much because they are not involved in the hookup culture on campus. Another reason that I am distanced from this culture is because my friends and I are in the honors program. The honors program students are generally less prone to participate in hookup culture. My friends are in the honors dorms with all honors students, so they do not see much hookup culture, although they know it is present.

Mia noted two factors. First, it was her own choice to "distance" herself from hookup culture. Second, she was surrounded by people who also "distanced" themselves. Mia was an honors student hanging out with other honors students and doing so in the honors dorms. Given her description of this context, I assumed that her reason and, by extension, her peers' reasons for rejecting hookup culture was that she valued academic success over hooking up, preferring to do well at one and to avoid the risks of the other.

Instead, when I asked her why she did not hook up, Mia gave a theological explanation. "I think, personally, people hook up out of the sense of not feeling fulfilled and are looking for love. They think they can find this feeling only this way, but I think that the only way you can feel true love is by turning to God." Mia was invoking a theological frame that says (a) because God created human beings in God's image and likeness and (b) because God is love, then (c) humans only find fulfillment in love. It is a perspective that has a long theological history, having origins in St. Augustine's phrase that "you [God] made us for yourself and our hearts find no peace until they rest in you," to modern figures like Dorothy Day, who noted that "We have all known the long loneliness and we have learned that the only solution is love."[4] Mia and those like her have taken this understanding of the human person as a creature made to love and have applied it to their relationships and those around them.

Mia's "made to love" frame appears widely available to students on Very Catholic campuses. It was alluded to in 25% of the comments from these campuses in answer to the question, "why do you think people hook up?"[5]

- Because they want to be loved and they do not know what true love consists in.
- They confuse sex with love and desire to feel wanted and loved.
- They are looking for love and happiness.
- Because they have self esteem issues possibly.
- Because it's a quick solution to feeling lonely, insecure, a lack of affirmation or feeling of self-worth.
- I think people hook up because they are looking to fill an emptiness in their lives that only God can fill. They are desperately looking for love, but they end up feeling even more empty after hooking up with someone.

While Anna's reason for rejecting hooking up culture included Mia's "made to love" frame, she added a new dimension to it.

People participate in hooking up because it is socially acceptable. It is what social media glorifies. I participated in it and am not proud of it. But everyone says it is fine. It's a reward system. Your friends praise you. If the person is of some status, you get even more praise. It does not matter if you talk later. It only matters if you got them for a night.

You can stop, but it is like a drug. You feel bad about yourself the first time and the second time, but, later, you're like, "this is great." The physical is not everything, but it means something. *We are made to love, and the physical makes us feel loved.* You can get out of it, but it takes time and patience and a strong desire not to be in it any more. If you don't have the desire, you will not stop. It is hard to stop, especially if your self-esteem is low. It is like drinking alcohol. Most people don't like beer or alcohol the first time. They acquire a taste for it. The second time is bad. The third time you feel great. . . . Yes, I have been involved in hookup culture before. I overcame it here. It doesn't have to be just physical. It can be emotional and spiritual before physical. This is a healthy relationship, the basis of a healthy relationship. You should be able to talk to someone.

Although Anna was from a different Very Catholic campus, she employed Mia's "made to love" frame. Yet, Anna had hooked up, unlike Mia, and had some insight into why it was attractive. Anna acknowledged that hooking up worked, a least somewhat, "because it means something." It seemed to touch on this deeper need for love. It was also supported by friends, through social rewards, where people get praised for hooking up, and especially for hooking up with the right kind of person. Finally, hooking up can also become addictive, like drugs or alcohol, because the physical experience is powerful. Even so, Anna eventually rejected it. She wanted something more, something emotional and spiritual, something closer to love.

Anna employed not only the "made to love" frame that Mia used but also a "conversion" frame. Conversion comes from the Greek word "to turn around" and is often used by Christians to indicate a change in one's life that leads them to more closely follow Jesus. It is a central piece of the gospel message, tied up with forgiveness, repentance, and new life. It finds expression in the life of St. Paul, who persecuted Christians before his conversion and, in more recent times, is explored in theology by Bernard Lonergan and in literature by Flannery O'Conner.[6] Building upon the "made to love" frame, Anna calls upon a "conversion" frame to talk about her past and her reasons for rejecting it. She found hooking up to be attractive—socially and physically—but it was not enough. She wanted something more, something that hooking up kindled but did not satisfy.

So, she rejected hooking up, not easily or thoughtlessly but because it did not fulfill her desire to be loved. The "made to love" frame helped her to identify why she felt "bad" about herself at first and what she wanted. The "conversion" frame gave her the ability to acknowledge her past, to own what she learned from it, and to choose what she felt was a direction that would better fulfill her. Anna added a pathway into the "made to love" frame for those who did not reject it from the beginning or came to it through experiences. The "conversion" frame provided an explanation for participating in hookup culture and the promise of something better, all without condemning oneself for hooking up.

The "made to love" and "conversion" frames are two pieces of the repertoire of frames and scripts used for relationships on Very Catholic campuses. While they are used to help guide relationships, they are also the two most widely employed frames on these campuses for choosing to reject, rather than embrace, stereotypical hookup culture. Students use them because, even on campuses where the majority of students do not participate in hookup culture, to reject hookup culture is still perceived as countercultural. Students see themselves in the context of the broader culture and so feel the need to explain their rejection of hooking up to any of their peers who ask and to themselves to understand why they are different. What is distinctive about students on Very Catholic campuses who do not hook up is that their reasons for not doing so are not academic pursuits or personal safety but Catholic faith.

Religion and Hooking Up

Ethan was very similar to Anna. They were both sophomores on Very Catholic campuses. They both rejected hookup culture and employed the "conversion" and "made to love" frames to do so. Ethan explained himself this way: "Hooking up means a one-night stand where you had sex with another person. I was involved in a lot of it in high school, before I had my slow conversion. Even before that, I thought hooking up devalued people. It was something precious and just given away to anyone."

Ethan was also like Anna in his understanding of hookup culture on his campus. He noted that it was not pervasive. "There is not a lot of those types of parties on campus. . . . I can think of only one party like that on campus. It was during regular visiting hours in a dorm. It lasted just an hour before being shut down by campus police. They said that the behavior was not consistent with the student code of conduct for the campus."

He also noted, again like Anna, that the subculture seemed to be linked to athletes but, after acknowledging that he was a football player, ultimately concluded that it had more to do with the campus Catholicism.

> It is a small enough campus, so everyone knows everyone. There is a very small hookup culture. My freshman year it was worse than it is now. Each semester is a little different. My freshman year the football team got 70 new players. They wanted a bigger team so gave more money, but only 27 of these guys are still here now. A good number of the people left because the place was too Catholic. Many of the guys on the football team left because there was not a big enough hookup culture. Only fifty to one hundred girls were willing. Hookup culture is something very small, limited to those on athletics teams.

Other students from Very Catholic campuses agreed with Ethan and Anna that the stereotypical hookup culture was primarily practiced by a small group of people who were not attracted to the institutional mission. In response to the question, "How would you describe hookup culture on your campus?," students wrote:

· While it [hookup culture] certainly does exist, it belongs to a minority of individuals on campus, perhaps 20% of the student body, mostly the non-catholics, although that should not be understood to say that all the non-catholics are engaged in the hook-up culture.
· It is not noticeable but done in secret/off campus.
· It's completely removed from the bulk of the campus, mostly central-ized around athletics and is a very small part of the campus. Many peo-ple are not even aware of it.
· It is local. The only people travelling to campus for college are those coming for its Catholic identity. The local people are here for the sports, so they go home on the weekend and they party off campus.
· People want sexual pleasure, and many young men and women feel that such behavior is "normal." Additionally, I personally feel that those who engage in the hook-up culture at [my institution] are almost delib-erately flaunting the university's policies on such things for their own self-gratification.

The quantitative data provide a little more precision to the nature of those who hook up on Very Catholic campuses. First, the statistics indicate that this group is small. If one takes the most general definition of hooking up, including instances that did and did not include intercourse, only 26% of students hook up. If one is more restrictive and counts only those hookups that included intercourse, the number is just 13%. In either case, the students were correct: it is a small group.

Second, unlike hookup culture overall, men are not the primary drivers of hookup culture on Very Catholic campuses. More precisely, on these campuses, gender is not a reliable predictor of hooking up. As I noted in chapter 1, the only demographic characteristic in my study that was a statistically significant indicator of hooking up was being a male. This correlation disappears on Very Catholic campuses.

Third, the students are likely correct when they say that the determining factor of who does and does not hook up is related to the Catholic culture. There are several pieces of data that point to this conclusion. First, one indicator for hooking up on Very Catholic campuses was being a non-Catholic (see table 3.2). This is not a claim about atheists, agnostics, and non-Catholic Christians in general. On Very Catholic campuses, non-Catholics did not differ very much from college students in general, hooking up at rates around 70%. The key difference is in the behavior of the Catholics. They are the vast majority who rarely hook up, and so typical hooking up stands out.

Residence hall policies are a second indicator that the prevalence of hooking up is related to the Catholic culture. The student comments indicate that those who hooked up did so off campus or were local students. As Ethan said, he could remember only one party on campus, and it was

Table 3.2 For Very Catholic campuses: "Including both instances that did and did not involve sexual intercourse, approximately how many times in the last year did you hook up?"

	Catholics (%)	Non-Catholics[*] (%)
0	77	25
≥1	23	75
Total	100	100

[*] This category includes non-Catholic Christians, atheists, agnostics, Jewish, Muslim, Hindu, Buddhist, and other.

N = 221 (Catholics = 207; non-Catholics = 14); P-value = 0.00.

Table 3.3 For Very Catholic campuses: "Visitation rules for guests of the opposite sex are enforced in the dormitories"

	Definitely true (%)	Somewhat true (%)	Somewhat false (%)	Definitely false (%)	Mean
Visitation rules for guests of the opposite sex are enforced in the dormitories	78	20	1	0	1.24

N = 236 (students who responded "Don't Know" were removed from this count. Percentages do not add up to 100% because of rounding).

shut down within an hour. This reality is also echoed in the institutions' residence hall policies themselves. Two of the key institutional structures correlated with students' perception of the overall religious culture are residence halls and visitation policies. Very Catholic campuses have single-sex residence halls only and limited coed visitation hours, either restricted to daylight hours or restricted to common areas. Added to this, students on these campuses indicated that it was "definitely true" that "visitation rules for guests of the opposite sex are enforced in the dormitories" (see table 3.3). Trying to hook up in these contexts would prove difficult, if not impossible. These dorms are not places for partying, drinking, and hooking up. Students would have to do so elsewhere—off campus and outside of the influence of the Catholic culture.

Taken together, the strong correlation between being Catholic and not hooking up, the students' perception that those not at college for the mission are hooking up, and residence halls not being conducive to hooking up, seems to indicate that the prevailing rejection of hookup culture is rooted in the religious culture of a Very Catholic campus. Plus, students tend to offer religious reasons for not hooking up, and the religious culture seems to be an essential contributor to the divide between rejecting and embracing hookup culture on Very Catholic campuses.

Opposing the Culture

Ideally, I would have interviewed students on Very Catholic campuses who hook up. This would have provided a better description of what they were doing, why they were doing it, and how they understood their relationships to their school's culture. However, none of the students from Very Catholic campuses who were willing to be interviewed were part of stereotypical hookup culture. Even so, the fact that those who rejected hookup culture have an account for those that do hook up was telling. Ethan gave the most thorough explanation.

> I am not entirely sure [why people hookup]. There are few people involved.... Some are doing it in direct rebellion. They were a little too forced into a certain way of living, so now recoil, live and let go. But they only last a semester and don't come back. Maybe their parents blamed the place for their behavior so did not send them back.
>
> Every freshman has a little rebellion. There are different kinds and degrees. My rebellion was TV. It wasn't that we weren't allowed on the TV. My dad just did not see the point of paying $1,000 dollars a month for cable. So my freshman year, I went through the first five seasons of *The Simpsons* while sitting on the couch eating chips. I gained thirty pounds, some from the chips and some from football. (I did not lose form, just my pants didn't fit the way they used to.)
>
> Smoking, smoking cigars, is huge here too. If I had a nickel for everyone who started smoking cigars.... It is just a problem that is out of control. I am originally from Pennsylvania and came from a large high school, 3,000, 4,000 students, and only 10 to 20 people smoked. Everyone knew who they were because they would go outside to smoke. Here, about a quarter of the people smoke, and most start during their freshman year.
>
> Rebellion is just natural. It just is different for different people.

Ethan, who was not part of stereotypical hookup culture, saw those who participate as rebelling. It was not an isolated rebellion, though, but a particular manifestation of the general spirit of rebellion on his campus. To put Ethan's explanation in my own terms, these students were enacting an "opposing" script—basically a course of action that is in opposition to what is typically expected.

On Very Catholic campuses though, an "opposing" script was most often used against the culture outside of the college or university. Anna described this use of the "opposing" script best, saying, "Hooking up has become part of our culture, and it's hard to resist the pressures of hooking up. Especially when the media and friends make hooking up seem like a fun, young, and reckless thing that has to be tried. . . . A large number of students here, as well as society in general, definitely create a pressure to act this way." She noted that the culture outside of her institution not only presented values in tension with her beliefs but also put "hard to resist" pressure on people to conform to it. Anna had participated in it for a while, but turned away from it. She now understood the broader culture as advocating for sex in ways that contrasted with her faith, so she opposed it.

Whatever one thinks about blaming the culture, Anna and those who shared her perspective were voicing something genuine, something true to their experiences. They noted that most of their peers did not value or act the way they do, especially when it came to sexual activity and faith. They did not, as Christian Smith noted, "use their Catholic faith as a key resource for arriving at any counter culture religious, social, or ethical commitments."[7] Instead, they mirrored the actions of those around them, most of whom were embedded in a broad cultural movement away from religion.[8] What Anna and those like her were voicing was their experience of "opposing" this perspective, of being different because they did use their faith to organize their life, including their relationships.

The result for those who strongly embraced their faith was the kind of opposition that Ethan described. The broader culture was perceived to be against religion, so these students understood being religious as opposing the norm. This broader culture said not to smoke, so students took up smoking. More to the point, in a culture where the expectation was to hook up, where everyone was assumed to be having sex, students rebelled by not hooking up. They employed an "opposing" script, and the prevailing hookup culture on a campus with lots of these students becomes one of rejection.

In other words, Ethan's explanation that those who hook up were rebelling actually said more about the prevailing rejection of hookup culture on his campus than about its stereotypical hookup culture. He was explaining the behaviors of so many students on Very Catholic campuses who were religious and did not hook up and, then, seeing those who hook up through his own experiences and those of his peers. Those who do hook up on Very Catholic campuses were just doing what typical college students do. Students like Ethan and Anna and Mia were the ones who are rebelling—using an "opposing" script—against the typical expectations of college students.

Conclusion

The repertoire of relationships frames—"made to love" and "conversion"—that provide reasons for not hooking up and the "opposing" script that guides the behavior to not hook up are the initial pieces for understanding the religious and hookup cultures on Very Catholic campuses. These places are pervasively Catholic, so one would assume that theological frames would be readily available. While the "opposing" script is not inherently Catholic, it fits well with the culture of Very Catholic campuses. The institution highlights its religion and attracts students whose religious commitments make them feel at odds with their peers.[9] These frames and scripts, though, are just one piece of the puzzle when it comes to understanding Very Catholic campuses and hookup culture. Their distinctive Catholic culture is critical.

4

The Evangelical Catholicism of Very Catholic Campuses

ALTHOUGH ETHAN, THE football player from a Very Catholic campus, was aware of the rebellious nature of students, himself included, he did not personally oppose the Catholic culture of his campus. He embraced it. In his friendly and free-flowing manner, he said, "I would describe the Catholic culture as strong compared to other campuses." He then proceeded to provide a number of reasons why this is the case. "The staff, especially the residence hall's staff, emulates and encourages Catholic values. This is not to say it is perfect. I would not say that. It is very good. It is tolerant. But it is not in your face.... There are also Catholic speakers from all different subjects, like art, psychology, science.... There are also campus-wide feast days.... The campus just tries to celebrate Catholicism but not force it in your face. It is part of the mission."

Mia, the honors student who rejected hookup culture, emphasized a different aspect of the Catholic culture on her campus. She said, "I would say we have a really good Catholic identity. Its funny, you can be walking around on campus and hear a conversation, we call them [university's name] conversations, where students or seminarians are having an in-depth theological discussion. I discuss faith among my friends in the cafeteria. We talk about it in theology classes. I like my theology classes as they really nourish my faith and spirituality."

Together, Mia and Ethan capture what defines the Very Catholic culture on their campuses. Ethan talked about how institutional structures reflected the school's religious identity while Mia noted that this religious identity could be found among the students. While institutional structures and socializing relationships are elements of almost every culture, the difference on Very Catholic campuses is that almost all of the students and institutional structures "celebrate Catholicism" and nourish "faith and spirituality." These campuses are places where every aspect of the culture radiates Catholicism, even if the university tries not to "force it in your face."

The Institutional Structures of Very Catholic Campuses

As Ethan continued to describe his campus, he noted concerts that featured Brahms and Celtic music and feast days that included special meals in the cafeteria. He mentioned worship, saying that "there is mass three times a day and adoration available, but they try to avoid guilt-tripping people. They try to promote Catholic culture, put it forward." Ethan even described in detail the visitation policies, "Take the dorms for example. They are not coed. They allow visiting hours mostly during the day and some evenings. On the weekends, visiting hours go until one in the morning. It is an open door policy. You have to keep your doors open when someone of the opposite sex is visiting. They encourage you to spend time with one another. If you want to have sex, they are saying just don't do it in the dorms. They encourage tolerance and openness." When Ethan thought of the Catholic culture, he thought of institutional structures.

This is no wonder. Institutional structures of Very Catholic campuses clearly support Catholicism. Residence halls are a good example. Most, if not all, of the residence halls are single sex. The policies governing visitation by members of the opposite sex do not allow overnight guests and limit the hours or location of all visits. Worship is another good example. On Very Catholic campuses, masses are offered at least once a day, and Sunday masses are always offered more than once.

Classes are a third example. Students at these institutions typically take three religion classes, all three of which pertain to Catholicism in some way. Moreover, on these campuses, 74% of the faculty is Catholic, which is significant in and of itself but is also indicative of how explicitly the schools support Catholicism. Less than 5% of all Catholic colleges and universities make known the percentage of their faculty who are Catholic. In my survey, every one of the schools where the majority of students classified it as a Very Catholic campus noted the percentage on its website. There were only a few Mostly Catholic and Somewhat Catholic schools that did so, and not nearly enough to estimate a reliable average. Whatever one thinks of this as a measure, the fact that Very Catholic colleges make such public proclamations, as well as the distinctiveness of their institutional structures, communicates the schools' emphasis on Catholic identity.

Students on Very Catholic campuses clearly grasp how these institutional structures support Catholicism. As noted in chapter 2, there is a clear correlation between how students classify their campus (either Very, Mostly, or Somewhat Catholic) and the perception of institutional structures. Students on Very Catholic campuses indicate that it is "definitely true" that Catholicism is talked about in class and among students, students take classes on Catholicism, there are lectures on Catholicism and opportunities for worship, and visitation policies are enforced (see table 4.1).

Table 4.1 Student perceptions of institutional structures
on Very Catholic campuses

Question	Definitely true (1) (%)	Somewhat true (2) (%)	Somewhat false (3) (%)	Definitely false (4) (%)	Don't know (5) (%)	Mean
Catholicism is talked about in the classroom	86.31	12.86	0.41	0.00	0.41	1.15
Students take classes on Catholicism	94.56	4.18	1.26	0.00	0.00	1.07
There are opportunities for prayer or worship	97.10	2.49	0.41	0.00	0.00	1.03
There are lectures about Catholicism	89.58	10.00	0.42	0.00	0.00	1.11
Visitation rules for guests of the opposite sex are enforced in the dormitories	76.76	19.50	1.24	0.41	2.07	1.32

N = 240.

If one runs through the list of student responses to the question "What aspects of life on your campus seem Catholic to you?" on the qualitative survey, the support of Catholicism by institutional structures—classes, masses, and dorms—were mentioned in 83% of the comments.[1] Students wrote:

- Daily Mass, Rosary Walks, Adoration, Availability of Priests, Way Church Teachings are integrated throughout Academics, Campus Activities, Service Outreach opportunities, Lack of Co-Ed Dorms....
- Class prayer, chapels in the resident halls, angelus prayer at 12 and 6, daily masses....
- The biggest aspect would be the fact that the Angelus is still prayed without fail at noon and 6 p.m. Also, almost any event begins with a prayer.
- We have chapels in every single dorm and one in the town. Mass is offered three times daily, confession several times a week.
- Mass, Adoration, sacraments, service opportunities, speaker series.
- The classes are definitely Catholic. We have a strong liberal arts core with every major, and the school's philosophy and theology departments are well known. Even classes in other disciplines are often taught with a Catholic perspective.
- Between the school and the church next door, there are fourteen Mass times and several hours of confession, daily.

As noted in chapter 1, institutional structures support and sustain a culture, in part, by promoting and sustaining certain frames and scripts and, as a result, making them accessible to a wide group of students. On Very Catholic campuses, institutional structures support certain kinds of behavior through two scripts. First, these campuses promote a "no sex before marriage" script. There are mainly single-sex dorms and limited visitation hours, and 77% of students said it was "definitely true" that "visitation rules for guests of the opposite sex are enforced in the dormitories." Ethan summarized this script well when he said, "If you want to have sex, they are saying just don't do in the dorms." Second, Very Catholic campuses support religious actions through "pray" and "worship" scripts. Seventy-nine percent of the students' comments explicitly mentioned prayer or mass as examples of the Catholic culture, and 97% of students in the quantitative survey said it was "definitely true" that "there are opportunities for prayer or worship." In addition to guiding behavior through scripts, these institutions promoted ways of thinking through a "faith and reason" frame. Faith was integrated into the academic curriculum. It can be found in the three required classes on Catholicism, the 74% of professors who are Catholic, and the 86% of students who indicated that it was "definitely true" that "Catholicism is talked about in the classroom."

The frames that guide thinking and the scripts that guide acting clarify the makeup of Very Catholic campuses. The academic curriculum is structured so that people understand their experiences through a "faith and reason" frame. This religious outlook extends into their relationships, so they often explain not hooking up through "made to love" and "conversion" frames. Connected to these ways of thinking are the scripts for acting. Students are encouraged to act on their faith by the "pray" and "worship" scripts and to live it in their relationships by the "no sex before marriage" script. While institutional structures on Very Catholic campuses promote this repertoire of frames for thinking and scripts for acting, they—like the institutional structures on all campuses—account for less than 25% of students' perceptions of the culture.[2] The students and their interactions are responsible for the rest. This freedom of students to choose is so essential that it constitutes another repertoire of scripts.

Freedom Scripts

Ethan's Very Catholic campus rang bells at the traditional times of noon and six, indicating to Catholics that it was time to pray the Angelus.[3] Even though the school and the majority of students were Catholic, this practice caused a problem. As Ethan explained:

> Last year there was an incident when the Angelus was played in the cafeteria, and, when it was, all the Catholics would stand up and sing it out of respect. This made the non-Catholics feel like they were being forced to pray. They felt like they should stand up when everyone else was standing up. I can understand. I mean, I am Catholic, and I love the Angelus, but sometimes I have only fifteen minutes to eat and get to class, so I am like, "Come on, this is my lunch." They took the complaint to the president. His solution was to move the Angelus outside of the cafeteria. Some complained that he was compromising the institution's Catholic identity, but he said, "We don't guilt people into prayer." This is how they promote the Catholic culture but don't shove it into your face.

As Ethan saw it, the institution was trying to find a way to encourage prayer, to support but not coerce it—not to "guilt people into prayer" and not to "shove it into your face." Ethan thought that they had struck a good balance, but, as even he noted, others felt differently. Of the third of the students who commented on balancing freedom and institutional priorities, half felt that their school supported the Catholic culture "without being overbearing or intolerant," and the other half felt the institution was "going downhill" because of its approach. As one student wrote:

> It seems though that the university is afraid of keeping its policies (or enforcing its policies) Catholic to the core for fear of "offending" or making non-Catholic students "uncomfortable." This is really quite unfortunate because the university sells to its students, the ones seeking a good Catholic university, as this intensely Catholic university. . . .

Whatever students believe about the correctness of their school's approach, their comments indicated an awareness of its attempts to simultaneously promote Catholic activities and students' freedom to choose to participate. As one would expect, this "freedom to choose" script is echoed in student comments. About 53% noted it—a few by writing that some students do not choose the faith and with most noting how students had opportunities to grow in their faith.

- Very Catholic, strong Catholic community, many opportunities to strengthen one's faith.
- The potential to grow in holiness is very present.
- The campus is very true to its faith identity without being overbearing or intolerant.
- You also have the administration, which is Catholic, although they let some things slide. In other words, the administration is not excessively restricting in order to ensure that everyone is living by Catholic values. This works out, though, because being serious about your faith is still a personal commitment and there is no pressure.
- In the end, I would say that this campus gives a lot of OPPORTUNITY to grow in your faith and be around people with Catholic values and lives. However, it is just that—an opportunity—and you are certainly free to choose otherwise and not face any pressure/judgment.

- Very strong. Involvement in the Faith is encouraged but not required to be accepted.
- There is church like every day, and the cathedral is right on campus basically. There are plenty of opportunities to become involved in Catholic-related activities and clubs.

When I interviewed Anna, she had a story exemplifying the "freedom to choose" script at her Very Catholic university. It was about the first time she visited the campus.

The Catholic culture is really, really phenomenal. I chose [my university] because of its identity. I have a story for you about it. When I was touring campus for the first time, I asked the lady from admissions if it was a party school. I didn't want one. She said, "You can come here to strengthen your faith or lose your virginity." It was that you can choose your own path here. The pressure to drink was low. The pressure to go to mass on campus was low.

While Anna was aware of this "freedom to choose" script, she also was aware that that did not mean the school was neutral.

There are talks once a week, or maybe it is once a month, I am not sure, called theology on tap. Last week, it was on exorcism. You could ask any question that you wanted. There is also daily mass. There are three masses a day. There is confession every day. You can just go to the priest, but they are also in [the church]. There is an athletics ministry. There is a youth ministry program. You go to [the local city] and serve the youth there. The students are very Catholic. There is perpetual adoration. There are chapels in every dormitory. . . . You have to intentionally choose not to grow in your faith.

Anna's story indicated how the "freedom to chose" script guided behavior on Very Catholic campuses. Typically, there is a distinction between two kinds of freedom—freedom *for* something and freedom *from* something.[4] Freedom *for* is the kind of freedom that emerges from learning a skill. People who learn to play the piano are then free to do so, whereas those who never learn to play are not free to do so. Freedom *from* is typically a freedom from restrictions. There are no laws restricting people from choosing to sign up for piano lessons. Whether they decide to do so is their own free choice. Very Catholic campuses emphasize freedom *for* in their "freedom to chose" script. To be more precise, they stress a "freedom for Catholicism" script. This does not mean that there is no "freedom to chose" script. There are students who are not there "for the mission" and who do not chose the Catholic faith, and these schools try to establish policies that do not coerce them. There is freedom to choose, but it is also clear that Very Catholic campuses emphasize choosing for Catholicism. They encourage students to pray and go to mass. The preferred choice is clear, even though the freedom not to choose it exists.

Together, these constitute the repertoire of "freedom" scripts that guide actions on Very Catholic campuses. Anna's and Ethan's stories about the "freedom to choose" script represent one type of "freedom" script. The institutional structures that support a "freedom for Catholicism" script represent another. The "opposing" script noted in chapter 3 is a third. Throughout Very Catholic campuses, then, there is an emphasis both on freedom and on choosing Catholicism. The institutional structures that support and sustain Catholicism condition the choices that students can make. They do not rob students of freedom, but they do support a culture that favors Catholicism and hinders its rejection. These institutional structures are not the only part of the culture that supports Catholicism, though—the students themselves also do so.

Evangelical Catholics

Throughout her interview, Mia consistently turned to her relationships with others, whether discussing her honors classes or her support for rejecting hookup culture. The same was true for her understanding of the Catholic culture on her campus. Several times, she mentioned how she overheard people talking about Catholicism, saying things like, "the conversations I overhear around campus definitely identify [the place] as a very Catholic school.... My friends and I call these moments 'only [on our campus] moments.'" Whatever aspects of her school she identified as Catholic, it always seemed to lead her back to the students, her peers and friends. Worship, for example, was about what students could do: "The great availability of the sacraments for all the students [on campus] allows them to practice their faith daily. With the chapels and the [the large church], you can go to a mass or confession almost any time of day."

Mia grasped clearly that, while Catholicism was supported by institutional structures, students and their faith made it *feel* Catholic. One way to

Table 4.2 Institutional classification and students'
Catholic self-identification

	Catholic (%)
The culture is somewhat Catholic	67.57
The culture is mostly Catholic	74.75
The culture is very Catholic	80.82

P-value = 0.01; N = 974.

Table 4.3 Institutional classification and faith shared by friends

	None (%)	Some (%)	Most (%)	All (%)
Very Catholic campuses	1	22	71	7
Other Catholic campuses	3	50	45	2

Very Catholic campus N = 246; other N = 763.

examine Mia's claims is through students' religious self-identification. On Very Catholic campuses, 81% of students identify as Catholic, whereas on Mostly Catholic campuses it is 75%, and on Somewhat Catholic campuses it is 68% (see table 4.2).[5] This should not be surprising. Given the institutional structures supporting Catholicism and the fact that information about these structures is publicly available, Catholic students, especially those personally committed to the faith, are likely to be attracted to Very Catholic colleges.

Because so many students are Catholic, Catholicism is more prominent in student relationships. Seventy-eight percent of students on Very Catholic campuses report that "all" or "most" of their friends share their faith. On other campuses, 47% of students share the same faith as "all" or "most" of their friends (see table 4.3). In addition, students on Very Catholic campuses also talk about Catholicism more. Whereas on other campuses, 79% of students say it is "definitely" or "somewhat" true that "Catholicism is talked about among students," and on Very Catholic campuses, this number goes even higher, with 98% of students indicating that this is true (see table 4.4).

Mia's sense that fellow Catholics surround her and that they are talking about Catholicism is correct. Very Catholic campuses have high numbers of Catholics, and so these Catholics are embedded in networks of Catholic

Table 4.4 Catholicism is talked about among students

	Definitely true (%)	Somewhat true (%)	Somewhat false (%)	Definitely false (%)	Don't know (%)	Mean
Very Catholic campuses	87.97	9.96	2.07	0	0	1.14
Other Catholic campuses	30.89	48.10	14.36	3.66	2.98	2.0

Very Catholic campus N = 241; other N = 738.

friends and find almost all the students on their campus talking about their faith. Thus, hanging out with friends, walking with classmates, or sitting in the dining room, students are most likely to be with Catholics and to be having conversations that include topics related to their faith.

Christian Smith notes that one of the key factors affecting religious involvement is the overlapping nature of adolescents' relationships.[6] When friends and parents are involved in religion, adolescents are more likely to be as well. In college, friends carry more influence than parents, so the density of a student's relationships—how people are friends with their friends' friends—will have an even greater impact on religious involvement.

Given this research about young adult friendships and religious commitment, we can predict that students on Very Catholic campuses will have high levels of religious participation, and that is exactly what one finds. Students on these campuses are committed to Catholicism and practice it regularly. On a scale from "1" being "Extremely Unimportant" to "5" being "Extremely Important," students indicate that Catholic teaching on God, Jesus, the Spirit, heaven, hell, the Eucharist, sacramental marriage, papal infallibility, and the Magisterium are all between "Somewhat" and "Extremely" important (see table 4.5). For most of these beliefs, students on Very Catholic campuses score only slightly higher than those on Mostly and Somewhat Catholic campuses. The real differences emerge only with the importance of beliefs on contraception, the beginning of life, the pope, and the Magisterium.

Students' religious practices follow a similar pattern. Using a scale from "1" being "never" to "6" being "daily," students on Very Catholic campuses go to mass more than once a week, pray privately and pray to the

Table 4.5 Comparison of Catholic beliefs of students on Very Catholic campuses and those on Mostly and Somewhat Catholic campuses

	God exists	Jesus is the Son of God	The Holy Spirit is God	Heaven is real	Hell is real	The Eucharist is the body and blood of Christ	Marriage is a sacrament	Contraception is wrong	Life begins at conception	The pope can speak infallibly on faith and morals	The Magisterium is a teaching authority
Very Catholic campuses mean*	4.47	4.43	4.44	4.45	4.36	4.44	4.44	4.11	4.42	4.25	4.28
Other Catholic campuses mean**	4.52	4.37	4.34	4.43	4.08	4.12	4.28	2.88	3.95	3.59	3.93

1 = Extremely Unimportant, 2 = Somewhat Unimportant, 3 = Neither Important nor Unimportant, 4 = Somewhat Important, 5 = Extremely Important.

* N = 226–227.

** N = 514–516.

Table 4.6 Comparison of Catholic practices of students on Very Catholic campuses and those on Mostly and Somewhat Catholic campuses

	Attend mass	Prayed privately	Volunteered	Attended a religiously affiliated group	Prayed to Mary or the saints
Very Catholic campuses mean[*]	4.67	5.45	2.71	2.80	5.18
Other Catholic campuses mean[**]	3.20	4.45	2.56	1.94	3.16

1 = Never, 2 = Once a Month, 3 = 2–3 Times a Month, 4 = Once a Week, 5 = 2–3 Times a Week, 6 = Daily.

[*] N = 225–233.

[**] N = 518–527.

saints several times a week, volunteer a few times a month, and attend a religiously affiliated group a few times a month (see table 4.6). For most of these, students on Mostly and Somewhat Catholic campuses are only slightly less active. They go to mass almost once a week, pray at least once a week, and volunteer at almost the same rate. The differences emerge in attending religious groups and praying to Mary and the saints.

What the similarities and differences indicate is a particular expression of Catholicism, what can be called "evangelical Catholicism." William Portier popularized this term in his seminal article, "Here Come the Evangelical Catholics."[7] Portier described shifts in Catholic demographics that began in the 1960s. He noted that, by and large, these movements led to the integration of Catholics into mainstream culture and the disappearance of many of the identity markers that had made them stand out, both in terms of beliefs and practices. However, he also noted sociological research that pointed to a small group of emerging "evangelical Catholics."

Evangelical Catholics, according to Portier, were highly committed to orthodoxy, actively engaged in worship and traditional religious practices, and enthusiastic about the church—especially the pope and the church's teachings.[8] More than this, though, they had a distinctive way of understanding themselves. While they knew their beliefs and practices were at odds with the broader culture, they did not become defensive or hostile.[9] Instead, they focused on witness and conversion.[10] They tried to live consistently

with their beliefs, understanding this as a kind of witnessing and consider-
ing it the best way to "preach" to others and promote conversion.

This evangelical Catholicism is an apt description of the Catholicism
of the majority of students on Very Catholic campuses. Evangelical
Catholicism implies behaviors that are reflected in the "pray" and "worship" scripts. Evangelical Catholicism also emphasizes traditional devotions like praying to Mary and the saints and daily mass attendance. It
emphasizes witness over preaching, an approach that dovetails with the
repertoire of freedom scripts. Just as evangelical Catholics attempt to live
consistently with their beliefs, students on Very Catholic campuses understand their relationships in light of their faith, using the "made to love"
and "conversion" frames, and act on this understanding by employing the
"no sex before marriage" script.

As a result, evangelical Catholicism is a way students are socialized on
Very Catholic campuses, helping them understand social expectations: frequent masses, prayers to Mary and the saints, trust in the authority of the
pope and the Magisterium, and beliefs that life begins at conception and that
contraception is wrong. It means not only identifying as Catholic but also
talking about it inside and outside of class. Catholic students will understand
much of this, being familiar with many of these beliefs and practices, and will
find plenty of support from others. Non-Catholic students will either need to
figure this culture out in order to be involved in campus life or find themselves on the outside looking in. Even if they are typical college students, they
will stand out on a campus where 81% of the students are Catholics and most
go to mass and pray several times a week. In other words, fitting in on a Very
Catholic campus means that one practices evangelical Catholicism.

It should not be a surprise, then, that on Very Catholic campuses, those
who are "not there for the mission" are small in number. They are neither
attracted to these schools nor have much social support if they choose to
attend. From the descriptions in the interviews, these students typically
want to play sports and graduate from college, but they do not employ the
relationship or evangelical Catholic frames for thinking and scripts for acting. If they hook up or drink or party, they tend to move these activities off
campus. Whatever is the case, those who are "not there for the mission"
do not integrate into the campus culture and hence do not fit in with the
typical students on Very Catholic campuses.

Yet, those who do not integrate are a minority. The majority of students are evangelical Catholics. Most of the students indicate that several
tenets of the Catholic faith are "extremely important" to them, and most

of these students also pray and go to mass "2–3 times a week." They find their own personal faith commitments shared by their peers and so can make friends and have non-hookup relationships more easily. This evangelical Catholicism is supported by institutional structures, and because evangelical Catholics are the majority, that support seems less like external pressure and more like welcomed encouragement of their personal religious commitments. This Catholic culture, sustained by students and the schools' institutional structures, is crucial for understanding how these campuses reject hookup culture.

From Not Hooking Up to an Anti-Hookup Culture

On all campuses—not just Very Catholic campuses—Catholic beliefs and practices are related to whether or not people hook up. Basic beliefs in God, Jesus, and the Spirit are correlated to not hooking up, as are "evangelical" Catholic beliefs on sexual issues and the authority of the church (see table 4.7). Catholic practices operate similarly. On all campuses, students who more frequently attend mass and pray hook up less (table 4.8). Other research has discovered similar correlations.[11] Religion affects hooking up, and the more religious students are—usually indicated by frequency of worship—the less they hook up.

The correlations for hookups that include intercourse follow a similar pattern but with a narrower set of indicators. For all campuses, stronger beliefs in the Eucharist, against contraception, and about life beginning at conception are correlated with less hooking up that includes intercourse (table 4.9). Also, for all campuses, more frequent worship and prayer as well as traditional practices like praying to Mary and the saints are linked to less frequent hooking up with intercourse (table 4.10).

These numbers indicate that strongly believed and frequently practiced Catholicism is related to not hooking up and evangelical Catholicism to not hooking up that includes intercourse. These connections should be expected—and not just because others studies have found similar connections between hooking up and religious commitment.[12] The "made to love" and "conversion" frames ease evangelical Catholics' negotiation of attraction and relationships. The "made to love" frame provides a way to understand desires for intimacy and sex and do so in terms of their faith: they are God-given desires for genuine and fulfilling love. Building upon the "made to love" frame, the "conversion" frame provides students a

Table 4.7 Catholic beliefs and hooking up (with or without intercourse)

		God exists***	Jesus is the Son of God*	The Holy Spirit is God**	Hell is real*	The Eucharist is the body and blood of Christ*	Contraception is wrong*	Life begins at conception*	The pope can speak infallibly on faith and morals*	The Magisterium is a teaching authority*
Hooked up in the last year	0	4.56	4.51	4.48	4.31	4.40	3.71	4.35	4.00	4.24
	≥1	4.54	4.34	4.33	4.07	4.11	2.75	3.86	3.59	3.84

1 = Extremely Unimportant, 2 = Somewhat Unimportant, 3 = Neither Important nor Unimportant, 4 = Somewhat Important, 5 = Extremely Important.

N = 683–686 (this number only includes Catholics as they were the only ones who were asked questions about Catholic beliefs).

* P-value = 0.00.

** P-value = 0.01.

*** P-value = 0.04.

Table 4.8 Catholic practices and hooking up (with or without intercourse)

		Attend mass*	Prayed privately*	Attended a religiously affiliated group*	Prayed to Mary or the saints*
Hooked up in the last year	0	4.24	5.20	2.56	4.42
	≥1	2.94	4.30	1.77	3.03

1 = Never, 2 = Once a Month, 3 = 2–3 Times a Month, 4 = Once a Week, 5 = 2–3 Times a Week, 6 = Daily

N = 677–680 (this number only includes Catholics as they were the only ones who were asked questions about Catholic practices).

* P-value = 0.00.

Table 4.9 Select Catholic beliefs and hooking up with intercourse

		The Eucharist is the body and blood of Christ*	Contraception is wrong*	Life begins at conception*
Hooking up that involved sexual intercourse	0	4.33	3.17	4.15
	≥1	3.97	2.54	3.64

1 = Extremely Unimportant, 2 = Somewhat Unimportant, 3 = Neither Important nor Unimportant, 4 = Somewhat Important, 5 = Extremely Important.

N = 313–314 (this number only includes those students who indicated that they were Catholics and had hooked up).

* P-value = 0.01.

Table 4.10 Select Catholic practices and hooking up with intercourse

		Attend mass*	Prayed privately*	Attended a religiously affiliated group*	Prayed to Mary or the saints*
Hooking up that involved sexual intercourse	0	3.94	5.21	2.85	4.13
	≥1	3.09	4.38	2.33	3.37

1 = Never, 2 = Once a Month, 3 = 2–3 Times a Month, 4 = Once a Week, 5 = 2–3 Times a Week, 6 = Daily

N = 313–314 (this number only includes those students who indicated that they were Catholics and had hooked up).

* P-value = 0.00.

way to understand how a desire for intimacy might overwhelm their faith commitments and how recovery is possible when this happens. The perspectives these frames provide are the foundation for the "no sex before marriage" script that guides behavior.

This connection between students' evangelical Catholicism and not hooking up does not explain the emergence of a prominent anti-hookup culture on Very Catholic campuses, however. Though cultures are built upon frames and scripts, they also include the sharing of these frames and scripts between people, a socializing that occurs because of this sharing and institutional structures supporting some of these particular ways of thinking and acting. The existence of a few evangelical Catholic students on any given campus can, if the conditions are right, generate a small anti-hookup culture, but they cannot make it the dominant culture of the whole campus. This requires other elements of a culture, and this is exactly what one finds on Very Catholic campuses.

Evangelical Catholic students on Very Catholic campuses are neither alone nor a minority. They are surrounded by other evangelical Catholic students. Collectively, these students typically do not hook up. They use the evangelical Catholic repertoire of relationship frames and scripts, thereby making anti-hookup culture the prevailing culture. Instead of incurring social isolation or marginalization for not hooking up, students find social acceptance. Even though they do not fit in with the culture at large and differ from typical college students, they easily fit in and understand the culture on their campus. As a result, evangelical Catholics and their rejection of hookup culture exist not as a fringe group but as the socializing force of the campus community. One student captured it well: "The Catholic Identity is quite strong. . . . I believe this is opposite of most universities, where the genuinely Catholic at most universities feel ostracized."

Along with this socializing aspect, the institutional structures of Very Catholic campuses sustain evangelical Catholicism and, in so doing, add further support for an anti-hookup culture. They do it partly through their policies. The curriculum and liturgical life encourage Catholic beliefs and practices while the residence halls and visitation policies facilitate the application of the faith to relationships. Evangelical Catholic students find their beliefs "resonating" throughout campus, amplifying their faith and its implications for hooking up and sex. These institutional structures also reinforce evangelical Catholicism as the glue that binds their culture. The explicit support of evangelical Catholicism attracts evangelical Catholic students to the school, and the majority of students on the campus end up being evangelical Catholics.

Thus, the Catholic culture on Very Catholic campuses sustains not a peripheral anti-hookup culture but one that is dominant and pervasive. While evangelical Catholics on other campuses might not hook up, they typically inhabit places where anti-hookup culture results in marginalization. On Very Catholic campuses, these individual students find networks of friends who not only accept them but also share their faith, and these students and their networks of relationships are intensified by institutional structures. The result is that each element reinforces the other to generate and sustain both a Very Catholic campus and a dominant anti-hookup culture.

5

Can Very Catholic Campuses Change Hookup Culture?

SADIE—LIKE OTHER STUDENTS I interviewed from Very Catholic campuses—was friendly, talkative, and happy with her college. In addition to thinking her campus' Catholic culture was strong and its hookup culture small, this sophomore also felt that romantic relationships on campus were in good shape.

> There are a lot of relationships on campus. Most are very chaste and very Catholic. The number they say is 80% of students find the person they are going to marry on campus.... Yes, relationships are happy ones overall. The chastity, the living a good solid relationship, doing activities that are Christian oriented, sharing their faith, all of these make them feel like they are becoming better. The students are always smiling.

Relationships seemed pretty ideal to Sadie. People were happy and chaste, more focused on marriage than on hookups—in short, living out the teachings of their faith. Should other colleges and universities foster these same kinds of relationships so they too can provide alternatives to hooking up and have students who "are always smiling"?

"I Met My Girlfriend on a Retreat"

Sadie proved aware not only of "happy" students in relationships but also how they got into them, "A lot of the time, it is just people meeting each other in classes together. It is a small school, so everyone knows everyone.

They start talking with someone of the opposite sex. There is no place to meet, so they just start talking at common activities." Sadie listed a number of these activities—including mass, swim club, cross country team, football, softball, student clubs, student government, and service learning—and concluded with, "Lots of people like something and do this, so they most likely meet each other doing it." Sadie continued by describing how people find relationships.

> People meet, they hang out, and then they date. A lot of time people set each other up. They say, "you two would be good together," so they go out on a date. This is probably the main way it happens. It happens a lot. One person is dating one person and their friends meet each other.... It is a small campus ... so someone always knows someone, and usually they are in your immediate friend group.

Sadie's description echoed that of Anna, the sophomore from a Very Catholic campus who had stopped hooking up in order to find more meaningful relationships. Both noted that relationships emerged not out of random or singular encounters but over time, through the networks of relationships on campus. Students met people through classes or extra-curricular activities, got to know each other, and, perhaps, dated or started a relationship. Ethan, the football player who saw the Catholic culture mainly through institutional structures, offered a good example of this process.

> Two friends of mine just got together this past semester. They were friends for three years, and, sometime after Christmas, they became something more than friends. Now they are already talking about marriage. People ask, "how can you talk about marriage after only six weeks?" But I tell them they have been in the same circle of friends since freshman year, the same six friends. So they have known each other for four years. This is the vast majority of relationships. They are friends first and then discover that they are more than friends.

What came out of these interviews was a pretty clear script for finding a relationship: a "hanging out" script. Researchers Paul Eastwick and Lucy Hunt have studied how people evaluate others' relationship potential.[1] Eastwick and Hunt noted that the typical assumption is that certain people have "desirable traits like commodities," and those with more of these traits are highly pursued and those with fewer traits less so.[2] Yet, what Eastwick and Hunt found was that relationships and desirability emerge out of a context where people get to know each other over time. They concluded that "romantically desirable traits actually appeared to be more relational than trait-like (i.e., consensual) across the contexts that we examined, and this difference between uniqueness and consensus was even more pronounced when people estimated how happy they would be with someone as a relationship partner."[3] In other words, people evaluated others' potential for relationships primarily by hanging out with them.

This "hanging out" script was used on all the campuses I studied. When students were aware that this script was available to them, they found it quite valuable. It provided for a different way of pursuing a relationship, one that was less ambiguous than relationship hookup culture, in which people feel compelled to pretend not to be interested in something more than hooking up when, in fact, they are. Hanging out provided an alternative script, another possibility for action that students might utilize, one that seemed effective.

The "hanging out" script differed on Very Catholic campuses though. Mason, who felt that Catholicism resonated throughout his campus, made this clear when he described how he met his girlfriend. "I think you hang out with people in different groups. I met my girlfriend on a retreat. . . . After hanging out for a while, I just asked her out." Ethan similarly explained that "they [students who are interested in each other] go to holy hour or church together. Schedules here can be wildly different, so you may not see someone for a week on accident. You can only meet together at dinner, adoration, and church. There is mass three times day, 7:30, noon, and 5:30 then dinner." Sadie gave the same description of how people get together, only briefer. "People just usually go on a walk or visit a chapel or go on a rosary walk." For Mason and many others on Very Catholic campuses, religious activities provided occasions for "hanging out."

This makes sense. On these campuses, masses were offered at least once a day and more than once on Sundays. Students at these institutions had to take at least three religion classes before they graduated, all three of which pertain to Catholicism. Students on Very Catholic campuses, on average, went to mass more than once a week, prayed privately and prayed to the saints several times a week, volunteered a few times a month, and attended a religiously affiliated group a few times a month. In addition, these students connected with one another through a shared evangelical

Catholicism. Very Catholic campuses emanated Catholicism, and this pervasive Catholic culture provided the majority of opportunities for students to get together, opportunities that interested them because of their own religious commitments.

Relationships as Courtship

As Sadie continued describing relationships on her campus, she noted that students took relationships seriously because, "they want marriage. The joke is that girls come here to get their MRS degree instead of the degree they are studying for. Every week there is a new engagement. About a quarter of the girls are here for this." The understanding that marriage is the goal of relationships consistently arose in my interviews with students on Very Catholic campuses. Ethan said, "The number of people who get married here is out of control. Seventy-five percent of the people met the person they are going to marry here." Mason said that "everybody is looking for someone to spend their life with. They might not think they are looking for marriage, but they are implicitly moving forward to marriage. They are getting closer all the time, and the time is preparation for marriage. . . . My girlfriend wants to be married, so we talk about it."

It seems that many on Very Catholic campuses understood their relationships as courtships. They tended to be committed, exclusive, and serious relationships, and students in these relationships were open to marriage, seeing it as the end result should they stay together. This "courtship" is a frame to understand relationships and is connected to the Catholic faith because courtship leads to marriage, and marriage is one of the few sanctioned relationships in Catholicism.[4] Students who understand their dating relationships with this frame imitated and moved toward marriage, a relationship recognized by and consistent with their faith.

The result of understanding relationships through their Catholic faith meant that students were guided by a "no sex before marriage" script on Very Catholic campuses. As noted in chapter 4, it was a script supported by institutional structures—single-sex residence halls and their visitation policies—but it was also seen in students' comments. The stereotypical script for college sexual behavior was hooking up—sexual activity without expectations of a relationship. Very Catholic campuses included an "opposition" script that meant many acted in ways that contrasted with the broader culture and so implied a "no sex before marriage" script. In response to the question "What are relationships like on your campus?,"

76% of the students contrasted relationships that are rooted in religion with those that are not.[5] They wrote comments such as the following:

- They differ with the individuals. Many of them seem exemplary Catholic men and women trying to lead each other toward God and discern His Will. Others do not seem exemplary.
- If they are good Catholics: Talking – Dating – Engaged – Married/ If not: talking – flirting – and the rest I don't know and don't want to know. . . .
- There are many respectful, nonsexual relationships between individuals on campus. However, there are still about 20% of the campus who engage in active sexual relationships.
- There are those who marry young, single [and] thinking about religious life, single who court, and those who hook up.
- I have witnessed some extremely faith-filled, chaste relationships and some very lustful relationships. From my perspective, it is about a 50/ 50 split between the two types.
- I believe there are many good relationships. Most of the actual relationships that take place (not just hookups) are present because of a mutual care between two people. Many are also built upon a shared love for Christ, and a desire to grow closer to Him with another person. Obviously, there are also less ideal relationships, as well as unhealthy ones.

From getting to know people through religious activities, to not having sex when they got together, and to pursuing marriage as the end game, almost every aspect of student relationships reflected Catholicism.

Should Every Campus Become Very Catholic?

Although living on a campus with a Very Catholic culture seems to make students happy, it would be very difficult to replicate on other campuses. As the Association of Catholic Colleges and Universities noted, only about "60% of incoming freshman at four-year Catholic colleges and universities self-identify as Catholics."[6] This is a far cry from the 81% of students who self-identify as Catholic on Very Catholic campuses.

Even if the number of students indicating that they were Catholic was higher, this does not necessarily mean that there would be more evangelical Catholics. In his *Young Catholic America*, Christian Smith studied Catholic emerging adults.[7] He created a typology of students that ranged from

apostates who abandoned their faith to the devout who resemble evangelical Catholics.[8] In the study, he found no devout emerging adults. For those
he interviewed, "none regularly attended mass, espoused well-expressed
Catholic doctrines, and evidenced the importance of their faith in their
daily lives."[9] Instead, Smith noted a gradual decline in religiosity among
most Catholics of this demographic group and concluded that emerging
adults "do not use their Catholic faith as a key resource for arriving at any
counter culture religious, social, or ethical commitments."[10] Without these
evangelical Catholic students, there can be no Very Catholic campus.

Even if there were significantly more evangelical Catholic students, there
are only a few Catholic institutions of higher education whose institutional
structures support this particular configuration of Catholicism. There are
approximately 260 Catholic colleges in the United States. The Cardinal
Newman Society publishes *The Newman Guide to Choosing a Catholic
College*, which "recommends Catholic colleges and universities because
of their commitment to a faithful Catholic education."[11] They list twenty
schools in this guide, making the approximate number of Very Catholic
campuses about 8%. In my sample of schools, 8% were considered to be
Very Catholic by the majority of students. If I used publicly available data
about each institution, the number of Very Catholic schools also comes
to 8%.[12] If I limit the institutional factors to just those affecting student
perceptions, the number is 6%. The point here is not to determine the
precise number of Very Catholic schools but that whatever the number is,
it is low, less than 10% of all Catholic schools. To support and sustain a Very
Catholic culture and its related anti-hookup culture, almost every Catholic
institution of higher education would have to reorganize itself, particularly
its residence halls, curriculum, and liturgical life. But even if they did so,
without evangelical Catholic students, the effort would be futile.

Finally, on top of these issues, even on Very Catholic campuses, students need more Catholic frames for thinking and scripts for acting. Even
though there are plenty of institutional structures supporting them and
the student body shares these beliefs, students need something more than
"no sex" and "get married."

Meaningful Relationships

For Mason, relationships provided certainty. "I think people are looking for certainty. They hate uncertainty. Hooking up is very uncertain,
so most people don't like it. A relationship removes this uncertainty.

You can be who you want to be. The relationship allows you to be truly yourself. You can't be yourself in hooking up because you are just being whoever you need to be to just have sex." The ability to be honest and not manipulative in a relationship emerged because it was "certain." Hookups typically presented a false or incomplete self because, from Mason's perspective, one was trying to use the other person, one does not know the other person's aims, one is insecure, or one does not know what will result from the encounter. Mason concluded by linking this "certainty" with faith in God.

> Religion affects relationships. People with strong morals are brought up and taught what is not appropriate. They teach you to look at the long term and what is good for you. Hooking up is so short term. . . . Catholic faith plays a big role. I was brought up and my girlfriend was taught and believes sex should be between two committed people, so we decided not to have sex. This strong faith takes uncertainties out of life. You know what to do. Without it, everything is "eat, drink, be merry." People might say they believe in God, but if they don't trust in God, then they will just go have fun because they can do it. With faith and trust in God, you step back. It is like you trust what you were taught, you trust in Jesus, and you are able to see that what the culture tells you is wrong.

The "certainty" for Mason provided a sense of direction, an ability to be yourself, and seek something more than what is immediate. For Mason, it was not just the "no sex," although that was part of it; it was the anchoring and security that faith provided that guided his relationships and his life.

Anna spoke about this dimension differently. She found that faith broadened her view of relationships. "Faith goes into making relationships good. Without faith, it is not good. Having faith in something higher helps you to realize that you are not the center of the world. You can think about something other than yourself." This broader view was essential to Anna.

> I would not date anyone that is not Catholic because it is so important to me. If I cannot share it in a relationship then I am not truly in a relationship. . . . If one is not a believer, then there is a divide. Where do you expect to find this middle ground? You can talk about things but not necessarily the part of your soul that matters. You do not connect mentally, emotionally, or spiritually—just physically.

Like Mason, who found that faith made him take a longer view of the relationship and enabled him to be more himself, Anna found that faith provided a wider perspective for people and relationships. It pushed her to connect beyond the physical, something she discovered that she desired after her experiences in hookup culture.

Both Mason and Anna said that religion helped them to achieve some meaning beyond the physical in their relationships. It was not so much that they felt that the physical was bad but rather that it was not enough. While the "no sex before marriage" script was part of this discernment, it also represented a belief that in relationships, you should be able to "be yourself" and able to "connect mentally, emotionally, or spiritually" with another. For Mason and Anna, the key piece was not so much a problem with sex but a problem of meaninglessness. They wanted something more.

What made Mason and Anna different from other students was not their desire for meaningful relationships but their choice not to hook up as a means of developing relationships. In stereotypical hookup culture, most people want something similar. Studies of hookup culture have found that the reason almost 90% of both women and men give for hooking up is that they want something meaningful from the experience.[13] The more people know and seem to care about each other, the better the experience seems to be.[14] In fact, the lack of something more is what often leads to regret. In their essay, "Hookups and Sexual Regret among College Women," Elain Eshbaugh and Gary Gute note, "When we controlled for age, religiosity, and other sexual-behavior variables, we found that two of the hooking up variables—engaging in intercourse with someone once and only once and engaging in intercourse with someone known for less than 24 hours—significantly predicted sexual regret."[15] The lack of knowledge and familiarity and the lack of a possible relationship suggested that people were unhappy about hooking up. They felt that the encounter meant nothing or that they were being used. Either way, it indicated that people wanted something more from the hookup.

The Problem of Exclusion

In stereotypical hookup culture, this pursuit of something meaningful is difficult. The frame for hooking up requires not having any expectations other than the hookup itself. If people want relationships, they must accept the assumption about hooking up and pretend that they do not want a relationship. If people reject hooking up, they have to accept some social marginalization. In both of these scenarios, pursing a meaningful relationship is difficult.

Very Catholic campuses also had expectations, and, even though they went in the opposite direction, this could still create problems of social exclusion. On these campuses, the "courtship" frame and the "no sex before marriage" script were widely shared by students. They could create expectations that it was not enough to have a meaningful relationship. One needs a Catholic relationship. Sadie noted this dynamic in her analysis of the different kinds of groups on her campus.

> People say there are two groups on campus. People here for the Catholic faith and people here for sports. I think there is a third group—strict Catholics. They are here for marriage. The strict Catholics are looking for strict Catholics to do faith stuff together. They agree to not have sex before marriage. They go to mass. They try to follow their faith in relationships. A lot of athletes are not in relationships.... The regular Catholics—the middle crowd—there are a lot of them in relationships. They are similar to the strict Catholics, just more social with others. They are friends with the athletes and the strict Catholics, friends with both crowds.

Sadie's groupings suggested the problem. The strict Catholics could cut themselves off from others, be less social, and, on a Very Catholic campus, this could up the stakes for the regular Catholics. This was problematic because Sadie's regular Catholics were actually evangelical Catholics, and the strict Catholics she mentioned were an even more select group of evangelical Catholics, a kind of hyper-evangelical Catholics. As in stereotypical hookup culture, this group could exert pressure on others as well as ostracize those who do not keep to their standards.[16] They could make the anti-hookup culture on Very Catholic campuses just as oppressive as the stereotypical hookup culture, marginalizing those who differ in what they want or how they behave.

This is why the "conversion" frame is so valuable. It provides a way for students to understand both their desires to live up the expectations of evangelical Catholicism and their struggle to do so. Ethan recounted two examples.

> Catholic individuals who maintain social standing by being good Catholics have been caught in the act of having sex.... One was

caught in the stairwell the other day having sex. I thought, "Go find a car at least." It was only eleven at night, so people were still going up and down the stairs. He at least should have watched a high school movie to find out where he should go!

Some people just make mistakes too. Two of my friends were in a relationship. They were trying to be chaste, and he was thinking about the priesthood. Then she got pregnant. Now they are getting married. He loves her, but it was just a mistake. People make mistakes. They are not perfect.

Even though Very Catholic campuses supported those who reject hookup culture, even though its institutional structures supported Catholicism, and even though students were socially rewarded for their religious faith, they still hooked up and had sex. The "conversion" frame provided a resource for understanding and not vilifying these students. Ethan's friends could be shown mercy and compassion instead of judgment and isolation, just as Anna's experience of hookup culture leading her to more meaningful relationships could become an example for others. The "conversion" frame enables students to acknowledge their past and its limitations as well as see it as what opens them up to a new way to live.

In doing so, the "conversion" frame can blunt the impact of marginalization. Without the "conversion" frame, the expectations for relationships on Very Catholic campuses can become a means for excluding people, from those who reject them to those who struggle to meet them. As Ethan noted, students "maintain social standing by being good Catholics." Yet the "conversion" frame carves out a space for these students by providing a way to understand their experiences. Instead of penalizing people socially, there is room for growth, learning, and change. Although it probably will not solve social exclusion completely, the existence of the "conversion" frame in the culture does create an alternative to it.

Can Very Catholic Campuses Change Hookup Culture?

Very Catholic campuses have a distinctive culture. Their institutional structures support the majority of the students' own religious commitment, and this faith is also shared between students. Together, this Catholic culture supports an anti-hookup culture and generates frames for understanding relationships—"made to love," "conversion," "meaningful relationships," and "courtship"—and scripts to know what to do for relations—"hanging out" and "no sex before marriage." Most important, though, students seem happy, especially with their relationships and Catholic culture. As long as they are attentive to the potential for exclusion, these Very Catholic campuses seem to be addressing a genuine need among their students.

How relevant is their example for other campuses and students? Initially, it seems, very little. Even if other campuses wanted to rework their institutional structures to match those of Very Catholic campuses, they would not find enough students to serve, or the students on their campuses would find the changes frustrating, problematic, or simply irrelevant. While replicating the culture as a whole would not work, the culture does suggest a way other campuses can address stereotypical hookup culture's tendency to overpower and practically eliminate alternatives. Those who want something other than a "sexual encounter without the expectation of a relationship" have few options, especially ones that do not include social marginalization. Moreover, many students want some kind of relationship, even if they are not looking for marriage. If some of the relationship frames and scripts from Very Catholic campuses—like the "meaningful relationships" and "conversion" frames and the "hanging out" script— became more broadly accessible, they would provide resources that students on other campuses seem interested in. Is there a way that students can become aware of and utilize these frames and scripts without having to transform the entire campus to make it Very Catholic?

Evangelical Catholic students are present on all campuses. It is their faith and the practice of it that makes them resist stereotypical hookup culture. Unlike on Very Catholic campuses, though, most of these students find themselves on the fringes of social life. Finding ways to support them would not only help these students but also provide a clear alternative to stereotypical hookup culture. The existence of an alternative has two effects. First, one alternative sets a precedent for the emergence of other alternatives. Second, one alternative also makes its repertoires of frames and scripts available to students who may not themselves be evangelical Catholics.

An easy way to provide this kind of support for evangelical Catholics and generate alternatives to hooking up is to create a residential learning community. Typically, students in learning communities take a coordinated sequence of courses, are supported by social networks, and link their academic work with these networks.[17] Residential learning communities are established in residence halls.[18] These communities usually house fifty or so students on a floor or a wing of a building.[19] This living arrangement supports individual students, and these students show greater engage-ment with the overall institution, with their peers, and their studies.[20] In other words, through these residential learning communities, students support each other and, by doing so, succeed individually and contribute to the broader institution.

These communities have several characteristics that suggest they would be highly effective in supporting a Very Catholic subculture and thereby combating hookup culture. First, residential learning communities are well established in higher education. More than 60% of the colleges and universities in the United States have residential learning communities.[21] Moreover, residential learning communities are found all over Catholic higher education. Loyola University of Chicago has learning centers for the environment, leadership, health, and service.[22] Marquette University has a Dorothy Day Social Justice Community.[23] Duquesne University orga-nizes their learning centers around themes such as love, citizenship, jus-tice, reason, and the earth.[24] This list goes on, but the point is clear. These institutional structures are already in place, so adding one more would be relatively easy to do.

Second, the structure of residential learning communities would help address three key aspects that could support and sustain a Very Catholic culture: residence halls, worship, and academics. The residential space would have to be single sex or have limitations on visiting hours. While this would support the "no sex before marriage" script, it is also the envi-ronment that gave rise to both Mason's and Anna's pursuit of relation-ships that go beyond the physical to something meaningful.

The residence halls would also make it easier to offer opportunities for prayer and worship. Opportunities for communal prayer—offered frequently—could be posted in these halls. Masses could be held in these areas, or opportunities to attend public masses together could be coordi-nated. Times for common prayer could be set up for those interested in participating. The space in a residence hall would make it easier to get the word out about these opportunities. While these are primarily activi-ties connected to the Catholic faith and desired by evangelical Catholic students, they also provide those opportunities for hanging out with other students and getting to know them. In addition to providing "pray" and "worship" scripts, it also suggests a "hanging out" script. This script is useful to all students because it provides an easy way to get to know someone, a clear alternative to hooking up, and need not be connected to a religious activity to be useful.

Finally, these residential communities would be accompanied by an academic curriculum. There would be a sequence of courses explicitly on Catholicism. They could overlap with or be added to the core requirements. It would not require a specific major but could be seen as supporting it or as an opportunity to grow and understand the faith. It might cut down on electives, but evangelical Catholics would probably already be seeking these kinds of courses. A curriculum would only make it easier for them.

In fact, this last component could be made available to everyone and not just those in the evangelical Catholic residential learning community. A couple of classes taken in common, even loosely organized and even without the residential component, still helps students connect with one another.[25] By providing a community of students who support each other's decision not to hook up, this more modest program could mitigate some of the social costs that come from not embracing stereotypical hookup culture.

The main point is that these residential learning communities on campuses that are not Very Catholic provide an alternative to stereotypical hookup culture and make its repertoire of relationship frames and scripts available on other campuses, and many of these frames and scripts would be helpful for students to pursue the kinds of relationship they desire in ways they enjoy. Even if they are not interested in either anti-hookup culture or courtship, many students are interested in meaningful relationships and feeling free to not hook up if they don't want to. The existence of alternative to stereotypical hookup culture might make additional alternatives seems more possible. Perhaps this is the key. One of the main difficulties with stereotypical hookup culture is the way it cuts off students' options. By providing alternatives, Catholic colleges and universities can open up the possibility for students to make the decisions that they want.

PART II

Mostly Catholic Campuses

6

Mostly Catholic Campuses Hooking Up the Most

"MOST PEOPLE SEEM to have the mindset of hooking up with little to no consequences." I had heard this comment so often that you would think I was doing my research among a bunch of grumpy old men, sitting around complaining about "kids these days." I wasn't, though. In this particular case, I was talking to Emily, a college senior on a Mostly Catholic campus. She delivered the line in a tone of exasperation and continued, "I just feel like everything is very causal among my peers. Very few of my friends are dating, let alone in serious relationships." It seemed like almost everyone I interviewed on Mostly Catholic campuses said the same thing. Everyone was hooking up, no one took relationships seriously, and this was disheartening. Most students wanted relationships, but they hooked up instead. It was just the culture, they seemed to say, even as they lamented it.

In fact, students almost universally disliked and disapproved of hooking up, especially casual and meaningless hookups. Virtually no one I interviewed from these campuses said anything good about hooking up; only two students out of seventy-four described it positively, writing, "It's decent" and "it is pretty strong." Most preferred to be in a relationship— maybe not an intense, heading-toward-marriage relationship, but something more than what hookup culture provided.

This dislike of hooking up made hookup culture on these campuses strange because more than half (55%) of the students indicated that they had hooked up in the last year, and 60% of these hookups included sex. This not only means that there are more hookups on Mostly Catholic campuses than on other kinds of Catholic campuses but also that these hookups include sex at rates far higher than colleges or universities in general. In other words, despite their disapproval of hooking up, students on Mostly Catholic campuses seem to have a very active hookup culture.

Hooking Up for a Relationship

Brandon, a senior, had been in student government all four years and, shortly before I interviewed him, had been crowned homecoming king. His personality and charisma meant that he was the kind of person who was known by everyone on his campus. But while one might assume that hookup culture is made for popular students like Brandon, he echoed Emily's frustration. "Everything today is like a one-night stand and getting what you want with the least amount of effort as possible. People want instant gratification and pleasure. They skip over the 'getting to know someone' or 'going out on a date.' It is 'friends with benefits' or 'no strings attached.' "

Brandon wanted something more than this, even if he could not quite find the exact word for it. Dating, relationships, being together, going out, getting to know someone, none of them seemed to work. Brandon used the terms interchangeably or piled them one upon the other throughout the interview, struggling to clarify what he meant. He did, however, have a sense of what this something more should be: "Being together with someone is something that shouldn't be just sexual in nature but a way to fit the pieces of yourself together. It should be an experience that helps you to learn about yourself. . . . You should eventually find that someone that completes you and you're able to trust in the end."

Emily had expressed this same desire in our conversation. She wanted something that was serious. As we talked, she used the term "dating" for it. To her, dating was a middle way, something more than the meaninglessness of hooking up and significant enough to lead to marriage. "Dating is the only way to find a future spouse. If you don't date and don't get to know someone, then you will never get married." Like Brandon, Emily wanted something more, something meaningful.

When I asked Emily to say more about what dating entailed or how a person would begin to date, her pessimism returned. She simply said, "I don't know. No one dates." Brandon seemed similarly resigned. "Sex is the major component in a relationship. It is how a relationship is centered." Finding someone that completed him and that he could trust seemed just too much to hope for. They both felt stuck in a culture that they did not really like but that seemed to be the only one available.

As my conversation with Brandon was ending, though, he said something that helped me to understand a bit better what was going on. In a kind of summing up of his whole line of thinking, he said, "People have the idea that being physically active between each other is the main point of relationships, that sex is the glue that holds a relationship together. Hooking up is just a way to get there." Stuck in hookup culture but hoping for something more, Brandon voiced how students on Mostly Catholic campuses were attempting to turn stereotypical hookup culture into a relationship hookup culture. There were no other markers and no definitive categories to indicate what Brandon and Emily ultimately wanted.[1] As a result, some physical, sexual activity became one of the few possible indicators of a relationship, so students hooked up in hopes of becoming more than friends. The physical was the "point" or the "glue" that made a relationship.

Many others echoed Brandon's and Emily's view that sexual activity was the way to initiate a relationship. Students felt that, while casual hooking up was bad, it was also the only way to begin a something-more-than-friends relationship and the only marker that distinguished a romantic relationship from a friendship. This came out clearly in written responses, with almost 20% of the comments echoing this "hooking up for a relationship" script.[2] As one junior female wrote, "In college, it seems that dating is initially a physical relationship and then the emotional and virtuous characteristics become active after a certain period of time. Pleasure is a prominent field of interest while building a worthwhile relationship based on love." Or, as another junior expressed it, "I believe that long-term relationships in college are based more on character, but I still think that people judge the seriousness of a relationship on physical acts."

The Relationship Hookup Culture of Mostly Catholic Campuses

Brandon and Emily provide us with a window into the hookup statistics on Mostly Catholic campuses. On the one hand, the rates of hooking up are much lower than the average. As noted in chapter 1, for colleges in general, about 70% of students hook up, but on Mostly Catholic campuses, only 55% of the students indicated that they had hooked up in the last year.[3] On the other hand, when these students *do* hook up, they are *more* likely than

typical students to have sex. While only 40% to 50% of hookups at all colleges involve intercourse, it is 60% on Mostly Catholic campuses.

On the whole, students on Mostly Catholic campuses express dislike
for and unhappiness about hookup culture. The statistics support this as
these students do not hook up as a frequently as students in general. Even
with this dislike, though, Mostly Catholic campuses do not have an anti-
hookup culture. More than twice as many students on Mostly Catholic
campuses hookup than those on Very Catholic campuses, 55% in comparison to 26%. While there are people who do not hookup on Mostly Catholic
campuses, their decision is not the norm, and the dominant culture does
not explicitly reject hookup culture.

Still, if students dislike hooking up, why are they more likely to have
sex when the do hook up? The higher rate of intercourse during a hookup
suggests students' attempts to use hooking up as a way into relationships.
Sex means more for students. They seek it out for emotional attachment,
to initiate or enhance a relationship, or to show affection for the other person.[4] These motives are even more pronounced when religion is involved.[5]
It appears what Brandon and Emily indicated in their interviews is correct: students want something more, something meaningful, in their relationships, and the physical is the way they show this.

That students are using sex to help build relationships is implied by
another peculiar factor on Mostly Catholic campuses. Only on these campuses is there a correlation between gender and hooking up with intercourse. In general, women are more hesitant to engage in casual sex. The
risks they face are typically higher than those for men, so, when women
do have sex, they do so usually in hopes of or in the context of committed
relationships.[6] This seems to be the case on Mostly Catholic campuses as
well. While they were still more circumspect than men, women still made
up 45% of those who hooked up and had intercourse (see table 6.1).

Finally, alcohol plays a different, or at least an additional, role in hookups on Mostly Catholic campuses. Alcohol has long been known as an
essential ingredient of hookup culture.[7] Without it, there might not be a
hookup culture at all. Its use enables people to overcome their aversion to
casual sex with unfamiliar people. In her *New York Times* article "Sex on
Campus," Kate Taylor captured the typical role alcohol plays in hookup
culture well when she wrote that, "Women said universally that hookups
could not exist without alcohol, because they were for the most part too
uncomfortable to pair off with men they did not know well without being
drunk."[8]

Table 6.1 **Mostly Catholic campuses: Gender and hooking up with intercourse**

	Did not hook up with intercourse (%)	Hooked up with intercourse 1 or more times (%)
Male	27	55
Female	73	45
Total	100	100

P-value = 0.00; N = 327. (This number reflects only the students who were asked and answered this question. It was only asked of those who indicated in the preceding question of the survey that they had hooked up but not if these included intercourse.)

Table 6.2 **For Mostly Catholic campuses, student estimates for how often, "When students hook up, they usually hook up with someone they already know"**

		Never or rarely (%)	Sometimes or often (%)	All of the time (%)	Mean
Drinking alcohol	Never or rarely	20	80	0	3.60
	Sometimes or often	3	94	3	3.98
	All of the time	3	82	15	4.09

N = 508 (those who answered "Don't Know" to either question were excluded from this count); P-value = 0.00.

On Mostly Catholic campuses though, alcohol did something else. When I surveyed students, I asked them both how frequently "Drinking alcohol" and "hooking up with someone they already knew" took place on their campuses. There was a clear correlation between these two questions (table 6.2). In fact, the more students agreed that alcohol was used on their campus, the more they thought students hooked up with people they knew. This suggests that alcohol was not just used to overcome anxiety about hooking up with a practical stranger but also to enable a sexual encounter with someone known.[9] In this scenario, it would appear that alcohol helps one express attraction or interest toward someone they already know, helping them overcome their fear of personal rejection but also deviating from the stereotypical hookup script, which implies no attachment.

Together, all these pieces of evidence suggest a relationship hookup culture. When asked, students express their dislike of hooking up, but they also acknowledge that hooking up is the only way to enter into the meaningful relationships that they desire. Statistically, they hook up less than is typical but are more likely to have sex when they do. They are clearly not rejecting hookup culture, but neither do they seem to be fans of meaningless hookups. They have more sex and see it as potentially something more. Finally, whereas alcohol often enables hookups between strangers, on Mostly Catholic campuses, it seems to be used as a way to bridge the divide between public expectations of no relationship and the personal desire for one. Comments, interviews, and statistics all point to a relationship hookup culture.

No Real Alternatives

Given that 89% of students from Mostly Catholic campuses agreed or strongly agreed that "hooking up is sexual activity between two people without expectations of a relationship," how can they, at the same time, see it as a way into a relationship?[10] Shelly, a senior, seemed to have this same question in mind. When I asked her about relationships on campus, she paused for a while before answering. "In my opinion, relationships today don't start in a traditional sense. I think there is no friendship to get to know each other first and mostly people rush into things. From a lot of relationships I've seen, I think there is a good majority based off of sex and more of the pleasures that they can give each other rather than truly loving each other. This is just what I've seen with people my age though." I could not tell if she was speaking about her own experiences or about the experiences of her friends. One thing that was clear, though, was that she did not see a lot of hope for these relationships "based off of sex." For her, the "hooking up for a relationship" script seemed precarious, almost doomed to failure, because it is too rooted in the physical.

Shelly, though, was not completely pessimistic. She did know of good relationships on campus. "Not all relationships are like that. I know a lot of people who have been in fully committed relationships with no problems and have been together for a while all because they love each other, not because of what they can get out of the relationship." Shelly was voicing an alternative, a different frame for understanding relationships. She went on to clarify the two possibilities she saw. "I think a relationship could be a good or a bad thing. If it isn't good, you'll keep the past with you next time you're with someone. If it is good, it allows people to know what love is." Her alternatives were stark—one bad and one good. You carried the bad one with you, and it negatively affected your subsequent relationships. The good one was perfect. It was where a person is loved and learns to love. This good, though, seemed almost like a dream to her. She could not articulate how one goes about finding a good relationship, so she simply reaffirmed what did not work: "If it starts off with pleasure, it will go downhill."

When I interviewed Allen, I immediately thought "football player." While he did confirm in his deep voice that he had come to college to play football, he had stopped playing after a knee injury his freshman year. Since then, he had focused on service along with his academics, so that by his senior year, he was president of the school's Habitat for Humanity club and finishing up his degree in sociology. He was friendly and funny, if a bit shy. When I asked him about relationships on campus, he said, half-jokingly, "I don't know. I've never had one." After a brief laugh, I asked if he was hoping for one. He said, "yes" but quickly added, "relationships are very scarce today. It's all about hooking up, which leads to bad relationships and consequences. I don't really want this."

When I pushed him on this by asking whether good relationships were possible on campus, he paused, thinking for a moment, before answering, "I suppose. It would be a lot of fun to really get to know another person, but other people get in the way. They can tear relationships apart because they give you advice on what to do and how to act." As he saw it, while relationships could be good, the campus culture made it almost impossible. You either had to start out by hooking up, which just resulted in problems, or relationships were torn apart by trying to live up to the expectations of others. As Allen saw it, the only way to avoid these problems was to opt out.

Allen and Shelly disliked hooking up and thought that starting a relationship with a hookup just caused problems. For them, the "hooking up for a relationship" script that was supposed to guide their actions did not work. Shelly voiced an alternative way of understanding a relationship based on love with a "fully committed" frame, while Allen took the other possibility of foregoing relationships altogether. Neither of these, though, were easy or practical alternatives for most students. Even if students wanted the "fully committed" relationship that Shelly described—and, to be sure, not all of them did—there was no clear way, no script, to enter into this type of relationship, other than hooking up. Allen's rejection of hookup culture came with a cost, as it always does. He had never had a relationship. While he did not seem socially marginalized, as so many who do not hook up are, he was unable to find a way to get to know someone. A seemingly unobtainable, committed relationship and being alone are not real alternatives for most students. They would rather hook up, especially with the hope of a relationship. Even if it did not make a lot of sense to hope for something more from a hookup, which by common understanding entails no expectation for a relationship, it was still the best option or, really, the least bad option.

What is missing is the possibility of just getting to know someone. This was driven home to me by a particularly reflective comment from Dale, a friendly junior from a Mostly Catholic campus. In the follow-up to my question about campus hookup culture, I asked Dale about the possibilities for relationships on campus. He replied, "I don't know. It used to be easier, I think. I talked to my dad once, and he said he would go on dates with multiple girls within a span of two weeks, without any serious thought to a lasting relationship. The dates were simply occasions of getting to know someone. My sisters overheard this and were shocked. They equated his action to cheating—going out with another girl while just finishing a relationship with another." Dale's comment captured the challenge of just getting to know someone. The only options seem to be Shelly's committed relationship, Allen's being alone, or Emily's and Brandon's hooking up, and, from Dale's sisters' perspective, Dale's dad was not hooking up or alone. He was cheating on all of these girls. They had no other way to categorize what Dale's dad had done. A "getting to know someone" script did not exist.

Struggling Against Expectations

Without anything like a "getting to know someone" script, sexual activity becomes one of the only ways to express interest or distinctively mark a relationship as something more than friendship. Given that the "hookup" script opposes relationships, those pursuing relationships have to fly under the radar, covertly trying to use the only available script to move themselves toward a relationship, no matter how poorly suited that script is. Students have to operate indirectly and implicitly with quiet hopes and desires for something meaningful. This is one of the reasons for the ambiguity of hooking up on Mostly Catholic campuses. Students are never quite sure if a hookup meant more and are also at a loss for how to develop a hookup into something more meaningful. Even though 89% of the students agreed or strongly agreed that "hooking up is sexual activity between two people without expectations of a relationship," when students on Mostly Catholic campus were asked to described hooking up, 64% of the comments mentioned its ambiguity.[11]

- "Hooking up today means anything the participants want it to mean."
- "In my opinion, I feel that today, everyone has different definitions of hooking up."
- "I think that the word 'hooking up' means so many different things to different people. I also think that it changes over time for people."
- "I think that there are several definitions of hooking up. It can mean that a person is single and with different people. It can mean an attempt to find someone to start a relationship with. It can also mean that two people are in a relationship."

This ambiguity heightens students' anxiety, and, when people are stressed, they rely more heavily on cultural repertoires of frames and scripts for security and guidance.[12] On college campuses, this means turning to the "hookup" script to navigate the confusion. In my interviews with students from Mostly Catholic campuses, it was the men who most clearly voiced both awareness of and frustration with these expectations for behavior. Steve spoke in a leisurely manner, like a California surfer, but was perceptive about hookup culture and himself. "In college, it is more about hookups and 'talking,' which often ends with awkward interactions following the encounters. I think it is viewed too casually. I find myself falling into certain societal traps, but, when it comes down to it, I always think almost too morally or sensitively than most guys in college do, which has its drawbacks a lot of the time. Nice guys finish last, you know." His meaning became clear as the interview continued. He felt guys were meant to sleep around and not care. If you did care, it meant you were less of a man, a "nice guy," and would relegate yourself to being "just friends" with girls. As he later put it, "hooking up is almost always about your social status."

Almost every college male I interviewed on Mostly Catholic campuses expressed a dislike for the idea that they were supposed to hook up and not care about others or relationships. They also admitted that they knew they would be marginalizing themselves from campus life by resisting this stereotype or not living up to it. As Steve put it, they thought "morally and sensitively" about their actions but still found themselves living up to the callous, sex-driven male expectations set out for them. They fell into these "societal traps" and played the role that the "hookup" script dictated.

In *The End of Sex*, Donna Freitas devoted a whole chapter to how social pressure affected men.[13] The problem that Freitas noted was that hookup culture was the "only game in town." While there were some men and some women who wanted to participate (and enjoyed it), most felt forced to do so. Freitas' insight here was that it was not just women who were forced into this culture but also men. Hookup culture did "not so much cater to heterosexual men and male desire" but rather to their anxiety about living up to the expectations about what "guys" should be: "Women experience glass ceilings just about every which way they try to move, but men face an emotional glass ceiling. We ask that they repress their feelings surrounding their own vulnerabilities and need for love, respect, and relationship so intensely that we've convinced them that to express such feeling is to have somehow failed as men; that to express such feeling not only makes them look bad in front of other men, but in front of women, too."[14]

Steve was painfully aware of this situation. Despite acting like a guy who enjoyed hooking up, he saw the situation differently. "I find that the hookup lifestyle makes people incapable of carrying on a sincere relationship that does not call directly for sexual interaction. It numbs them in a sense, as I see it. I think it's too superficial and gets in the way of actually finding a good person that can be a counterpart." Despite all this, though, Steve still felt the pressure to participate. "I do understand where the temptation comes from though, hooking up and having little regard for other's feelings.... I try not to walk into a situation without anticipating something will be significant." Steve seemed stuck in the situation and saw no other way to pursue relationships. He knew what guys were supposed to act like, and it fed into the "hookup" script, and both of these were part of the socializing aspect of the culture that created pressure to conform. As well as he knew this culture and as often as he conformed to its expectations, he still did not enjoy doing so. So, as it typically happened on Mostly Catholic campuses, he positioned himself to be open to something more, something "significant," when he hooked up. He employed the well-known but barely acknowledged "hooking up for a relationship" script.

How does a hookup culture emerge in which the only way to develop something meaningful is to pretend that you do not want something meaningful? This is where the religious culture of Mostly Catholic campuses comes in. As Gianna (from chapter 2) said, people on these campuses "are very nice," and their campuses are "very hospitable." Students are socialized into this kind and welcoming attitude, bonding them together and providing a kind of safety net. The Mostly Catholic culture is not a Catholic culture that enforces explicit principles about sexual behavior. Instead it provides some common assumptions about how students should treat each other. To fully understand how this culture supports students' pursuit of something meaningful but also traps them in the ambiguity of a relationship hookup culture, we have to turn to this particular religious culture.

7

"Nice" Catholics, "Safe" Hookups

IN A SINGLE comment, Riley, a senior, captured the key paradox of Mostly Catholic campuses: "There is a big division on campus between those who are really into their faith, they call them the God Squad, and those that are not. The God Squad is a bit intimidating and hard to get into. They seem exclusive, and it is hard to bridge this gap. Everyone else might go to church every week, but they're also the people who party the hardest. They do what they want until 7:00 PM mass on Sunday. Most people seem like this."

Riley's "division on campus" is a peculiar one. At first glance, it might seem as if she divided her campus into evangelical Catholics like those on Very Catholic campuses and those who were not. But, in fact, everyone in Riley's two groups was religious. It was between those who were "really into their faith"—the God Squad—and others who "go to church every week." The actual division Riley noted was between students who did and did not "party." The weekly mass goers were also "the people who party the hardest," a Party Squad. They lived in a Catholic environment, one that surrounded but did not hinder hookup culture.

How does a culture where almost everyone went to church regularly and where some were "really into their faith" support a hookup culture? None of the typical explanations worked. It was not a simple case of hypocrisy. Nor was it students interested in the "college" experience before "real life." Finally, it was not that the students had abandoned the religion of their upbringing now that they were on their own. When I surveyed and interviewed students on Most Catholic campuses, I discovered little evidence for these interpretations. Students found the Catholic culture embedded throughout their daily life and were typically happy about it. This culture supported the students but, in doing so, also supported the hookup culture that most of the students disliked.

"The campus is very Catholic. It is very warm and welcoming."

Since both the God Squad and the Party Squad seemed to be religiously committed, I pushed Riley to describe the Catholic culture of her campus more broadly. She said that "the religious values are talked about in every class, by priests and professors. The campus also seems to treat you like a family. It is a small campus, so you get to know people. I went on a trip over spring break with some friends and stayed at this guy's house who I barely knew. It was great. He was nice. His parents were nice. It was during Lent, so some of us went to church together, like four or five of us, not everyone. There were nine or ten of us." While Riley noted Catholic values were "talked about in every class," the focus of her comments was on people and the way they treated each other. The Catholic culture, when it came down to it, was more about how people related to each other, welcoming them in and treating them like family.

Penny's view was similar. She was a typical junior, comfortable at her school and just beginning to be a bit nervous about her post-college plans. When I asked her about the Catholic culture of her campus, I was expecting a typical list of classes and campus activities. Instead, she said, "The campus is very Catholic. It is very warm and welcoming. It has clearly set out guidelines that are no secret. They are not hiding their Catholic identity. You see it in lots of places, in the pro-life club and the Relay for Life. You also see it in the nature preserve. They preserve beauty and history here. They keep buildings, even condemned buildings, for emotional reasons. Other campuses would destroy them." For Penny, yes, the school had Catholic "guidelines," but that was not what made it Catholic. It was the atmosphere. The campus was warm, welcoming, full of beauty and history. For Penny, being on a Mostly Catholic campus meant being in a place where the environment as a whole reflected Catholicism.

Together, Riley and Penny provided a good understanding of how students on Most Catholic campuses saw their religious culture. They did not refer primarily to the rules and regulations. Rather, they thought of how people treated each other, and how students, professors, and staff all interacted. These networks of relationships gave the campus its feel and created a Catholic culture that was "warm and welcoming." Gianna, whom we met in chapter 2, called this Catholic culture, simply, "nice."

This perspective was backed up by the written descriptions of students on these campuses. An overwhelming number of students (83%) indicated that the Catholic culture was strong, writing comments like, "Catholic and relaxed atmosphere," "Very strong and rooted in Catholicism," "It is very strong," "Strong in its traditions," and, "I believe the Catholic identity is very welcoming and calm."[1] Of these comments, 31% explained that the culture was strong because of the people on campus or their daily interactions with others.[2] Students wrote:

- [The college] is a small, tight-knit, Catholic community. Even though there are students here who do not identify as Catholic, EVERYONE embraces the friendliness and closeness of the community.
- "I would say we have a definitive Catholic identity. The spirit of campus is strong, and, just by looking around at the campus and the people, you can tell the spirit of God is working through everyone to make it the best campus it can be!"
- "The Catholic identity is very prominent in everyday college life on campus."
- "Noiseless, small, peaceful, and full of the western culture. Actually, for an international student, I feel very good when I stay on campus. Very good for studying."

Even the few negative comments confirmed that Catholic culture permeated daily life. As one student wrote, "It's very present. Most of the time it is an annoyance in day to day routines."

Students, on the whole, seem to be friendly, hospitable, and welcoming in their daily interactions with one another. It is how people are expected to behave. A "be nice" script guides them, and it is key to understanding how students are socialized in the campus culture. They are not required to accept or convert to the beliefs of Catholicism so much as expected to treat others with respect and kindness. The Catholic culture is "strong" because students act—or are assumed to act—according to this script.

Obviously, being nice is not exclusive to Catholicism, but, on Mostly Catholic campuses, being Catholic implies that one *should* be nice. This connection between niceness and Catholicism seems to be the result of a predominately Catholic student body. The vast majority of students (69%) self-identified as Catholics, and 52% of these Catholic students indicated that all or most of their friends were also Catholic.[3] On average, these students indicated that the beliefs that God exists, Jesus was God's son, the Holy Spirit is God, and heaven exists were "extremely important" to them (see table 7.1). Moreover, they typically attended mass

Table 7.1 Catholic beliefs of students on Mostly Catholic campuses

	God exists	Jesus is the Son of God	The Holy Spirit is God	Heaven is real	Hell is real	The Eucharist is the body and blood of Christ	Marriage is a sacrament	Contraception is wrong	Life begins at conception	The pope can speak infallibly on faith and morals	The Magisterium is a teaching authority
Mostly Catholic campus mean	4.51	4.35	4.33	4.45	4.11	4.10	4.27	2.96	3.93	3.62	3.96

1 = Extremely Unimportant, 2 = Somewhat Unimportant, 3 = Neither Important nor Unimportant, 4 = Somewhat Important, 5 = Extremely Important.

N = 422–423 (only Catholic students answered these questions).

Table 7.2 Catholic practices of students on Mostly Catholic campuses

	Attend mass	Prayed privately	Volunteered	Attended a religiously affiliated group	Prayed to Mary or the saints
Mostly Catholic campus mean	3.16	4.43	2.51	1.94	3.15

1 = Never, 2 = Once a Month, 3 = 2–3 Times a Month, 4 = Once a Week, 5 = 2–3 Times a Week, 6 = Daily

N = 422–423 (only Catholic students answered these questions).

almost weekly, prayed several times a week, volunteered, attended religious groups, and prayed to Mary and the saints at least once a month (see table 7.2). It is no wonder that the differences in the student body that Riley noted were not religious because almost everyone and almost everything seems Catholic. Students overwhelmingly think the campus is strongly Catholic, even the few who don't like that fact. The result of having a majority of Catholic students with strong Catholic beliefs is that the "be nice" script is understood to be an expression of Catholicism. This situation is also the case with the other dominant script of being "nonjudgmental."

"It was a non-judgmental zone."

When Riley first mentioned the God Squad, I assumed she was in some ways dismissing and judging them since, as she said, they were "a bit intimidating and hard to get into." I thought she was using them as an example of students who stuck out from the welcoming and nice Catholic culture. As she continued to describe the Catholic culture though, she said, "I went on ... retreat. It was a bit of an introduction to the God Squad. But it was great. It made me take my faith seriously. It was a nonjudgmental zone. As long as God was the focus, it did not matter. It was all good." My early impression gave way to a sense that the God Squad was not judging others, but they were just deeply into their faith. Riley did not judge them as they did not judge her. In fact, she articulated what seemed to be widespread on Mostly Catholic campuses: they were "nonjudgmental zones."

Being nonjudgmental was a recurring theme in students' written comments. One of the frequent ways students characterized the "warm and welcoming" Catholic culture was by how it accepted people. Thirty-three percent of Catholic students' comments noted this factor explicitly:[4]

- "It is strong but not pushy."
- "While there isn't anyone pressuring you to be Catholic, if you are, then you are encouraged to practice and fulfill your faith."
- "The Catholic identity on our campus is strong. But our campus is also very welcoming of those who are not Catholic as well."
- "It is strong, and I feel that the community here is strong, and that even non-Catholics are welcomed by the Catholic community here."
- "The campus has a very Catholic atmosphere and community. Everyone is very friendly and supportive of one another. However, if you are not Catholic, there is no pressure for you to conform. The campus is very accepting of all people."

These comments were not restricted to the Catholic students. The non-Catholic students made similarly explicit comments about acceptance 35% of the time.[5] These students wrote, for example:

- "I am not Catholic, but I feel as though Catholic identity is very strong but also welcoming."
- "I would say our campus finds our Catholic identity important but also is a relaxed atmosphere that is not that strict."
- "There are a lot of Catholics on campus, but they are open and nice to non-Catholics."
- "I would say that this school is only as Catholic as you desire it to be. As an atheist, I have not found religion to be 'shoved down my throat' while attending this school...."
- "There is a Catholic identity on campus, but it is not forced upon you."

Perhaps Penny captured it best when describing her best friend. "My best friend is not religious. She was raised Catholic but doesn't believe the stories in the Bible. They are just too fantastic for her. (I am fine with that. If I wrote down all that has happened to me, I am sure people would think it was too fantastical in twenty years.) She doesn't really feel out of place . . . just not committed. She is not sure if she wants to commit to it. Lots of people are like this. They are just not sure and don't know if they want to commit."

Communio *Catholicism*

Penny, like so many others, knew that people had different beliefs, and she was "fine with that" just as others felt that the campus was "welcoming," "not pushy." Religion "is not forced upon you" or "shoved down [your] throat." This "nonjudgmental" script for acting reinforces the students' description of the Mostly Catholic culture. It was not primarily understood as a set of rules to be followed. It was understood as a way to treat people. First, it was a "be nice" script: welcoming others and being kind to them, treating them with respect. Second, it was a "nonjudgmental" script. Students knew that not everyone thought and acted as they did, so they tolerated and accepted these differences. They knew they did not need to feel ashamed or hide what they believed, especially if they were Catholic, but they were also conscious neither to shove what they believed down others' throats nor use their beliefs to judge others as inferior.

The Catholic perspective of these students is a *communio* Catholicism.[6] *Communio* comes from the Greek work *koinonia*, which means something like fellowship, joint participation, sharing in common, and community. The term has been used to describe the understanding of the church that emerged at the Second Vatican Council. The council highlighted the multiple relationships that make up the church: the relationship of humanity to God, the relationship of believers to each other, the relationship of Catholics to non-Catholics, and the relationship of those living on earth and those living in heaven.[7] As an explanation of the Catholic Church, it makes relationships foundational, even if it acknowledges different types and roles for different kinds of relationships. As the Second Vatican Council's *Declaration on the Relation of the Church and Non-Christian Religions* notes, "One is the community of all peoples, one their origin, for God made the whole human race to live over the face of the earth."

Students on Mostly Catholic campuses were socialized into *communio* Catholicism. In part, this was because 69% of the student body self-identified as Catholic and, on average, affirmed most Catholic beliefs to be important to them and attended mass almost weekly. In addition, *communio* Catholicism found expression in the way students were socialized to treat others well. In the interviews and written comments, students didn't measure their peers against conformity to rules, the do's and don'ts. Instead, they viewed each other as part of the campus community. They ate and lived together, and, while they each had their differences, these were not reasons for isolation or marginalization. The cultural norm was to be kind and welcoming. Students were to "be nice" or, at the very least, be "nonjudgmental." Students were aware of how their peers treated each other, and this created pressure to adopt these scripts and became the way students integrated into the campus culture. The result of students' acceptance of these expectations was the evaluation of the campus culture as "strongly" Catholic.

Institutional Structures

This *communio* Catholicism was also supported by institutional structures. Ninety percent of the colleges and universities that students identified as "Mostly Catholic" on the quantitative survey had Catholic presidents. Each of these schools had a chapel where mass was said at least once daily and at least twice on Sundays. Each had a campus ministry that was staffed, on average, with nine people and an office of service learning that was staffed, on average, with two people. Finally, every student had to take at least two classes on religion before graduating, at least one of which was explicitly on Catholicism. This institutional support for Catholicism carried over into the daily lives of students. Those on Mostly Catholic campuses overwhelmingly indicated that it was "definitely" or "somewhat" true that Catholicism was talked about in the classroom and talked about among students, that students took classes on Catholicism, that there were student religious groups, that there were opportunities for volunteering, prayer, and worship, and that there were lectures on Catholicism (see table 7.3). The result was a Catholicism expressed in student relationships and supported by institutional structures.

This institutional support for *communio* Catholicism was present throughout campus life except in one respect. Students indicated that it was between "somewhat true" and "somewhat false" that dormitory visitation rules were enforced and that it was between "somewhat false" and "definitely false" that programs on sexual behavior occurred in the residence halls (table 7.4). In fact, students on Mostly Catholic campuses indicated that residence hall policies regarding visitation were enforced less than alcohol or drug policies.

While in theory, this might look like an inconsistency, in practice it was not. Institutional structures are not independent of the culture but rather arise from and sustain it. Since students are one of the main influences of the culture on campuses, they also influence institutional structures. On Mostly Catholic campuses, this meant a thorough support of Catholicism, a support that might feel more like shoving Catholicism "down their throats" if it were on different campuses with students who

Table 7.3 For Mostly Catholic campuses, student perceptions of Catholic characteristics

Question	Definitely true (1)	Somewhat true (2)	Somewhat false (3)	Definitely false (4)	Don't know (5)	Average
Catholicism is talked about in the classroom	50%	43%	5%	1%	1%	1.60
Catholicism is talked about among students*	34%	47%	14%	4%	2%	1.94
Students take classes on Catholicism*	71%	25%	4%	0%	1%	1.36
There are student religious groups*	85%	12%	2%	0%	2%	1.22
There are opportunities for volunteering	90%	8%	1%	0%	1%	1.14
There are opportunities for prayer or worship	92%	7%	1%	0%	0%	1.10
There are lectures about Catholicism	65%	25%	4%	1%	5%	1.54

N = 600–602.

* Equals 101% because of rounding.

were less open to Catholicism. Yet when it came to the residence halls, especially around issues pertaining to sexuality, these institutional structures felt weaker to students. It might seem as if Mostly Catholic campuses could take measures to strengthen their enforcement of visitation rules and offer more programming on sexual activities, but this would assume that students were open to it or desired it. This does not seem to be the case. Students hook up and use a "hooking up for a relationship" script, and the institutional structures reflected these activities, as well as the students' Catholic faith.

The Catholic Culture Making Hooking Up "Safe"

Josh, a junior, echoed Riley's and Penny's description of Mostly Catholic campuses. When I asked him to describe the Catholic culture of his campus,

Table 7.4 For Mostly Catholic campuses, student perceptions of aspects of residential life

Question	Definitely true (1)	Somewhat true (2)	Somewhat false (3)	Definitely false (4)	Don't know (5)	Average
Visitation rules for guests of the opposite sex are enforced in the dormitories*	38%	29%	15%	11%	8%	2.22
Drug rules are enforced on campus	57%	26%	9%	3%	5%	1.72
Alcohol rules are enforced on campus*	42%	36%	13%	7%	3%	1.94
There are programs in the dormitories about sexual behavior*	13%	18%	25%	21%	24%	3.26

N = 599–600.

* Equals 101% because of rounding.

he said, "I would say the Catholic culture is strong. The reasons being there are lots of people that go to mass, and there are lots of students that are Catholic. I also see it lived out on campus in person-to-person interactions." What made the place seem Catholic? Catholicism was everywhere, and it was reflected in students' daily lives and in their person-to-person interactions. The religious culture was strong and relational. No surprises there.

As the interview moved forward, Josh told me a story about something that had been bothering him for more than two years. "My freshman year, my pod mate was a solid dude through and through. He got up early to study. He wasn't Catholic, but his faith was important to him. (I don't know his denomination.) Then, after a tough week, he came back and said, 'I am going to get mine tonight.' I was surprised because it seemed so disconnected from what he was like. It stuck with me. Sometimes it makes me think that 70% of people here are hooking up."

This event clearly unsettled Josh. He seemed to glimpse up close with his roommate—who was a "solid dude," whose "faith was important to him," and who "got up early to study"—a disconnect between religious convictions and sexual activity. Josh recognized personally what Riley noted more broadly. There are students—Riley said most students—who "go to church every week" but are "also the people who party the hardest."

Josh and Riley noted the tension between religious commitment and hooking up. This disconnect was not the result of students abandoning their faith, however. Students on Mostly Catholic campuses indicated their beliefs in God, Jesus, the Holy Spirit, heaven, hell, and the Eucharist were "extremely" or "somewhat" important to them, went to mass almost weekly, and prayed several times a week. "Faith is important," as Josh said. Everyone went to church, even the Party Squad. In fact, this indicates why stereotypical hookup culture was not the dominant culture on Mostly Catholic campuses. Although these students were hooking up, only 55% indicated that they had done so in the last year, and this relatively low rate was linked to the fact that so many went to mass so regularly. The more often students attended mass, the less often they hooked up, both in general (table 7.5) and in instances that included intercourse (table 7.6). Since 69% of the students were Catholics who, on average, attended mass almost weekly, there was not a stereotypical hookup culture.

Yet students' Catholic faith was not expressed in conformity to the church's sexual teachings. Mostly Catholic campuses did not have an anti-hookup culture as they did on Very Catholic campuses. Mostly Catholic campuses did have what Riley termed the God Squad and others students described in their written comments as a "small group of extremely devout students" or "a small percentage of the student body" to which the "strong" Catholic culture seemed confined. This group of students exhibited the key markers of evangelical Catholicism. They indicated that the beliefs "contraception is wrong," "The pope can speak infallibly on faith and morals," and "the Magisterium is a teaching authority" were "extremely important"

Table 7.5 **For Mostly Catholic campuses, mass attendance and hooking up**
"Approximately how many times in the last month have you attended mass?"

		Never (1)	Once a month (2)	2–3 times a month (3)	Once a week (4)	2–3 times a week (5)	Daily (6)	Mean
"Approximately how many times did you hook up in the last year?"	0	21	20	21	73	24	22	3.69
	≥1	47	46	41	63	10	4	2.79

N = 391; P-value = 0.00.

Table 7.6 For Mostly Catholic campuses, mass attendance and hooking up with intercourse

"Approximately how many times in the last month have you attended mass?"

	Never (1)	Once a month (2)	2–3 times a month (3)	Once a week (4)	2–3 times a week (5)	Daily (6)	Mean
Hookups that involved sexual intercourse	0	15	13	14	36	9	3	3.22
	≥1	34	34	30	31	1	1	2.50

N = 221; P-value = 0.00.

to them, and also attended mass more than twice a week on average. Of these students, 88% had not hooked up in the past year.[8] These evangelical Catholics were highly committed not only to the church's teachings in general but also to the church's sexual teachings, bringing them to bear on their relationships. Thus, they rarely hooked up. Whereas on Very Catholic campuses, these were the vast majority of students, on Mostly Catholic campuses they were a minority, making up at most 15% of the student body. They still fit into these campuses as their preferences for personal faithfulness over preaching to others fit well with the "nonjudgmental" script, but they did not make up the dominant culture.

The tension on Mostly Catholic campuses can best be explained by the distinctive way in which *communio* Catholicism supports the relationship hookup culture. Students did not employ the church's teachings on sexuality. They rarely mentioned them in writing or in interviews and ranked many of these teachings as lowest in importance among all the church teachings I asked them about.[9] Even if students wanted to follow the church's teachings, they did not see how they could get to marriage or even have a relationship without utilizing the "hooking up for a relationship" script. The alternatives were either being alone, like Allen, or desiring a committed relationship with no idea of how to pursue it, like Shelly (both students were discussed in the preceding chapter).

Yet, students didn't abandon Catholicism and pursue meaningless hookups. Instead, students were socialized into a *communio* Catholicism and so put a clear priority on people and relationships. Students assumed—rightly or wrongly—that others were kind, welcoming, and hospitable, acting according to the "be nice" script. This script set expectations for respect—though not directly for sexual behavior—between people who hook up. Hooking up was made "safe" by students who were expected to "be nice" and use "hooking up for a relationship."

Even if the students failed to transform hooking up into something meaningful, the "nonjudgmental" script provided a kind of safety net. Students were not shamed or ostracized but rather found understanding. Friends were sympathetic and supportive, even if the hookup never resulted in anything more and even when the students were unhappy with themselves for doing it. Riley and Josh both noted the importance of friends. Continuing her comments about the Catholic atmosphere of campus, Riley said that "there is always someone around to help, somewhere, like a guidance counselor, and they are there all the time. You don't have to wait for an appointment. You can just walk up to a priest or friend for help." Josh said that Catholicism affects relationships because "you find friends with similar beliefs and they provide support for you."

An Achilles Heel

When I asked Chelsey whether or not the Catholic culture affected hookup culture, she responded adamantly that "it does." Given the forcefulness of the answer, I anticipated some explanation of the positive impact religion made on hooking up. Instead, Chelsey's answer was troubling. "Hookup culture is under the radar. It is sneaky. When I visited some of my friends from high school at another college, it was all out there. People would talk about it in public, out loud. Here, people don't talk about it. It's a small campus, so people know who hooked up or can figure it out. People sit at the same table with the same group of friends all the time. My friends on their campus are all sitting at different tables in the cafeteria all the time. And they just talk out loud about hooking up. It's wide open, bigger and louder than here. The ratio might be the same; just here it is not talked about in public."

Chelsey's answer revealed an Achilles heel on Mostly Catholic campuses. As supportive of students and relationships as the religious culture was, it provided students no way to critique or change the hookup culture that the majority was unhappy with. Chelsey's "don't talk about it" script, even if it was not widespread, was an example of how the *communio* Catholicism allowed hookup culture to dominate the social scene. Being nice and nonjudgmental meant not criticizing others, especially for hooking up. As a result, it became almost impossible to critique hookup culture because it sounded like one was critiquing one's friends and peers and therefore being judgmental. Tolerance was expressed through silence rather than through respect, which left hooking up as the unquestioned way to enter into relationships. It was assumed to be the way things are. Alternative ways of pursuing relationships—ones that might better serve what students wanted—were ignored or pushed to the sides. Students consistently indicated that they were unhappy with hookup culture and wanted something meaningful, but they felt stuck in the situation. The culture that emerges on Mostly Catholic campuses supports students but also is a kind of adaptation to the problem instead of resolving it. The situation might seem intractable except for the fact that students themselves are already developing alternatives. The challenge is to find ways to support and make others aware of what students are already doing. Mostly Catholic campuses need to give students what they want.

Follow the Students' Lead

STUDENTS NEED HELP, right? They don't particularly care for hookup culture, but it seems to be the only way to find relationships. The *communio* Catholicism of Mostly Catholic campuses seems to support it, providing more of a safety net than an alternative. Students seem stuck in a situation they want to change but cannot. Are they powerless? Helpless? Not really. Students on Mostly Catholic campuses utilize all kinds of scripts to find relationships. They use them to bend hookup culture toward relationships but also as alternative ways to meet people and get to know them. Students just need to be more aware of what they are doing so that these alternatives can be out in the open, widely utilized, and not result in social marginalization. Students want alternatives to hookup culture, and some students are devising them. Their schools need to encourage these alternatives.

Are There Relationships on Campus?

Both Allen and Shelly (from chapter 6) expressed interest in having a relationship, but neither seemed to know how to go about finding one. Allen didn't have relationships. Shelly, after describing fully committed relationships, only knew how not to have one. "If it starts off with pleasure, it will go downhill." Within relationship hookup culture, where the script "hooking up for a relationship" is rarely acknowledged and the desired outcome is unlikely, it might seem like there are very few relationships on Mostly Catholic campuses. Perhaps, as so many have suggested, dating is dead.[1]

Penny, the junior from chapter 7 who described the culture of her Mostly Catholic campus as "warm and welcoming," portrayed a more complex situation. "Actually, there are sort of four groups: a small group in committed relationships, a group in or looking for relationships, a group hooking up, and a group that doesn't care at all about it. They are busy with schoolwork or friends or club activities. I think that most people are looking for someone to start building a life with, someone they can trust and is loyal."

Students' written comments supported Penny's perspective. A large majority of them—almost 80%—indicated the existence of committed relationships on campuses.[2] The comments also suggested that those relationships took different forms. In response to the question, "what are relationships like on your campus?," students identified roughly three groups. The first group had entered into fully committed relationships. As one senior male wrote, "At least in my personal clique, relationships tend to be strong and long lasting. I myself have been dating the same person for more than three years currently after meeting them here, and I know a number of people who are in similar situations." A sophomore female echoed this writing, "Most that I see, or perhaps that I surround myself with, are generally healthy, defined relationships. Often I see couples going to mass together, hanging out together with friends, a balance of personal and social time."

The second group was made up of students who hooked up, a group of students that contrasted with those in fully committed relationships. These students wrote:

· I see a lot of solid, stable relationships. Such as those that I have met during freshman year and still speak with as a junior that have the same significant other. But there are those in which you see them holding hands, etc. with someone different every couple of weeks.
· Most relationships on campus are serious and will eventually lead to marriage. Other relationships are more as I would call it "flings" or "high school" relationships.
· The majority of people who actually are in real relationships seem to be very happy and committed to one another. I've noticed that people who get into relationships here are often in their relationships for a very long time. So although the hookup culture seems to be a very prominent thing on campus, relationships are not taken lightly around here.

The final group was often portrayed as occupying a middle ground. They were students who had "casual" or short-term relationships. They were neither hookups nor were they heading toward marriage. As one senior, a female, wrote: "Some [relationships] are solely for the physical hooking up and out of pleasure or lust. The other extreme is the people who meet early on, start to date, and by their junior or senior year are engaged and then married after graduation. It is the fast lane to a marriage that many grads are involved in. Some relationships are in the middle, though not as common." Others described these middle relationships this way:

· They vary a lot. There are very committed couples and causal partners.
· I think it's hard to generalize. I've known people who just hook up, people who've had several relationships that weren't very serious, and people who've been in serious relationships for long periods of time.
· All over the place. Some are so serious and married or engaged, others are barely dating, and some don't date but hookup.
· They either last 2 weeks or 2 years and not much in between.

Hooking up was not the only option. Students knew about hookups, of course, but many also knew Shelly's "fully committed" relationship frame. There was also a middle way—the "casual partners," "barely dating," and "relationships that weren't very serious"—that indicated a "casual" relationship frame. The first two seem particularly prominent, coming up in student comments and interviews about hookup culture. The third exists, but barely; there was "not much in between," and it seems to be disparaged as not "very serious." Student descriptions of it sound like Dale's sisters from chapter 6, who felt like their dad was cheating when he went on dates with different women in the course of a few weeks. There seemed little room for a "getting to know someone" script or a "casual" relationship frame. This marginalizing of a middle way was not the only challenge facing relationships on Mostly Catholic campuses, though.

Relationship Anxiety

Riley, who noted a God Squad and a Party Squad, was equally perceptive in her observations about relationships. She began by discussing hookup culture.

College is also fun, especially freshman year. You meet new people, you're at a new place, everything is exciting. It is the best part of freshman year. It loses its appeal your junior or senior year. I think if you were on a big campus, like 10,000 people, it would be like freshman year, so maybe there is more hooking up there. . . . People really hope for a physical and spiritual connection. Just a physical connection loses its appeal so quickly. People are social, they want more, but it is hard to go against the norm [hooking up]. I don't know how it became the norm. It's college. It's only four years, so you need to live a little while you can.

While this is a good description of relationship hookup culture, Riley continued by noting how these dual forces—one for something that is both physical and spiritual and one for the norm of hooking up—created precarious situations for relationships. She said,

A friend of mine had a boyfriend for four years, and then she just kissed another guy. She said she didn't know why and regretted it, but she was curious. It was like the Adam and Eve story where Eve was just curious about the apple.

Students' written comments seem fraught with worries about similar kinds of occurrences. Some worry about situations almost exactly like Riley's friend, writing that they knew people "who have their partner cheating on them." There was worry about abuse, "There are many relationships and I have yet to see any type of abusive or negative relationship between people. I'm sure it happens, but I have not been exposed to it."

Two concerns came up slightly more frequently. The first was an anxiety about sex becoming too important, more important than people and relationships. Students wrote statements like: "There seem to be a variety of relationship structures, but some definitely involve hooking up, although these may not even be true relationships." Or "some [relationships] are good and strong. Others are strictly pleasure." Or "few true relationships based on love and quality emotions; and more so based on physical attraction and a 'what can I get out of this' mindset." The second anxiety was on the opposite extreme—a concern that the relationship would become too important. Gianna, who described her Mostly Catholic campus as "nice," voiced this anxiety briefly during her interview, saying, "Some people do their things. They interact with other people. Some people give up their friends to seek out relationships but not many." Other students wrote, "There are either very serious couples who spend every minute of every day together, and then there are friends and friends with benefits" and "people are way too involved with their significant other and lose touch with their friends."

These comments are best read cumulatively instead of individually. There was not one worry that was mentioned significantly more frequently than the others. Together, however, these worries appeared in 15% of the students' comments and suggest a latent anxiety about relationships within hookup culture.[3] Students were not naïve and so recognized that relationships are precarious, even if they saw good ones around them. They knew there was ambiguity and risk in a hookup culture and with the "hooking up for a relationship" script, but they also knew that there was risk in pursuing and having a relationship on a college campus. Students worried about finding someone but also about being deceived or used or betrayed. How does one negotiate between the vulnerability needed for a relationship and the potential dangers that accompany such vulnerability?

Middle Way Scripts

Riley neither dismissed nor condemned hookup culture. She knew its limits, that hookups were strictly physical when people wanted something both physical and spiritual. Yet, she also knew that in order to develop a relationship, a person had to become vulnerable and take risks. What did she do? "Usually, you hook up with people if you want to find a relationship, but there is no one set way. People use alcohol or texting to start. It is easy to hide behind them. Being vulnerable is scary. You don't want people to cheat on you, and you don't want to waste your time with people. So you start off safe. I used a joke once. I read a book about 'parallel eating,' so I asked a friend if he wanted to go to the cafeteria and parallel eat."

Riley's "parallel eating" script was pretty clever. If she asked the guy to go to a restaurant, that was a pretty serious step, indicating an advanced level of commitment in a relationship that was beyond what she wanted. If she just found him in the cafeteria and sat next to him, it would not clearly indicate anything. So, she found a middle ground, directly asking him to eat next to her in the cafeteria. Her approach navigated between "not a date" and "not saying anything" in order to communicate "I'd like to get to know you better." It was a "hanging out" or "getting to know someone" script and allowed just the right amount of vulnerability. As clever an approach as it was, Riley's parallel eating was not unique.

Several people found ways to use a "hanging out" script. Penny noted that people drew upon their network of friends to find people to hang out with. "First, people start to mingle with the friend group of someone they like. It is a small campus, so you almost always know someone who knows someone. Sometime you just date your friends. Sometimes your friends say, 'you two should go out,' so you do. I think it is rare for people without connections to just start dating." Others used student groups, having classes together, studying, sports (both varsity and intramurals), and frequenting certain low-key bars to employ a "hanging out" script. The key seemed to be finding ways to talk and get to know someone through the typical occurrences of college life. This enabled people to share a little of themselves, be a little vulnerable, but also not risk too much. Like Riley, these approaches found the middle ground between a formal date and opting out of relationships altogether.

Gianna recognized that texting was a different way people got to know each other. "Being on a small campus helps because you have connections. If you tell your friend you like a person, they will say, 'I know him from class,' and then they can talk to a friend and can talk to the guy, and you can meet him to talk and then text." Gianna's understanding of texting did not imply a contrast with other "hanging out" scripts but rather saw it as a complementary one. Students enjoyed each other's company after having met through friends or at a club or in class, and these conversations expanded out from these particular places and times through technology. Through texting, people "hang out" between "hanging out" and negotiate between asking someone out on a formal date and doing nothing.

Despite the typical assumption that it isolates people, texting can benefit relationships. Just as Gianna noted, students often text as a way to get to know each other and figure out if they like each other long before they enter into any kind of serious relationship. After people meet in person, they can carry on a relationship by text, which provides some shielding as people become more vulnerable. People can use texting to indicate and strengthen attachment to each other even after relationships start. Of course, texting has its limits. It is not good for dealing with difficult topics, fighting, making apologies, and breaking up. Later in the interview, Gianna noted this when she said, "People will text and meet, and the meeting is awkward. Couples can text all the time but cannot talk in person." Penny seemed to grasp the same problem, "Texting, IMing through Twitter or Facebook is big. It is the stage before dating, 'talking.' It is hard to talk on the phone or in person." Even with the risks though, texting is clearly one of the "hanging out" scripts that students employ.[4]

Although not a "hanging out" script, discussions of relationships inevitably mention making them "FBO" (Facebook Official). Gianna notes it as one of the most obvious ways to know whether someone is in a relationship,

"I know lots of relationships on campus. I know a couple who just got engaged. They are around. You see the people together or you ask about them or you check Facebook. Sometimes you find out through word of mouth and sometimes you find out through Facebook." The particular value of the FBO script is that it is one of the few ways of publicly declaring a committed relationship. Its advantage is that it is a clear marker, one that is easy to use and admits of little ambiguity. While students so often feel that it is a bit ridiculous to have to use social media to formalize a relationship, they also recognize that not doing so inevitably raises questions about whether one is in a relationship. Without other scripts for declaring a relationship, it becomes difficult to avoid the FBO script.[5]

Together, these scripts make up a relationship repertoire on Mostly Catholic campuses. From previous chapters, students are guided by the "hookup" and the "hooking up for a relationship" scripts. Off to the side, though, are the "hanging out" scripts that are employed in the cafeteria, through networks of friends, during campus activities, and by texting. There is even a declaration of a relationship script enacted through Facebook. The difficulty is that only those scripts associated with hooking up appear widely shared between students and so make up the socializing aspect of the culture. The others are not. If they were, students would have a number of ways to get to know people other than hooking up. As it is, students are socialized into a relationship hookup culture, and this culture pushes other frames and scripts to the side. Students, like Riley, are left to create their own alternatives, or discover some through their small pockets of friends.

Follow the Students' Lead

Mostly Catholic campuses can provide support for these alternative relationship scripts and, in so doing, make them more likely to be shared and used by students. It should be possible for these colleges to do so because the students themselves have already done the difficult work. They have created a repertoire of relationship scripts. These provide genuine alternatives to hooking up for those who desire them. Without students as the catalysts, institutional structures would be tasked with doing more of the work and would inevitably struggle. They are poorly suited to act alone, and, when they do, their actions often come across to students as imposed, officious, or dictatorial. To understand this, just imagine the student fallout from changing visitation policies to make them more restrictive or adding courses to the core curriculum. Even if institutional structures were able to successfully overcome this challenge, their influence on the campus culture would pale in comparison to what students and their peers could accomplish themselves. When students have taken the lead in generating alternative relationship scripts, though, institutional structures can do what they were meant to do: support and sustain useful frames and scripts of the associated culture. This is a much easier task and more likely to succeed.

Mostly Catholic campuses can also help because of their *communio* Catholicism. This socializing force sets expectations for students to "be nice" to each other and to be "nonjudgmental" of people and their behavior. These scripts mean that people are disposed to being tolerant of new approaches to relationships and the people who employ them. In addition, *communio* Catholicism emphasizes the interrelatedness of students. While these characteristics are the reason why *communio* Catholicism supports relationship hookup culture, they are also what would enable it to support alternatives. Kindness and tolerance pave the way for alternative scripts, and student connectedness enables them to be easily shared.

One clear example of how to utilize this potential is the Healthy Relationship Seminar, a program that won the Association of Student Affairs at Catholic Colleges and Universities' 2015 Student Activities Award.[6] Mary Collins, the vice president for student affairs at Saint Vincent College, and Bob Baum, the director of student affairs, invite twenty students to gather, once a month, for a semester, over dinner, to discuss topics related to relationships. During the meals, there is a "speaker." Although the "speaker" is a professor, she or he is not to lecture but facilitate a discussion or activity meant to engage students and get them talking about relationships on campus. The hope for each session is to have students take the lead.

The topics include friendship and romance, unhealthy relationships, the influence of families, pornography, and the teachings of the Catholic Church. In one session, there is a "values auction" where students receive a set amount of fake money and bid for certain values that they desire for a partner. The list includes attributes like "belief in God," "sense of humor," "good job," "smart," and "likes to travel." After all the values have been auctioned off, students discuss why they bid the way they did, what they thought about what they acquired, and what does it mean for understanding good and healthy relationships.

Another topic is a "fake date" with another member of the group. The facilitators pair students randomly and take them to a local restaurant for a meal. The couples sit together and carry on a conversation over the course of a meal. The event usually happens halfway through the semester so that students know each other a little but not completely. Part of the exercise is to help young people develop conversational skills, and part of it is to manage the anxiety of talking to someone new. Afterward, students are brought back together to talk about the event, the stresses, and conversation strategies.

A final activity addresses beginning and ending relationships. Students are asked to brainstorm scenarios that occur around asking someone out and breaking up. These are written on a piece of paper and put into a hat. The "speakers" of the session begin by pulling out a scenario and acting as if they were in it. Because the improvisation is meant to explore how to handle the situation, it is neither enacted only once nor just by the facilitators. Scenarios are repeated. Everyone makes suggestions. Students become the principal actors almost immediately, and, after each scenario, everyone discusses what would and would not work and what they would and would not try.

As can be seen from these examples, the intention is to get students to talk and make them think about what they want, what makes a good relationship, what is campus life like, and what scripts work. Obviously, this requires students who are willing to participate in these kinds of activities, and this is why the program begins with invited students. Inviting students also enables the group to be representative of the campus as a whole. They are attentive to gender, race, majors, and sexual orientation. It also helps to ensure that the meetings are safe spaces for students to have honest and difficult conversations about hooking up and relationships on campus.

If it stopped with these invited sessions, the program would be effective in making students aware of alternative relationship scripts, but it has been expanded. During residence life training, staff go through an abbreviated version of the Healthy Relationship Seminar and are encouraged to develop programs that might work with their residents. They have encouraged former participants of the seminar to share the work with their friends or run variations of the program on their own or with their clubs and student organizations, in effect turning it into an "open source" program. Recently, they have also expanded the program to include an open enrollment for those who have heard about the program and would like to participate.

The Healthy Relationship Seminar is an example of how Mostly Catholic campuses can suggest a response to stereotypical hookup culture's propensity to suffocate anything other than hooking up. The seminar shows that alternatives can exist, alternatives that students desire, by just listening to and supporting them. It does not entail any kind of explicit denunciation of hooking up or new policies aimed at hooking up. Instead, the Mostly Catholic campuses indicate that listening to students and recognizing their different desires—some for hooking up, some for relationships, and some for something in-between—can be effective for providing alternatives to the stereotypical hookup culture. Of course, not all campuses are like Mostly Catholic campuses, and just as few are like Very Catholic campuses. What works on these campuses might not work elsewhere. What about those places with a different Catholic culture, ones less bound up with students' own faith and relationships? What about campuses where stereotypical hookup culture dominates? Welcome to Somewhat Catholic campuses.

PART III

Somewhat Catholic Campuses

9

Hooking Up for a Few, Relationships for a Few, and Nothing for the Rest

HARPER WAS THE first person I interviewed from a Somewhat Catholic campus. When I began my interview with her, it quickly became clear that this was a different kind of culture from the other campuses I had visited. When I asked students on Very and Mostly Catholic campuses what hooking up meant, they typically responded by saying something like "people get together, do something, and then go their own ways." It was a general response, with specifics left out. When I asked Harper what hooking up meant, she was direct. "It means anything from fingering or a hand job to sexual intercourse. Usually, I assume it means sexual intercourse."

It was not so much the explicitness that gave me pause, but that it came from Harper, a friendly sophomore, who seemed to enjoy her Catholic campus, even though she was a committed Protestant. This explicitness was unusual during interviews with students from Very and Mostly Catholic campuses. With Harper, though, it seemed perfectly normal. This was what it was, her tone implied, just a statement of fact. Stereotypical hookup culture was simply the reality on her campus. It was the way things were, so students, even students like her who did not participate in it, took it for granted. When I asked if hooking up was part of her culture, she replied,

Yes, definitely. It is on campus and off campus. People go together to other people's dorm rooms. Most of the time, when they are done, they just go back to what they were doing before they hooked up. When I was a freshman, I would see girls I didn't know on the floor. I assumed they hooked up with the boys on the floor. I knew most of the girls on my floor, and these girls would be dressed the way they were out last night, and their hair and makeup would be a mess. It also happens off campus. There are lots of houses off campus. This is where the majority of the parties are and where people go to party and drink. They go to the parties to drink, relieve stress or whatever, and they take home whoever they can.

On campus, off campus, Harper felt like everyone around her was hooking up. She was not sad or upset so much as detached—just describing what it was like. It was the culture surrounding her, even if she was not a part of it. She was not alone in thinking this, though.

Cole, a sophomore from a different Somewhat Catholic campus, offered the same matter-of-fact accounting of hookup culture on his campus:

Hookup culture is very present. We are a small campus, 2,000 students, 90–95% residential. Everyone knows everybody. They spend a lot of time together, especially in the dorms. Then, on the weekend, guys go out with guys in a group and girls go out without girls in a group, and they go to a party off campus. I wake up the next day and my roommate is with a girl in my room. They go out in groups and pair up at the party.

It turns out Cole did not participate in hookup culture. He was a Catholic—a "practicing Catholic" as he explained, different from "Catholics in name only"—so he didn't hook up. He saw it up close though, with his roommate. Much like Harper, Cole felt surrounded by hookup culture, a culture in which he did not participate. The view that everyone was hooking up was echoed by every student I interviewed from a Somewhat Catholic campus. These students felt that this is what college was, even though they were not part of it.

Everyone and No One Hooks Up

In response to the question, "does hookup culture exist on your campus?," 90% of the students indicated in their written responses that it did.[1] Within this group, they described hookup culture in one of four ways, all of which assumed the presence and prominence of hooking up. First there was a group, about 25%, who reflect the views of Cole and Harper, resigned to a prominent hookup culture even though they were detached from it.

- I can't really say, but I would assume hookup culture exists everywhere.
- It's hard not to have it on any campus honestly. It's the world we live in now, which is really disappointing.
- I am mostly oblivious to it. But it is generally through friends of friends and networks.
- Just as much as any other state or private school. A fair amount of the student body is not about the hookup culture, but being a virgin here definitely means being part of the minority.

There was a second, very similar group, one that affirmed the prominence of hooking up without specifying their relationship to it. They made up 40% of the comments.

- It's definitely prevalent among certain groups of students. Also, it's certainly closely tied in with alcohol use.
- It happens a lot because of the location and atmosphere of our campus surroundings.
- Every party, every weekend.
- It happens every weekend, among many students.
- [My campus] is a huge party school. With that being said, it is normal for people to go out on the weekends, get drunk, and bring some one back to their room. It is also normal for people to be hook-up buddies or friends with benefits. The hookup culture is prevalent on [my] campus.

A third group of about 20% wanted hookup culture to be more prominent.

- Pretty sad, there isn't a whole lot of (hooking up) in our campus.
- It's not as prominent as it would be at a state party school.
- Hookup culture is limited because of the number of students on the campus.
- Risky because you see the same people every day.

A final group of about 15% focused on the division on their campus between some who hooked up and others who did something else.

- Some people experience the normal college hookup, while others refrain. I would not say it is swayed as one way more strongly compared to another.
- I would say our campus is similar to most environments where there are a large number of young adults in an unsupervised setting. There is no pressure to behave in any particular way, and there are people who abstain from hooking up as well as people who oftentimes hook up, and a spectrum of behaviors.

Regardless of the particular perspective, every one of these views suggested the existence of hookup culture, one that was active. At the same time, they all implied a disengagement from it. The first group disliked hooking up, the second made no commitment to it, the third group complained about the lack of opportunities to hook up, and the fourth acknowledged that only some participate in it. Students from all four groups pointed to the existence of hooking up. Like Cole and Harper, they felt as if hooking up was everywhere. But few indicated that they themselves were hooking up. So is everyone hooking up? Or no one?

Stereotypical Hookup Culture

Most of the students on Somewhat Catholic campuses understood hooking up to mean "sexual activity between two people without expectations of a relationship," with 87% of the students indicating that they "agree" or "strongly agree" with this definition.[2] While high, this level of agreement is almost exactly the same with students on Very and Mostly Catholic campuses. It is an affirmation that no matter what kind of Catholic campus, most every student understood what hooking up was. The "hookup" script, whether students employed it or not and whether they approved or disapproved of it, was everywhere. It was part of almost every student's experience and part of every campus culture.

When asked how often hooking up occurred and how often hooking up involved intercourse, students on Somewhat Catholic campuses indicated that it was between "sometimes" and "often" (see table 9.1). In comparison, this means that students estimated the frequency of hooking up on their campus almost the same as those on Very Catholic campuses

Table 9.1 For Somewhat Catholic campuses, "For the following statements, please estimate how often the particular behaviors occur on your campus"

	Never (%)	Rarely (%)	Sometimes (%)	Often (%)	All the time (%)	Mean
Hooking up that does not involve sexual intercourse	8	3	28	36	24	3.65
Hooking up involving sexual intercourse	4	3	31	39	23	3.75

N = 108 (those answering "Don't Know" were excluded).

Table 9.2 Comparison of Very, Mostly, and Somewhat Catholic campuses estimates of frequency of hooking up

Scale = 1 – Never, 2 – Rarely, 3 – Sometimes, 4 – Often, 5 – All the Time

	Very Catholic average	Mostly Catholic average	Somewhat Catholic average
Hooking up that does not involve sexual intercourse	3.62	4.07	3.65
Hooking up involving sexual intercourse	3.02	3.81	3.75

Somewhat Catholic hooking up N = 108; Mostly Catholic hooking up N = 529; Very Catholic hooking up N = 195; those answering "Don't Know" were excluded from these counts.

and lower than those on Mostly Catholic campuses (see table 9.2). This is a bit strange. In written comments, 90% of the students on Somewhat Catholic campuses indicated that hookup culture existed and was prominent. Those interviewed felt like they were surrounded by it, but students' estimates as a whole were more modest. They point to a twofold perception: hooking up was everywhere, though not a lot of people were participating in it. Even though people consistently overestimated the number of students who were hooking up, the estimates on Somewhat Catholic campuses still suggested more modest participation.[3] So, while students were aware of the "hookup" script, affirming that hooking up existed on their campuses, they only thought that it actually happened "sometimes."

Table 9.3 Comparison of percentage of people hooking up on Very, Mostly, and Somewhat Catholic campuses. "Approximately how many times did in the last year did you hook up?"

	Somewhat Catholic (%)	Mostly Catholic (%)	Very Catholic (%)
0	55	45	74
≥1	45	55	26
Total	100	100	100

Somewhat Catholic campus N= 132; Mostly Catholic campus N = 571; Very Catholic campus N = 221.

The actual numbers of those hooking up provide one final piece to understand the hookup culture on Somewhat Catholic campuses. Students did hook up. Forty-five percent of the students indicated that they had hooked up in the last year (table 9.3). While it is not quite as low as the 26% who do on Very Catholic campuses, it is noticeably lower than the 55% who hook up on Mostly Catholic campuses. If one compares this to the overall estimates of college hookups (70%), it is significantly lower. There were students hooking up, but they were not the majority of students.

If one employs the narrower definition of hooking up as including sexual intercourse, Somewhat Catholic campuses still stand out. These campuses had the highest percentages of those having sex when they hooked up, with 68% of the students indicating that they had sex during a hookup. Mostly Catholic campuses were lower, with only a little more than half, 55%, having sex during a hookup, and Very Catholic campuses had the lowest rates of intercourse in a hookup, with only 48% doing so. Yet students on Somewhat Catholic campuses were also the most likely to hook up with sex only once (table 9.4). While some seemed willing to hook up and have sex, there was a large minority who tried it once and not again. For them, it seemed unappealing and so was not repeated.

On Somewhat Catholic campuses, students feel that hooking up is pervasive. They said this in interviews and wrote it in comments. They overwhelmingly insisted that hookup culture existed on their campus, and they were clearly familiar with the "hookup" script. Yet their actual participation rate of 45% contradicted this perception. The rates were low. Even the perception of these rates, which people typically inflate, was low. How does a culture seem to be everywhere even when only a few participate?

This is almost a perfect characterization of stereotypical hookup culture. First, it is a given, the accepted norm on college campuses. As was seen by

Table 9.4 Comparing Very, Mostly, and Somewhat Catholic campuses
for those who indicated that they hooked up with intercourse

	Somewhat Catholic (%)	Mostly Catholic (%)	Very Catholic (%)
0	32	40	52
1	20	15	10
≥2	48	45	38
Total	100	100	100

Somewhat Catholic campus N= 60; Mostly Catholic campus N = 328; Very Catholic campus N = 67.

Daniel in chapter 1, his participation in hooking up without expectations of a relationship needed no explanation. His behavior was what was expected of college students. As the norm, stereotypical hookup culture is what all students have to contend with even when they don't want to participate and even when they do not, in fact, participate. It is why anti-hookup culture and relationship hookup culture are both responses to the assumed default of stereotypical hookup culture. Second, stereotypical hookup culture rarely engages the majority of students. Many people do not actually participate. Many of those who do participate do not want to do so or want something other than a meaningless hookup. There are usually only a few people both practicing and enjoying stereotypical hookup culture, but these few are enough to make stereotypical hookup culture the campus norm.

Thus, Cole's and Harper's perspectives captured the stereotypical hookup culture on Somewhat Catholic campuses. Even though they do not participate, they experienced it. They saw hooking up in their own dorms and even in their own rooms. They felt surrounded by it, even though most students were not hooking up and even though the rates of hooking up campuses were the lowest of any except the Very Catholic campuses. Stereotypical hookup culture dominated Somewhat Catholic campuses, so students had to accept the behavior of those around them without questioning it. As the students said, "hookup culture exists everywhere," and it "is normal for people to go out on the weekends, get drunk, and bring someone back to their room."

Justifying (Not) Hooking Up

When I asked her why she thought people hooked up, Harper captured this sense of normalcy for hooking up, saying, "Everyone prefers hooking up. . . . Lots of students are just like living it up. 'We're young and we should enjoy it.'" Even though Cole said he didn't participate in hookup culture, he implied that it was normal behavior, at least for men, "I think they want the sexual experience. It's needed for late teens to early twenties. I think, from the male perspective, they don't want commitment. It's pure sexual desires. Males don't want to get bogged down by one girl when there are so many other fishes in the sea. I think women have a sexual desire as well, but I think they want commitment more than men do. I don't really understand why they participate in hookup culture. They are a mystery to me. Maybe they just want the sexual experience as well."

Both Cole and Harper articulated a "what college students do" frame to understand the pervasive stereotypical hookup culture. It was the idea that hooking up was what was expected. College students are young, and college is perceived as a time to be carefree, a period during which there are no consequences, no risks. When I asked students why people hook up, the number one reason was some form of this "what college students do" frame, with 48% of the students writing something like:[4]

- Easier to hook up in college and students are away from home
- They want sex without commitment
- Because sex is fun and fulfills a basic human need. That's why I do it anyway.
- I think as a generation, we are more likely to view hooking up as a natural response to being on a college campus environment, and we are more accepting of people who hook up than previous generations may have been.
- Sexual urges and the freedom of being away from home. There's so much temptation on a college campus, and college students want the sexual pleasure without the work of a relationship.

Of course, this assumption that stereotypical hookup culture was just "what college students do" meant that anyone who differed risked being marginalized, so students either suffered social isolation for not hooking up or bent and twisted stereotypical hookup culture to their own ends. Harper noted this dynamic clearly in her interview.

I think that hookup culture makes it harder to find meaningful relationships. I listen to my mom's stories. Lots of her friends went to college. They all met someone in college, had a relationship in college, and found someone to marry in college. Today, this is not easy to do.

If you don't find someone in college, then it is much later. I think the average age of marriage is like twenty-five, and I think it is because it is so hard to find anyone to marry in college. No one is looking to get married in college, and hookup culture does not make it easier. People are not looking for compatible people that could lead to marriage. They are just looking for someone to hook up with. . . . There is almost a prejudice against marriage in college. My boyfriend and I have been together for more than a year. We are thinking about the future and our plans, so we have talked about marriage. No one thinks this is ok. They say, "why would you get married?" It is like a prejudice against early marriage. No one is looking for serious relationships.

Harper felt that relationships, especially serious ones like marriage, were frowned upon. She called it "prejudice." It was not the norm and so pushed to the side.

Harper had to justify her difference, explaining why she did not hook up. "Me, personally, I always think of the consequences. Drinking to the point where you don't know what is going on. . . . I scare myself in thinking about the consequences. The consequences are real. You don't know people and don't know if they have health problems. You can always get pregnant. If you are too drunk to understand, that is not good." The form of Harper's response was typical. For those who don't hook up, there is a reason why hooking up is riskier than social marginalization. For Harper, it was the health risks of hooking up—disease or pregnancy. Eleesha in chapter 1 indicated she did not hook up because it violated her conscience and risked her future plans. Mia on a Very Catholic campus believed hooking up did not fulfill people who were "made to love" by God. What all of these people shared was an explanation of why they stood outside the norm.

Those who do not hook up have to explain to themselves and others why they are different, and the reason often includes an explanation of why hooking up is not appealing to them. This negative assessment of hooking up was the second most frequent kind of explanation given by students on Somewhat Catholic campuses for why students hook up. Twenty percent of students wrote some form of a "problem with hooking up" frame.

· They hook up because they are lonely and need someone to talk to or listen to.
· Because they either don't have the right morals or don't respect themselves or others enough.

- Because there are lonely, they are experimenting, and they just don't care.
- Drunk, pleasure, friends with benefits, lacking that close bond with someone else, making up for something they don't have.

These written statements all point to a perception that something is amiss and that these young people are hooking up for bad reasons. These students saw in hooking up a misplaced desire for love, or a compromising of morals, or a fulfilling of some need that could be better met in some other way. These statements say less about why students do hook up and more about why students do not. They are akin to the risks that kept Harper from hooking up, indicating (a) the need to give reasons for not hooking up and (b) the kinds of reasons students give for doing so.

On Very Catholic campuses, there was a clear set of frames—"made to love" and "conversion"—that were widespread and readily available to help students understand the purpose of relationships. This made their rejection of stereotypical hookup culture easier. On Mostly Catholic campuses, there was a "hooking up for a relationship" frame that people employed to bend hookup culture to their own ends. On Somewhat Catholic campuses, there was some variation of a "problem with hooking up" frame among students that helped them justify not hooking up. Still, this frame does not seem to be widely shared. It was mentioned less than half as often as the "what college students do" frame. Stereotypical hookup culture dominated and so established the socially accepted ways to behave. Its frame—don't expect anything from hookups— and script—go to parties, get drunk, hook up—are shared among students so that they know how they are supposed to behave. These behaviors are the default expectations, and, as a result, the "problem with hooking up" frame's influence pales in comparison to that of stereotypical hookup culture. This became even clearer in my interview with Jackson.

Hooking Up for a Few, Relationships for a Few, and Nothing for the Rest

Jackson was in the same situation as Harper and Cole. He felt that stereotypical hookup culture dominated his campus, noting its pervasiveness by saying that people hook up "because of social expectations and peer pressure. It's a vicious circle. It starts, it happens, it's expected, and this draws others in." Jackson did not participate and, as a result, provided a negative assessment of it, one that suggested an intentional justification for being different. He said:

> Hooking up means that a person with some amount of romantic interest did something that they will later regret. Hooking up implies no long-term commitment. It implies sex, a one-night stand. In my group of friends, it does not exist. In certain cliques, in certain social circles, it does. It is "inbreeding." It is just the popular, athletic, drunk every night, poor grades, not attending classes circle.

Despite the expectation that people should hook up, Jackson was in a relationship. "Some people are single. Some people are just here for sports or school. Some people are here for long-term relationships, and they find it here. You get what you are looking for. I started dating Leslie my freshman year, and we are still dating." A senior when I interviewed him, Jackson had been dating his girlfriend for almost four years.

Jackson stood out because he was one of the few students on a Somewhat Catholic campus who indicated that he was in a relationship. Like Cole and Harper, who felt that few were interested in relationships, students' comments suggested that relationships were only found among a small portion of the student population. Only 20% of the students gave positive responses to the question, "what are relationships like on your campus?" [5] The rest (80%) indicated that although relationships existed, they were not the norm. These students wrote:

- There are relationships, but mostly hookups.
- Dating relationships are not that popular on campus. Very few people date other people here. It's mainly just a group of guys hanging out with a group of girls, with sexual activity between the groups.
- There are couples who are easily identified on campus. But the majority of students, in my opinion, do not seek relationships. A lot of people have told me, "We are still young. I need to live it up while I can, and that means not getting in a relationship with anyone."
- Relationships in general are not very common and are not very serious or responsible.

While there did seem to be a few relationships on campus, the numbers did not indicate they were abundant. On Somewhat Catholic campuses, the only demographic factor correlated with hooking up was gender, and

**Table 9.5 Gender and hooking up on Somewhat
Catholic campuses**

	Males (%)	Females (%)
0 hookups in the last year	65	47
1 or more hookups in the last year	35	53
Total	100	100

N = 131; P-value = 0.04.

this correlation suggested that being a woman meant one was more likely
to have hooked up (table 9.5). Based on the broader research about gender
and hooking up, this correlation provided some support for a relationship
hookup culture, as women more often than men want a relationship out
of hooking up. In his research, Justin Garcia found that "65% of women
and 45% of men reported that they hoped their hookup encounter would
become a committed relationship."[6] Moreover, Garcia found that 51% of
women and 42% of men explicitly asked about relationships after hooking
up.[7] Lisa Wade and Caroline Heldman found that women want to hook
up with those whom they at least were "in-like" with if not "in-love" with.[8]

This is a very tenuous claim for a relationship hookup culture, though,
and it is further attenuated by the statistics on hooking up that included
intercourse. While gender was correlated with hooking up in general, it
was not correlated with hooking up that included intercourse. For students who had intercourse during a hookup, those were most likely to
do so only once. This is often a sign of regret, a sense of being used and
feeling like the act was meaningless.[9] Usually, sex occurs on a regular or
ongoing basis within the context of a relationship.[10] If it were a relationship hookup culture, sex might indicate greater intimacy or commitment
in relationships. For this to be the case, though, there should be some indication that people were hooking up and having sex with individuals they
were interested in. On Somewhat Catholic campuses, however, there were
no correlations between hooking up with intercourse and any factor that
might point to greater intimacy, factors like "hooking up with someone
known." Everything suggests that people who had sex during a hookup
adhered closely to the "hookup" script of having no expectations afterward.

Thus, there is little to no indication of a widespread relationship
hookup culture. The students knew of relationships on campus but typically thought they were few and far between. Jackson and Harper had

relationships, but they felt out of sync with everyone else. They had to explain being different to their peers as well as explain why they were not interested in hooking up. Jackson's friends had different priorities than the "inbreeding" group, and Harper thought of the risks. This was, in part, because stereotypical hookup culture was the norm, and deviating from it was risky, often incurring the social penalty of isolation and marginalization. People can resist hookup culture, but because stereotypical hookup culture was seen as the norm, even if few actually participate in it, those who opt out would be unlikely to publically deviate from it.[11]

The result is a strange mix. In comparison to Mostly Catholic campuses and colleges in general, not many students were hooking up on Somewhat Catholic campuses, even though stereotypical hookup culture prevailed. Most (55%) do not participate in it. There were relationships, but nothing indicated that relationships were widespread. Students seemed left with few options. Hooking up for a few, relationships for a few, and nothing for the rest. Stereotypical hookup culture on Somewhat Catholic campuses suffocated other alternatives, allowing for little deviation.

In the comments, one student wrote, "I personally don't like the notion of 'drunk' sex, but if two people consensually decide to be sexually active, then nobody should be able to tell them they're wrong." One just wishes that this same level of tolerance would be extended to those who wanted alternatives to hooking up. Wanting a relationship or not wanting to hook up should be as acceptable and easily enacted as "drunk" sex.

10

Catholicism: There if You Want It but Not in Your Face

JACKSON DID NOT hook up, believing that it reflected a lack of seriousness befitting a college student. As noted in the previous chapter, he thought hooking up was for the "popular, athletic, drunk every night, poor grades, not attending classes circle." Although he did not hook up, and neither did his friends, it wasn't for religious reasons. Jackson said he was agnostic "at best." Why did he come to a Catholic school? "[My school] gives a lot of money to come here, and that is a good reason to come." When I asked him about his interactions with the Catholic culture of the campus, he explained it this way, "If you want to be involved, you can be. If you're just here for academics, it's ignorable. It's not all-encompassing. This has not much changed since I started here." He sounded almost exactly like Brooklyn (from chapter 2), who said that the Catholic culture on her campus "is there if you want it but is not in your face. There are things available if you seek them out."

Cole was a very committed Catholic, a "practicing" Catholic as he called it, on a Somewhat Catholic campus. He seemed disappointed in his campus Catholic culture. When I asked him to describe it, he said,

> I have to say when I came to campus I thought it would be Catholic. I am Roman Catholic, and I assumed everyone would be Roman Catholic and the culture would be overwhelmingly Roman Catholic. It turns out the culture is like any other campus, Catholic or state school. My college is about 45% Catholic but most of those are Catholic in name only. On Sunday nights, the chapel is almost empty. Only a certain percentage of people practice their faith. Most

don't. Some actually lose their faith. Hookup culture is very present but the Catholic culture not so much. The university's campus ministry is very active, but it is just for those who are interested in it. It is just for those who seek it out. It is not an evangelical campus.

Jackson and Cole were not alone in thinking that the religious culture on Somewhat Catholic campuses was available for those who were interested in it but avoided by those who were not. In response to the question, "How would you describe the Catholic identity of your campus?," about 30% of the students' comments affirmed the presence of a Catholic culture:[1]

- I feel it's very strong and true.
- As a Catholic school, we focus on the values the church holds throughout the curriculum.
- It is very dominant in everything around campus.
- It is pretty heavy with the different classes we have to take.
- Very Catholic.

However, most students on Somewhat Catholic campuses (57%) felt that this Catholicism was mostly just in the background of campus life.[2] Their comments were something like the following:

- There are pictures and statues around campus, but the religion isn't incorporated into teachings.
- They do not push being Catholic.
- About half of the student population is Catholic, but it is not forced or pushed upon students.
- It is present, and sometimes professors preach a little too much. But we also have freedom to be who we want to be.
- While many students strongly participate in the Catholic faith, there are just as many that do not.
- [My campus] certainly gives students opportunities to pursue their Catholic faith, but it is not widely taken advantage of.

Although Jackson and Cole were coming from contrasting religious perspectives, both their perspectives captured what so many other students experienced as the religious culture of Somewhat Catholic campuses. It was present but rarely affected the daily lives of students. It was "there if you want it but is not in your face."

Institutional Catholicism

It is not that Somewhat Catholic campuses had no institutional structures supporting Catholicism. They did, even if they were not as prominent as on other Catholic campuses. Mass was offered once during weekdays and once on Sundays, whereas Mostly and Very Catholic campuses offered mass daily and several times on Sunday. Somewhat Catholic campuses had one required class on Catholicism in the core, whereas Most Catholic campuses had two and Very Catholic campuses had three. There were few limits on coed visitation on Somewhat Catholic campuses, like having nonvisitation hours limited to less than five hours a day, having limits just on freshmen, or enforcing them only if an issue arises with a roommate.[3] By contrast, Mostly Catholic campuses had more limits on visiting hours, and Very Catholic campuses allowed very little in room coed visitation, if any. Somewhat Catholic campuses typically had no single-sex residence halls. Mostly Catholic campuses had a few single-sex floors or dorms, and Very Catholic campuses had almost all single-sex residence halls. Even with these differences though, students on Somewhat Catholic campuses still felt the religious culture. Their average perceptions for institutional structures like taking classes on Catholicism hovered around "somewhat true," opportunities for worship around "definitely true," and enforcement of visitation policies around "somewhat true" (see table 10.1).

Students also saw the Catholic culture in other ways. Cole said he experienced it in a variety of places.

> Other campuses hand out condoms. We don't. It would be diametrically opposed to the mission. There are crosses in every classroom.... It is in the core curriculum and requires three religion classes. There are ones on Catholic values. There is one on the intellectual journey.... We take the study of religious texts and delve into the Bible, Hebrew Scriptures, and the Qur'an.

Student comments corresponded closely with Cole's perspective. What students noted most frequently were the crucifixes in the classroom and the presence of priests or nuns teaching, with 66% of the comments including these factors.[4]

What frustrated Cole, though, was that he came to campus looking for a Catholic culture, but once he arrived, felt like it was in the background and his peers were not interested in it.

Table 10.1 **For Somewhat Catholic campuses, "How true are the following statements about your college or university?"**

	Definitely true (%)	Somewhat true (%)	Somewhat false (%)	Definitely false (%)	Mean
Students take classes on Catholicism	65	30	4	1	1.39
There are opportunities for prayer and worship	91	8	0	1	1.10
Visitation rules for guests of the opposite sex are enforced in the dormitories**	37	30	14	20	2.16

N = 137 for each row (those who answered "Don't Know" were excluded).

** Equals more than 100% because of rounding.

They [the core curriculum religion classes] do not have a good repu-tation. People just want to get them out of the way. They don't like Gen Ed requirements in general. They don't see how they fit into their careers, so they just want them over. The science requirement, they don't like more. The religion requirement, people understand it's just part of the mission and agreed to take it when they came here, so they just want to get it over.

The main difference in Jackson's view was that he was comfortable with Catholicism being in the background, whereas Cole was disappointed by it. Apart from this difference in opinion, Jackson provided a strikingly similar description as Cole.

It [the Catholic culture] is integrated and separate. There are service projects and mass, but if you don't look for it, you're not aware of it. The identity of the college is there but is not overbearing. The priests teach and walk around. There are crucifixes in every room. There are works of art everywhere. There is religious art all down the hall-ways, not in the dorms though. There are crucifixes in the dorms.

The Catholic presence was there. There were priests and crucifixes. Still, it was easy to avoid. Like Cole's peers, Jackson knew the place was Catholic, and he tolerated that, but rarely did he seem interested in it.

Jackson's view probably represented the majority of students' views on Somewhat Catholic campuses. Unlike students on Very Catholic campuses, where 83% noted prayer and worship as signs of the campus' Catholicism, only 47% of the students on Somewhat Catholic campuses noted these aspects. Unlike Mostly Catholic campuses, where 31% of students noted how people treat each other as a sign of the Catholic culture, only 10% of the students on Somewhat Catholic campuses noted it. In other words, students noted Catholicism mostly in terms of crucifixes hanging on the walls and less in the actions of students. Typical student responses to the question, "What aspects of life on your campus seem Catholic to you?" were:

- There really isn't too many aspects of Catholic teaching around the school. The masses are not mandatory (thankfully), and there isn't a strong push for religion.
- Just the chapel.
- Crosses in classroom, that's all, nothing else.
- There are friars on our campus.
- The fact that we have to take a ton of religious based classes just to graduate.
- Well there is the church and the religious classes as well as several religious clubs. Then on the other side of things, there are the drunken weekends with random hookups and of course drugs. Seems pretty Catholic to me no?

Every student seemed to know the campus was Catholic and could identify aspects as Catholic. Mainly, though, these aspects were institutional structures. Classes, crosses, and clergy: these three seemed to be most indicative of the presence of Catholicism, a presence clearly in the background. Before making any judgment on this institutional support for Catholicism, whether good or bad, one should be aware that these structures closely reflect the students and their preferences about the faith.

Not Part of Daily Interactions

Students on Somewhat Catholic campuses were religiously diverse (see table 10.2). A high percentage of students were Catholic, with 67%

Table 10.2 For Somewhat Catholic campuses:
Students religious affiliation

Christian—Catholic	67%
Christian—Protestant/Christian—Other*	15%
Atheist, Agnostic, Other**	15%
Other Religions***	3%

N = 144.

* Those who indicated Christian—Others were asked to specify. Answers included nondenominational, Lutheran, Episcopalian, Baptist, Presbyterian, Methodist, and Apostolic.

** Those who indicated Other were asked to specify. Answers included: none, spiritual but not religious, and pagan.

*** Other religions included Buddhism, Hinduism, Islam, and Judaism.

identifying as such, but they also had a large number of non-Catholic Christians at 15% and a large number of atheist, agnostic, and unaffiliated at 15%. They also had a few students (3%) affiliated with other world religions.

This diversity also existed among the Catholic students. In general, Catholic students indicated that beliefs like "God exists" and" Jesus is God" were between "somewhat important" and "extremely important" for them (see table 10.3). These students also, on average, attended mass two to three times a month, prayed a little more than once a week, and volunteered a few times a month (see table 10.4). By comparison, the Catholic beliefs of students on Somewhat Catholic campuses were very similar to students on Mostly and Very Catholic campuses, and they engaged in Catholic activities a little more than students on Most Catholic campuses and a little less than students on Very Catholic campuses. While one might expect the students to be less committed to Catholicism, they seem pretty typical for the campuses I surveyed and perhaps even for Catholic students in general.[5]

Not all the Catholic students were like this, though. Most of the beliefs and activities noted in tables 10.3 and 10.4 result from the majority of students indicating the same level of importance for beliefs and the same level of frequency for activities. The distribution is a bell curve. However, when one gets to some of the evangelical Catholic beliefs and activities, the average is different. It is lower than the other

Table 10.3 For Somewhat Catholic campuses, "How important are the following Catholic beliefs for you?"

Extremely Unimportant 1, Somewhat Unimportant 2, Neither Important nor Unimportant 3, Somewhat Important 4, Extremely Important 5

	Somewhat Catholic campuses	Mostly Catholic campuses	Very Catholic campuses
God exists	4.57	4.51	4.47
Jesus is the Son of God	4.43	4.35	4.43
The Holy Spirit is God	4.36	4.33	4.44
Heaven is real	4.35	4.45	4.45
Hell is Real	3.91	4.11	4.36
The Eucharist is the body and blood of Christ	4.21	4.10	4.44
Marriage is a sacrament	4.28	4.27	4.44
Contraception is wrong	2.47	2.96	4.11
Life begins at conception	3.95	3.93	4.42
The pope can speak infallibly on faith and morals	3.16	3.62	4.25
The Magisterium is a teaching authority	3.40	3.96	4.28

Somewhat Catholic campuses N = 93; Mostly Catholic campuses N = 422–423; Very Catholic campuses N = 226–227. Those who answered "Don't Know" were excluded from these averages.

Table 10.4 For Somewhat Catholic campuses, "Approximately how many times in the last month have you. . . ."

Never 1, Once a month 2, 2–3 Times a month 3, Once a week 4, 2–3 times a week 5, daily 6

	Somewhat Catholic campus	Mostly Catholic campus	Very Catholic campus
Attended mass	3.36	3.16	4.67
Prayed privately	4.53	4.43	5.45
Volunteered	2.81	2.51	2.71
Attended a religiously affiliated group	1.97	1.94	2.80
Prayed to Mary or the saints	3.24	3.15	5.18

Somewhat Catholic campus N = 94; Mostly Catholic campus N = 422–423; Very Catholic campus N = 226–227.

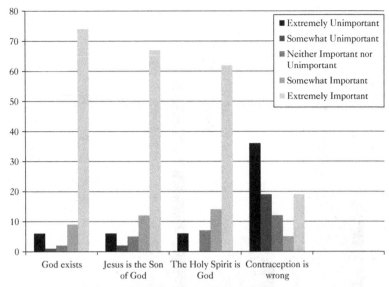

FIGURE 10.1 Catholic students on Somewhat Catholic campus: Importance of Catholic beliefs

beliefs, and it emerges from extremes at two ends, a bimodal distribution. For the distinctive evangelical Catholic belief that "contraception is wrong," there is a divide between 38% of the students who find it to be "extremely unimportant" and 21% who find it "extremely important" (see figure 10.1). While most students have similar rates of attending mass, praying privately, and volunteering, those praying to the saints are divided between 37% who "never" do it and 25% who do it "daily" (see figure 10.2). Finally, while most Catholic students on Somewhat Catholic campuses attend mass almost weekly, about 19% of students go to mass more than once a week and about the same percentage "never" go (see figure 10.2).

This subgroup of evangelical Catholic students is just one form of Catholicism on Somewhat Catholic campuses. They make up about 20% of the Catholic population, but there is also a group of Catholic students, a little less than 20%, who indicate that their beliefs are important to them, though they do not attend mass. This means that there is another 60% of Catholics who are not evangelical Catholics but do believe and regularly attend mass. Together, these different groups represent the 67% of the student population on Somewhat Catholic campuses. These students are complemented by 15% of the students who are Protestants, 15% who are atheistic, agnostics, and unaffiliated, and 3% who identify with other

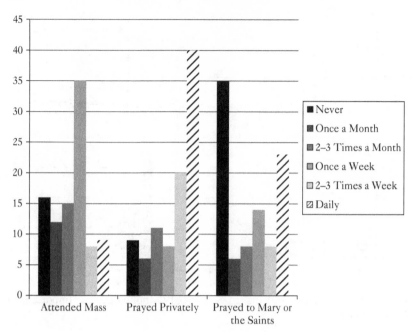

FIGURE 10.2 Catholic students on Somewhat Catholic campus: How frequently they engage in Catholic activities

religions. Such diversity suggests that the Catholic culture is not a social-izing force on Somewhat Catholic campuses. It is not something bringing students together.

This becomes apparent when you look at student interactions sur-rounding Catholicism. First, the more Catholic friends Catholics have, the more they feel that the campus is Catholic. On average, Catholic students on Somewhat Catholic campuses said that only "some" of their friends shared their Catholic faith, whereas on Very Catholic campuses, the most common answer was "all" and it was "most" on Mostly Catholic cam-puses (see table 10.5). Second, students on Somewhat Catholic campuses believed that the statement, "students talk about Catholicism," was some-where between "somewhat true" and "somewhat false," whereas students on Very Catholic campuses indicated that it was "definitely true," and stu-dents on Mostly Catholic campuses said that it was "somewhat true" (see table 10.6). Finally, on Somewhat Catholic campuses, students indicated that the statement, "Catholicism is talked about in the classroom," was "somewhat true," whereas those on Mostly Catholic campuses said it was more between "definitely true" and "somewhat true," and those on Very Catholic said it was "definitely true" (see table 10.7).

Table 10.5 Institutional classification and shared faith (Catholic)

	How many of your friends share your religious beliefs? (Catholic)				
	None	Some	Most	All	Mean
Somewhat Catholic campuses	1	47	45	0	2.47
Mostly Catholic campuses	4	198	212	9	2.53
Very Catholic campuses	1	42	168	16	2.88

Somewhat Catholic campuses N = 141; Mostly Catholic campuses N = 423; Very Catholic campuses N = 227.

Table 10.6 Catholicism is talked about among students

	Definitely true	Somewhat true	Somewhat false	Definitely false	Mean[*]
Somewhat Catholic campuses	27	72	24	6	2.13
Mostly Catholic campuses	201	283	82	21	1.86
Very Catholic campuses	212	24	5	0	1.14

Somewhat Catholic campuses N = 127; Mostly Catholic campuses N = 587; Very Catholic campuses N = 241.

[*] Those who answered "Don't Know" were excluded from the average.

Table 10.7 Catholicism is talked about in the classroom

	Definitely true	Somewhat true	Somewhat false	Definitely false	Mean[*]
Somewhat Catholic campuses	58	67	7	4	1.68
Mostly Catholic campuses	300	261	30	6	1.57
Very Catholic campuses	208	31	1	0	1.13

Somewhat Catholic campuses N = 137; Mostly Catholic campuses N = 602; Very Catholic campuses N = 241.

[*] Those who answered "Don't Know" were excluded from the average.

All of these factors help illustrate the distinctiveness of Somewhat Catholic campuses. There are Catholics. Most go to mass, pray almost weekly, and their Catholic beliefs are important to them. Others indicate many of the Catholic beliefs are important to them but do not go to mass, and still others are evangelical Catholics who go to mass several times a week. Beyond this diversity is the broader religious diversity of the campus that includes Protestants, atheists, agnostics, the unaffiliated, and those who belong to other religions. As a result, networks of friends include more religious diversity, and Catholicism will not be what connects them to one another. Without this common Catholicism, it is unsurprising that students, on the whole, do not typically talk about Catholicism among themselves and in the classroom. Catholicism is around but usually in the form of crucifixes on the walls and priests and nuns who teach. It does not seem to be part of students' daily interactions. Students indicated that this made their campus "somewhat" Catholic, and it is a distinctive configuration of Catholicism.

Accompanying Catholicism

Somewhat Catholic campuses tend to be of one of two types. They are either large universities with more than 9,000 students or small colleges, founded by a women's religious order, with enrollments of fewer than 4,000 students. The former represented 20% of the Somewhat Catholic schools in my survey, while the latter represented 80%. These types of campuses might sound different in their descriptions, but they have some striking similarities in their student populations because of the history of Catholic higher education.[6]

At the end of the nineteenth and beginning of the twentieth century, most Catholic colleges and universities were in need of money. Around 70% of Catholic colleges had shut down.[7] To fix this situation, what are now many of the larger Catholic schools took several interrelated approaches. They scaled back their explicit Catholic identity in order to become eligible for federal aid.[8] As a result of this change, many more students could afford Catholic colleges and universities, and these schools responded by admitting more students generally, and more diverse students. More of the 42 million Catholics who, by 1960, were rising in economic status could go to and pay for Catholic higher education. The schools were able to accept those returning from World War II who sought out college education with the help of the G.I. Bill.[9] Finally, these institutions began accepting women.

While this last move was just one part of the large Catholic universities' expansion of their enrollments and resulting fiscal stability, it had a ripple effect on small Catholic colleges founded by women's religious orders. Susan Poulson and Lorett Higgins note that many women applied to these formerly all-male institutions because they were viewed as more prestigious. As more and more women attended them, fewer and fewer women went to women's colleges. The result was that almost half of the women's colleges closed their doors, going from 300 institutions in 1960 to 146 in 1973.[10] Like the larger institutions, these smaller colleges had to rework their missions to attract students and survive. They chose to serve "a more diverse student body, including large numbers of adult and non-Catholic students" and promoted a "career orientation" for education.[11] The result was that large Catholic universities and small Catholic colleges founded by women's religious orders both survived by scaling back their overt Catholic identities and admitting a more diverse student body.

This reconfigured Catholic identity for both kinds of schools focused less on Catholic formation and more on service to others. It is an accompaniment Catholicism. Accompaniment is a term favored by Pope Francis. He likens it to what Jesus did with his disciples on the road to Emmaus.[12] The disciples did not recognize the resurrected Jesus as they were walking to the city of Emmaus. They told him of how they had hoped Jesus was the messiah but now doubted because he had been killed. Jesus then explained to them how the scriptures predicted this as they proceeded to walk. The story culminates when, after this day of walking and talking, the disciples invite Jesus to have dinner with them. While they did not recognize Jesus until they sat down to eat, it was the accompaniment that led them to extend the invitation. They could have ended the conversation then and there, but, by accompanying them, Jesus led them to faith. Accompaniment means this walking with people, being available to them. In doing so, the hope is to open up others to the faith all the while allowing them the freedom to go their own way and to avoid the faith if they desire.

Paragraphs 169–173 of the encyclical *Evangelii Gaudium* is, perhaps the most official exposition of accompaniment Catholicism. Pope Francis indicates that accompaniment is a way of leading people to Christ. It does so not by explicit and direct teaching and preaching but by being sympathetic, steady, and reassuring to others. Patience and prudence are two of its key virtues. Listening is essential because it "is an openness of heart which makes possible that closeness without which genuine spiritual encounter cannot occur." This approach is slow and deliberate, operating with the notion that "Reaching a level of maturity where individuals can make truly free and responsible decisions calls for much time and patience." In summary, the idea is that accompaniment of people in love raises the chances that they will advance in the Christian life.

This is an apt description of the religious culture on Somewhat Catholic campuses. Catholicism is present, available and there if you need it, but it is not "in your face." The crucifixes are there. The priests and nuns are teaching classes. The college's Catholicism is accompanying the students but is clearly neither judging nor proselytizing them. The Catholic culture is there when needed, for those who "seek it out" and, through this presence, implicitly hopes to lead people to Christ. These Somewhat Catholic schools make students aware of Catholicism but also respect those who do not want to hear it. It is an excellent approach for Catholic schools with diverse student populations and a portion of students who find the Catholic culture, "Obnoxious. I wish it were more secular." It seeks to make Christ present but also respects students' freedom to go their own way.

Somewhat Catholic Campuses and Hooking Up

When I asked Cole if Catholicism played a role when students were deciding whether or not to hook up, he gave me a two-part answer.

> Individuals' religious beliefs affect their interactions in relationships. Couples are centered and strong in their Catholic faith (or whatever faith they've chosen). They are more than likely to choose to abstain from sexual intercourse. Those without faith are more likely to have sexual intercourse.
>
> There are also two groups of Catholics as I see it, Catholics in name and Catholics in practice. Some are only Catholic in name, and go to church when their parents are around. Catholics in practice participate themselves, go to mass on their own. In my opinion, Catholics in name are more apt to participate in hookup culture. Catholics in practice do not participate.
>
> I don't think the Catholic culture affects hookup culture though. The people who participate compartmentalize school and personal life. They study all week, and when Friday night comes, they put their religion book in their backpack and go off to the party and do whatever they want to do.

The first part of Cole's answer was that sometimes students' faith made a difference in hooking up. "Practicing" Catholics did not hook up, but Catholics "in name" did. The second part of his answer was that the Catholic culture did not have an effect. It was "compartmentalized" to certain aspects of campus, in the background of students' daily interactions.

Jackson's answer to the same question had both of these parts. "I know Catholics who claim they are really devout and do the most un-Catholic things. I know atheists who do things that are very rational. For some people, it [Catholicism] does matter. For some people, it doesn't matter. For those that came because the place was Catholic, they find it. For other people, Catholic means nothing."

Harper, who had provided one of the most detailed descriptions of hookup culture, also gave a similar answer.

> No, in my opinion, no. The Catholic culture doesn't have an impact. I know a lot of people that are part of the biggest ministry clubs on campus and take a leadership role in those clubs. Thursday, Friday, Saturday, they go out and have sex with people without being in a relationship with them or without being married to them. I know one guy that was in this ministry club and got three girls pregnant. Sadly, two had abortions and the third had a miscarriage, but this same guy was big into the club and good friends with the friars. . . . I don't think the Catholic culture has any effect.

Jackson, Cole, and Harper all felt that the only factor affecting whether students hooked up was their own individual choices, sometimes supported by their faith and sometimes not. The Catholic culture seemed far removed from students' decisions.

The quantitative data reflects this disconnect between the Catholic and hookup cultures. On Somewhat Catholic campuses, the residence halls and visitation policies, opportunities for worship, and classes on Catholicism did not correlate with hooking up. Students' perceptions of the culture were not predictive of hooking up. The degree to which students talked about Catholicism inside and outside of classes did not correlate with hooking up. The number of Catholics on campus and their network of relationships did not correlate with hooking up. In short, neither institutional structures nor students' perceptions of the Catholic culture correlated with hooking up.

Table 10.8 For Somewhat Catholic campuses, hooking up and importance
of "contraception is wrong"

		Extremely unimportant (%)	Somewhat unimportant (%)	Neither important nor unimportant (%)	Somewhat important (%)	Extremely important (%)
Hooked up in the last year	0	30	18	12	6	32
	≥ 1	50	25	16.67	2.78	5.56

N = 86; P-value = 0.05. Those who answered "Don't Know" were removed from this calculation.

Table 10.9 For Somewhat Catholic campuses, hooking up and mass attendance

		Never (%)	Once a month (%)	2–3 times a month (%)	Once a week (%)	2–3 times a week (%)	Daily (%)
Hooked up in the last year	0	9.80	7.84	17.65	35.29	11.76	17.5
	≥ 1	27.78	19.44	11.11	38.89	2.78	0

N = 87; P-value = 0.01.

The only factors on Somewhat Catholic campuses that seem to affect hooking up were the students' own faith. In particular, it was specific evangelical Catholic beliefs and practices that were predictive of hooking up. The more important the belief "contraception is wrong" was to students, the less they hooked up (see table 10.8). The more frequently students attended mass, the less they hooked up (see table 10.9). As Cole, Jackson, and Harper indicated, for some students, their faith affected their decision about hooking up. For others, it did not. Accompaniment Catholicism seems to have little direct impact.

Again, this does not mean that because of accompaniment Catholicism there was rampant hooking up. While hooking up was not as rare as it was on Very Catholic campuses, those on Somewhat Catholic campuses hooked up far less than the best estimated rates of hooking up at all colleges and universities. They even hooked up less than students on Mostly Catholic campuses, who felt like their campus was more Catholic. To be sure, stereotypical hookup culture was present, but its dominance did not mean that the majority of students hooked up. Instead it meant that the "hookup" frame and script was the dominant way of thinking about sex and relationships. Very Catholic campuses had an anti-hookup culture to provide an alternative choice, and students on Mostly Catholic campuses developed scripts to pursue relationships. Without widespread alternatives, students on Somewhat Catholic campuses had no easy way, no readily usable frames and scripts, to pursue something other than hooking up. As bleak as this seems however, Somewhat Catholic campuses do offer some resources for providing alternatives to stereotypical hookup culture, and—as on Mostly Catholic campuses—they come from the students.

II

Supporting Students

BROOKLYN, THE SOPHOMORE who described her Somewhat Catholic campus as "there if you want it but is not in your face," echoed much of what others had said. What makes the place seem Catholic? "There are crucifixes in every classroom. We have nuns on campus and teaching classes." What is the hookup culture like? "It is a pretty big campus, so there are a lot of parties. So hookup culture is huge. When you mix college students and alcohol that is just what happens. I would say about 70% of the people participate in hookup culture." Does that Catholic culture affect hooking up? "If people are involved in campus ministry, it might affect them. Otherwise, it does not have any effect. I see people go to mass on Sunday and see them hooking up the days before. People that do participate in the religious culture participate in hookup culture."

Like everyone else I interviewed from Somewhat Catholic campuses, Brooklyn felt as though the Catholic culture was in the background, an accompaniment Catholicism, having little effect on daily life or hooking up. Stereotypical hookup culture was still the social norm, with students like Brooklyn overestimating the number of students who hooked up, thinking it was 70% when the actual number was 45%. There were a small number of evangelical Catholics, what Cole called "practicing" Catholics, who did not hook up because of their faith. Most, however, neither pursued meaningless hookups nor rejected hooking up all together. What did they do?

"Every Kind of Romantic Relationship"

When I asked Brooklyn about alternatives to hookup culture on campus, she started to paint a complicated picture.

I think about 55–60% of the girls are looking for relationships. Only some guys look for relationships. It's mostly girls. There are a few that are not looking for relationships at all. They are busy partying, being regular college kids. Some are not ready for relationships. They are focused on school or athletics.

The boys usually find someone to date because they are athletes. They can be in a relationship or hook up. They can hook up with girl athletes, but the girls don't have to be athletes. Everyone is interested in athletes. It just depends on who is looking for what.

A lot of time people start sleeping with someone, then they start to like each other and take it to the next level. Then they end up dating more typically. I think this is more true for girls. They get attached, emotionally attached, and want more attachment. There are a few people just looking for a date.

My friends do it differently. My one friend found someone she was interested in, and they became interested in each other, then they started dating. Most of my friends don't date though. I live in a suite with six girls. They were all raised in church, and chose not to have sex. They were raised that way. We talk about relationships and our decisions. We support each other.

There are probably few better descriptions of the social scene on Somewhat Catholic campuses than Brooklyn's. Other than the stereotypical "hookup" script and the "what college students do" frame—or as Brooklyn said, students just "being regular college kids"—there were no standard scripts and frames for people to connect with each other. Some girls wanted relationships. Some boys wanted relationships. Some boys and some girls wanted to hook up. Some athletes wanted to hook up. Some athletes wanted relationships. Some wanted neither but focused on school. Some hooked up and then became couples. Others talked and then became couples. Others, like Brooklyn and some of her friends, didn't date at all, equating sex with dating and not wanting to have sex. There was no one way to a relationship, and hooking up may or may not be a route to a relationship. There were no other shared frames and scripts. The divisions did not break down by gender or academics or athletics. Yet none of these alternatives to hooking up rose to prominence, and so not one created an alternative to stereotypical hookup culture. The latter was the norm, even if many did not participate.

In response to the question, "what are relationships like on your campus?," student-written comments reflected a similar lack of common relationship frames and scripts.

- It depends. They range from "no sex until marriage" to friends with benefits to people that are married. Basically every kind of romantic relationship exists here somewhere.
- I think formal relationships are nonexistent. I would say it is more common to just hang out with someone and "talk" to them.
- Some are just friends with benefits, others are long-term boyfriend/ girlfriend.
- There are people who are in steady, stable relationships as well as people who hook up with a different person every week, people who are single, and people who are in a not-relationship relationship.
- There are a few monogamous couples on campus, but a lot of relationships consist of "hook-ups" or people with significant others from off-campus.
- Some people are dating, some are "talking," some are married, some want casual hookups, some want drunken hookups.

On Somewhat Catholic campuses, one could find examples of "every kind of romantic relationship." The student above noted: a "no sex until marriage" crowd, friends with benefits, married couples, people who are talking, long-term boyfriends/girlfriends, single people, casual hookups, drunken hookups, monogamous couples, and not-relationship relationships. This is an amazing diversity but one that raises a question: How does it exist when stereotypical hookup culture is considered the dominant culture? How do students find alternatives when it is assumed that "being regular college kids" means hooking up?

Finding Alternatives

One alternative to stereotypical culture is rejecting it. Like so many who do so, Brooklyn had a "problem with hooking up" frame to justify the cost of not hooking up. It came out when she explained why she thought others did so.

It is just what college students do. [Pause] Lots of girls have a hard time respecting themselves. They want attention. They lack morals.

Everyone is doing it, so they hook up. There are no sororities or fraternities on campus, but athletes usually have parties. Then the upper classmen are hooking up, so the underclassmen do the same thing.

She believed hooking up was the norm, evoking a "what college students do" frame. Yet she described those who did it as struggling with self-respect, in need of attention, lacking morals, and going with the crowd. Not wanting to be any of these kinds of people, she did not hook up or even date. "I am not in one [a relationship]. I don't want to have premarital sex, so I am saving myself for marriage. I don't want to be in one now." Her beliefs, both her Protestant beliefs about sex and her own about hookup culture, made her decide not to hook up. She was not completely isolated, though. As noted earlier, Brooklyn lived "in a suite with six girls. They were all raised in church, and chose not to have sex. They were raised that way. We talk about relationships and our decisions. We support each other." Her personal religion helped her to choose against hooking up, but her small circle of friends supported her and helped her to live out that faith.

Committed relationships offer another alternative to stereotypical hookup culture. Jackson came to his campus because of the money they offered him. He found a relationship through band. "You find someone with similar interests. It's impossible to find someone without similar interests. So you go to student groups and hang out and find someone similar. I met Leslie [his girlfriend] in the marching band." It was through a small community with similar interests that he found someone, and, by the time of our interview, he had been dating her for four years. Moreover, as noted in chapter 9, Jackson's group did not hook up. "In my group of friends, it does not exist. In certain cliques, in certain social circles, it does." While they have different beliefs and different interests, Jackson and Brooklyn both negotiated relationships in and through a small circle of friends, a small community that shared and supported their beliefs. Brooklyn found it in the dorms, and Jackson found it among his group of friends with a common interest in music.

Harper found her relationship in a similar way. She and her boyfriend had been dating for a year and were even talking about marriage. They met through their academics. "Here, people find relationships through common interests. People who have a common major have common classes together. It's a small school, so you get to know people."

By now the pattern seems clear, people get to know each other over time through common interests.[1] In fact, Cole provided a clear summary of it.

A lot of people meet because they have the same academic majors. This means they have the same study habits, the same classes, and the same professors. Some people have the same group of friends and meet that way. Some study together in the library and grow together. People start to have the same groups of friends in the dorms. Men are on one floor, and women are on the floor below, and they just start hanging out together. People also meet through clubs and activities. Clubs, activities, and the classroom, that is how most people find relationships.

The only other small community not covered by Cole was athletes. Brooklyn mentioned them explicitly. Jackson said, "The hookup culture is the smallest set. The hookup crowd is mostly athletes, but not the reverse. Not all athletes hook up." Harper mentioned it as one of the small communities people find relationships in, saying, "People meet each other through club activities, sports, ministries. They use these to meet someone to have a relationship with."

The problem on Somewhat Catholic campuses is that even though students are clearly developing any number of scripts to pursue alternatives to hooking up, those scripts do not seem to be widely available. On Mostly Catholic campuses, students found ways to "hang out" instead of hook up, and these alternative scripts were bolstered by a *communio* Catholicism, which also connected students through "be kind" and "nonjudgmental" scripts. On Very Catholic campuses, most of the students were evangelical Catholics, and this common approach to the faith generated and supported their rejection of hooking up as well as their "hanging out" script around religious activities. On Somewhat Catholic campuses, though, accompaniment Catholicism resided mostly in the background of students' lives. It was not a socializing force and so did not facilitate the sharing of frames and scripts among students. Without this, the way Brooklyn resisted hooking up and Jackson and Harper found relationships were known only by their friends. Stereotypical hookup culture's tendency to marginalize all other relationship frames and scripts was not tempered, and students were left with fewer choices and less freedom in their pursuit of relationships. Students on Somewhat Catholic campuses seemed mostly resigned to this situation—hence the "what college students do" frame—and occasionally became angry about it, such as when Jackson likened the hookup culture to "inbreeding."

If there is to be any change in the dominance of stereotypical hookup culture on Somewhat Catholic campuses, institutional structures have to be strengthened to support students.[2] Athletics, academics, residence halls, and clubs are known to shape students' lives and integrate them into the campus culture. Brooklyn, Jackson, Cole, and Harper show that these institutional structures can help students generate and find alternatives to stereotypical hookup culture. Campuses do not have to directly promote alternatives to hooking up but can, by strengthening their institutional structures, foster alternative frames and scripts.

Promoting Scripts through Residence Life and Clubs

As Brooklyn noted, residence halls were critical to her rejection of hookup culture. She lived in a suite with other girls who shared her Christian background. They "talked about relationships." They generated a small anti-hookup culture by valuing their Christian beliefs over hooking up and pulled together to limit the social cost of doing so. They "support each other." The result was a group of friends who seemed happy and able to sustain an alternative to stereotypical hookup culture.

Student groups functioned similarly. Jackson was able to find his girl-friend Leslie through marching band, even though it had nothing explic-itly to do with relationships. Student organizations like marching band provided ways for students to gather and, in doing so, supported each other's ways of thinking and acting. Bound together in common interests or activities, they share frames and scripts that are useful for navigating social life on campus.

Jackson's and Brooklyn's experiences indicate how students can use clubs and dorms to pursue alternatives to stereotypical hookup culture. For them to be able to do so however, residence halls and student groups need to be supported in particular ways. Clubs work well if students direct them.[3] They foster academic success, give students experience in leader-ship roles, and, of particular interest here, help students foster mature relationships.[4] Student groups become ways for young people to socialize, come together, and carry out changes.[5] Residence halls are similar. They are places where students come to feel as though they belong to and fit into the campus life.[6] For this to happen though, campuses' approaches to residence life need to follow what the Association for Student Affairs at Catholic Colleges and Universities has recommended. They emphasize that residence halls should not dictate the academic or religious lives of students but instead should create spaces and programs that encourage students' moral, spiritual, and professional growth.[7]

Colleges' and universities' support for these institutional structures should not turn into control over them. If it does, these positive effects disappear. Residence halls lose their ability to support students if they are primarily understood as places to sleep or revenue streams for the college.[8] Students will disengage, believing that their activities won't make a difference or that they are pawns of the college.[9] Clubs also lose the effectiveness if colleges and universities view them primarily as venues for job preparation.[10] Students will then join several groups for no purpose other than to be able to list them on their resumes.[11]

Support for student groups might mean providing them with financial resources, access to meeting spaces, ways to recruit members, and avenues for promoting their activities. Support can also mean taking measures to ensure that clubs do not reflect economic class stratification, one of their perennial problems.[12] For the residence halls, this might mean finding ways to foster friendships in the dorms and support those networks of friends that emerge. Residential learning communities (as noted in chapter 5) and the Healthy Relationship Seminar (chapter 8) are good examples. Whatever form this support takes, though, supporting residence halls and student groups leads to greater student connectivity and so greater cultural sharing between students. With more institutional support, Jackson's and Brooklyn's scripts might become more accessible and more viable choices for other students.

Developing Scripts through Academics

Harper found her relationship through the classes that come from a common major. Shared time is important, but academics can offer more. This came to me clearly in a conversation I had with Bill Hisker, professor of management and chair of business at Saint Vincent College. He devised an assignment for his business ethics class that required students to attend a party but not drink. They were to pay attention to what they observed, write it down, and comment on it. His idea was to help students understand the social scene a bit more by stepping outside of it. He was careful with this assignment. He did not want it to turn into a paper that made fun of students or mocked them. Instead, he wanted them to analyze what was going on by assessing the reasons, both personal and social, that motivated people's actions.

He explained that the assignment originally started as a way for students to think about corporate culture and analyze its effects on people's behavior but soon realized it became personal for students. As he explained it to me, "I never told them what they should think or how they should analyze it. My only concern was that they used the ethical tools I had been discussing in class. What I found, though, is the tools that had been so abstract and only relevant for life after college suddenly became very useful for them in college. They started asking themselves what was going on and why it was going on."

Kerry Cronin did something similar. In summarizing one of her first talks on dating, she said:

> When my faculty friends and I first decided to give a talk on dating and relationships, we met for weeks ahead of time, trying to anticipate all the controversial questions that might come up. We thought, "They are going to ask us when they should have sex." When the Q&A period started, we were on pins and needles expecting difficult questions that might be pointed and controversial.
>
> The questions we got were not of that kind at all. I'll never forget the girl who stood up and asked, "How would you ask someone out on a date?" I started to answer abstractly and philosophically. Holding a notebook, she stopped me and said, "No, what are the words?" Another woman stood up and said, "You talk about sending signals, and I think I am sending signals all the time, but I have no idea if anyone can read them." A young man from across the auditorium said loudly, "We can't read them." It was a fun exchange in which students were speaking to each other about very practical things.[13]

Cronin realized that the students were struggling with very practical concerns. As a result, she devised a dating assignment.[14] She required students to ask someone out personally, not through technology, on an "old-fashioned" date. The date was to last between forty-five minutes and an hour and a half, be planned out, have no physical interactions, and be completed before ten in the evening. She generated other requirements that were meant to ensure that the students talked to one another during the date and that unnecessary anxiety was lessened. After the date, students were required to write an essay reflecting on it.

These examples are not meant to imply that every class should have a relationship unit or push professors to be dispensers of relationship advice. Instead, they are examples of the potential of academics to engage students and, by doing so, bring about alternatives to hookup culture. Cronin and Hisker are, first and foremost, engaged in effective pedagogy. By taking the tools of their classes and applying them to students' lives, they are employing what Ken Bain, in *What the Best College Teachers Do*, calls a WGAD—Who gives a damn?—principle.[15] This principle means that professors demonstrate how the material in their course is relevant to the lives of their students, helping them to understand why what they learn in class is important for reasons other than the grade they get. Attention to this question often results in students caring more about the material and learning it better.

This increased engagement of students is valuable for destabilizing the dominance of stereotypical hookup culture. Hisker's assignment highlights how academics can provide tools for students to analyze the college culture in order to figure out what they believe to be good and bad or better and worse. He provided them with critical thinking tools that could, if applied to hookup culture, question its pervasiveness and help students discern what they desire. Cronin's assignment complements this, providing a serviceable "dating" script that was a viable option for students.

This direct engagement with hookup culture is not the main point, however. The primary aim is to engage students intellectually. By employing a WGAD principle, a class can draw students in and enable them to apply what they have learned to their daily lives. Students will be set up to expand their repertoire of relationship frames and scripts by developing new ones and borrowing from others. As relationships are a frequent and important concern of students on college campuses, students' expansion of frames and scripts will almost inevitably occur.

Athletics and Removing Harmful Scripts

While athletics are a key way students connect with each other and find support, they also frequently add more problems than they solve.[16] Other than fraternities and sororities, athletic teams are the primary communities where coercive hookup culture is perpetuated. They are the groups of students most likely to drink excessively and engage in risky behavior.[17] Male athletic teams are also the ones most likely to engage in sexual assault.[18]

The relationship between athletics and assault is not straightforward. There is an image of masculinity, one that values aggression and that operates in these groups, and there is social pressure from peers to conform to this image.[19] This socializing suggests particular frames and scripts for how men behave. Just because they exist does not mean everyone acts on them, but their availability and social support (with the addition of alcohol) raises the chances that they are acted upon. It is this dynamic that has led people to talk about "rape culture": a culture where sexual assault becomes normalized and accepted.[20]

To respond, colleges and universities need policies that promptly respond to accusations, protect the rights of those involved, punish those who commit assault, and protect those who bring accusations.[21] In addition, colleges and universities need to attend to the socializing aspect of this coercive hookup culture. They need to find ways to have athletes themselves rework the culture. Having male student athletes become aware that most of them actually do not like violence and prefer meaningful relationships is essential. So is realizing that the understanding of men as violent and lacking in empathy is a frame that few want to conform to and that hides numerous other frames for understanding manhood. Finally, new scripts need to be introduced so that athletes know how to oppose sexual assaults and intervene when they see it occurring.[22]

By taking these approaches, and others that prove useful, campuses can remove these scripts—or at least greatly obstruct their use—so that coercive hookup culture is hindered or, better, halted. It requires the direct approach of institutional structures but also the indirect approach of supporting students in changing the culture. It requires a strong stance against physical coercion and is needed for the safety and respect of all those victimized by it. This stand against sexual assault is needed in and of itself, but, by taking a stand against physical coercion, it can help make social coercion equally problematic. The introduction of a "no coercion" frame could easily be used against the social coercion of stereotypical hookup culture that isolates or marginalizes people for not hooking up. By removing coercive hookup culture and challenging the coercive aspect of stereotypical hookup culture, alternatives to hooking up would arise, be used, and be shared by students.

Accompaniment Catholicism Can Help

Although accompaniment Catholicism is not a socializing force among students, it is well suited to promoting institutional structures in the ways suggested above and, by doing so, supporting students' alternatives to stereotypical hookup culture. Accompaniment Catholicism suggests that the way to Christ is an enduring presence that patiently listens to people and so fosters their "free and responsible decisions."[23] This might lead to supporting students in residence halls and clubs as they attempt to foster greater connections between them and greater sharing of their various relationship frames and scripts. Assignments like those mentioned above would fit well within this framework as they do not directly insist on partic- ular types of relationships but provide tools to help students develop their own frames and scripts for relationships. Accompaniment Catholicism would call for attending to those victimized by coercive hookup culture as well as male athletes who feel pressure to conform to it.

Accompaniment Catholicism also restrains Catholic colleges and uni- versities. Because it calls for listening first, it mitigates against dictating too much from the top down and thereby neutralizing the effects of dorms and clubs. Academic curricula flowing from accompaniment Catholicism would be cautious not to directly advocate for or critique certain relation- ships and behaviors—not wanting to judge students—and instead favor an approach that enables students to utilize course material in ways that are most meaningful for them. Accompaniment Catholicism would also assume that, in order to thwart coercive hookup culture, students must take the lead in working for change.

Finally, accompaniment Catholicism does not mean that anything goes. It is directed toward Christ—not primarily through preaching, which would not be well received in a religiously diverse context, but through actions that attend to and care for students, especially those who are in need. Accompaniment Catholicism would ensure that clubs do not become pockets of class division. Through academics, it would fos- ter student-generated questions about what is good and bad, right and wrong. Finally, it would necessitate preventing sexual assault as contrary to human dignity.

Even though accompaniment Catholicism is not a socializing force on Somewhat Catholic campuses, it is well equipped to help students. It need neither convert nor preach to students. Instead, it focuses on patience and respect as a path to what is good and right. If Somewhat Catholic campuses fully embrace their accompaniment Catholicism, they will strengthen their institutional structures so that they support students, students will in turn become more connected to one another, and their alternatives to stereotypical hookup culture will be more readily shared.

Conclusion

FOUR BENEFITS OF FAITH

SEVERAL YEARS AGO, one of my students sat in front of me looking for some practical advice about relationships in the guise of doing "research on sexual ethics." I began this study in hopes of finding some help for him and other students like him. I have not sought to provide moralistic help, telling students what they should or should not do, but rather have tried to provide an understanding of their campuses and the cultural resources that are available to them. I focused on Catholic colleges and universities in part because so much research indicated that religion did affect sexual activity and implied that religiously affiliated colleges and universities could also be places where help might be found. By listening to students on these campuses, I found four main benefits to faith.

Catholic Campuses Reveal the Coercive Potential of Stereotypical Hookup Culture

All cultures have a socializing aspect. People pick up the frames and scripts of a culture so that they learn how to function in it. They need to know what is expected of them so they can fit in and cooperate with others. Often this is helpful. Students learn how to register for classes at college or how to behave during a job interview. Sometimes it can be harmful. Those who do not understand or cooperate with a culture's frames and scripts can be marginalized or isolated.

Stereotypical hookup culture has a socializing aspect. Its frame (hooking up is sexual activity between two people without expectations of a relationship) and its script (to hook up, one goes to a party, drinks, finds someone, interacts physically—which can range from kissing to sex—and then has no further contact with that person) are meant to enable students to negotiate sex, attraction, and relationships on their campuses. Stereotypical hookup culture sets expectations for students so they know how they are to behave. Students have the freedom to accept, reject, or change these frames and scripts, but doing so risks being socially marginalized or isolated.

Catholic campuses draw attention to the fact that this socializing aspect is often coercive. Even though the majority of students on Catholic campuses do not hook up, they still felt the expectation to do so. It is the social norm, even if it is not the statistical norm, and so pushed every other alternative to the margins of social life. This was true on all types of Catholic campuses. Even on Very Catholic campuses, despite the fact that 74% of students did not hook up, they still had to justify that decision—often through the "made to love" and "conversion" frames—despite being supported by their peers and campuses' institutional structures.

The situation was similar on Mostly Catholic campuses. It was not that they rejected hooking up—55% of the students on these campuses indicated that they had hooked up in the last year, the highest rates of the three campus types—but they did have to explain why they used it as a way into relationships. Even though they knew, according to the hookup frame, that they were not supposed to want relationships, they did want them. They developed a "hooking up for a relationship" script with the hopes of a "casual" or "fully committed" relationship. Even as they did so, they were acknowledging the coercive aspect of stereotypical hookup culture. Since they could not expect a relationship to result from a hookup, they shielded themselves from the risk of pursuing one by utilizing "be nice" and "nonjudgmental" scripts derived from their *communio* Catholicism.

Even on Somewhat Catholic campuses, the propensity of stereotypical hookup culture to dominate students' understanding of sex, desire, and relationships was apparent. Most students on these campuses did not hook up but felt as if they were among the few who did not. They felt mostly isolated and resigned to this situation. Few seemed happy about it. Whereas alternatives existed at other types of schools—Mostly Catholic campuses had a relationship hookup culture and Very Catholic campuses had an anti-hookup culture—Somewhat Catholic campuses had none. They found ways to "hang out" and have relationships, but nothing that provided a significant alternatives to stereotypical hookup culture. Students believed hooking up was all there was.

Because the majority of students on Catholic campuses did not hook up, the potential for stereotypical hookup culture to become coercive was apparent. It cut across what students wanted, pushed alternatives to the margins of social life, and isolated those who did not participate. Deviations from the hookup frame and script had to be justified, and, even then, students risked social isolation by not following them. Awareness of the coercive potential of stereotypical hookup culture, one that becomes apparent on Catholic campuses, is not a story of woe or pity for students. It is just the stage for the second benefit of faith.

Catholic Campuses Reveal That Students Can and Do Shape Their Campus Cultures

In the midst of stereotypical hookup culture, students on Catholic campuses developed alternatives. They found ways to pursue what they were interested in, whether it was "hanging out," having "casual" relationships, choosing "fully committed" relationships, or "courtship." Students developed their own frames and scripts to create alternatives to stereotypical hookup culture. Despite the way hookup culture socialized students and penalized them for not cooperating, students still exerted their own freedom to pursue what they desired.

This ability of students to influence their culture came out clearly on these Catholic campuses. It can be seen in connection with individual students' Catholic beliefs and practices. Catholic students with the markers for evangelical Catholicism—beliefs in the teaching authority of the church, practicing traditional devotions, and attending mass more than once a week—typically choose not to hook up, regardless of whether they were on Very, Mostly, or Somewhat Catholic campuses. These evangelical Catholic students would not hook up even if that decision left them on the fringes of social life.

Students' ability to influence their culture was also seen in the communities that they formed. Students found friends in the residence halls who shared their preferences. They joined clubs with people who had similar interests. They ended up hanging out with those who had the same major and found those who had similar views on relationships. They shared frames and scripts and so generated alternatives to stereotypical hookup culture. Some of these groups were smaller, like Harper's friends in her residence hall. Some were larger, like the marching band where Jackson met his girlfriend. But whatever their size, these communities of students created alternatives to stereotypical hookup culture.

Nowhere is the influence of students clearer than on Mostly Catholic campuses. There, students shared a *communio* Catholicism, with most students indicating that Catholic beliefs were important to them and that they attended mass and prayed regularly. These students wanted something more than a "no-strings-attached" hookup, something between a "casual" relationship and a "fully committed" relationship. They developed these frames for understanding relationships, as well as the "hooking up for a relationship" script and further drew upon their religion to provide them with some protection. Their *communio* Catholicism bound them together like a family, and, as a result, they felt compelled to "be kind" to each other and "nonjudgmental." Together, out of their shared faith, they could pursue what they desired, and, as they did so, they transformed stereotypical hookup culture into a relationship hookup culture.

Students' impact on the culture can also be seen through institutional structures. On the one hand, the limits of institutional structures point toward students' role in influencing the culture. While the academic curriculum, the policies of residence life, and the opportunities for worship all affected students' perception of Catholic culture, they account for less than 25% of it. The rest results from students' faith and that of their friends and peers.

On the other hand, institutional structures amplified students' impact on the culture. Through their policies in the residence halls and religious activities, Very Catholic campuses supported the evangelical Catholicism of the majority of students. The students chose not to hook up and supported each other in this decision, but the restrictions on coed visitations, single-sex residence halls, and the pervasive Catholicism all reinforced the anti-hookup culture of these campuses. On Somewhat Catholic campuses, students used clubs, residence halls, and academics to connect with other students who had similar views and interests. Students used these institutional structures as places to "hang out" and possibly form relationships and, as a result, expanded individuals' preferences into that of small groups of students.

Students are clearly not just passively compliant in the face of the socializing aspect of stereotypical hookup culture. They can and do shape their campus cultures. The main limitation seems to be their lack of awareness of this ability. If they knew how powerful they were, they could significantly alter their culture. While they probably do not want to eliminate stereotypical hookup culture altogether, they do seem to want alternatives to it, especially ones that do not result in students being marginalized. They could adjust the campus culture to provide a wider array of choices for students regarding how to pursue relationships and what kinds of relationships are possible. Students have already done most of the groundwork for this, which is the third benefit of faith.

Catholic Campuses Reveal Alternatives to Hooking Up

Given that stereotypical hookup culture on Catholic campuses socializes most students into a culture that they do not desire, and given that students can and do shape their campus cultures, it should not be surprising that students develop repertoires of frames and scripts that help them establish alternatives to stereotypical hookup culture.

There are frames that provide ways to understand different types of relationships and, in doing so, enable student to imagine different possibilities. On every campus, there is clearly the hookup frame. Beyond this, though, there is the "casual" relationship noted by students on Mostly Catholic campuses. There were also those pursing "meaningful" relationships in contrast to hooking up. Shelly noted her desire for "fully committed" relationships, and on Very Catholic campuses "courtship" emerged as a way to think about relationships. This variety of frames opened up possibilities for relationships, helping students figure out what they desired or, if they were in a relationship, what was going on. They also indicated that hooking up was only one possibility among many for dealing with desire and attraction.

While students noted these frames, many struggled to figure out how to pursue a particular type of relationship. Shelly and Allen from a Mostly Catholic campus believed that hooking up did not lead to a committed relationship but struggled to articulate what might lead there. If one attended to students on all three types of Catholic campuses, there are numerous scripts that suggest ways into any number of different types of relationships. There was a "hanging out" script that on Very Catholic campuses centered around religious activities but on Mostly and Somewhat Catholic campuses was found in student clubs, academics, residence halls, and even in the cafeteria. Students also used their networks of friends to make connections and "hang out" with people they wanted to get to know. Dale, on a Mostly Catholic campus, reflected on his dad's experience of college, and it suggested a casual script, some way of "getting to know someone." Perhaps Kerry Cronin provided a "dating" script on her campus through her dating assignment. On Very Catholic campuses, there was the "no sex before marriage" script to use as a guide, and students on Mostly Catholic campuses noted how Facebook provided an official declaration of a relationship. Students could still hook up and even use the "hooking up for a relationship" script, but they also had countless alternative ways to get to know someone, alternatives embedded in almost every aspect of campus life.

While these frames and scripts are not unique to Catholicism, on these campuses, it was in and through the Catholic culture that they arose and were shared. Coming from Very Catholic campuses was the idea that relationships were important because human beings were "made to love." It meant that people should not take advantage of others but should instead respect them and show kindness. Even so, when people got caught up in the culture, there was a "conversion" frame that noted the difficulty of loving self and others well and that failure did not mean eternal condemnation. In addition to this, Mostly Catholic campuses situated the fragile pursuit of relationships in a *communio* Catholicism that emphasized care for others. In hooking up and relationships, students were to be "be nice" and "nonjudgmental" toward each other. These Catholic cultures provided anchors for the frames and scripts that students developed and, in doing so, facilitated their sharing. The influence of students was amplified by the religious culture of their campus, a dynamic that suggests the final benefit of faith.

Catholic Culture Affects Hookup Culture Up,
but Not in Simple or Straightforward Ways

Whenever I told people about this project, they would draw upon their perception of Catholicism's sexual teachings and ask, "Does Catholicism stop hooking up?" There was no easy way to answer this question. On Catholic campuses, the cultures differ between evangelical, *communio*, and accompaniment Catholicism. They were all Catholic but with important differences among them. On top of this, there was not just one kind of hookup culture. There were at least four. Moreover, although stereotypical hookup culture dominated campus social life, most students on Catholic campuses did not participate in it. They used hooking up to pursue relationships, or rejected hooking up to preserve their faith, or gave up on relationships because they didn't want to hook up, or even ignored hooking up to find relationships through their friends and peers.

While there was no easy answer, the Catholic culture taken as a whole did alter the dynamics of hooking up. The students, their faith, their friendships, and the institutional structures of the campus each contributed to the emergence of a different kind of hookup culture. If the majority of students were evangelical Catholics, their friends were evangelical Catholics, and the institutional structures supported evangelical Catholicism (as on Very Catholic campuses), then the result was an anti-hookup culture.

If the majority of students went to mass weekly and indicated that their Catholic beliefs were important to them, if Catholicism was discussed in the classroom, and if visitation rules did not appear to be strongly enforced (as on Mostly Catholic campuses), then what emerged was a relationship hookup culture. Catholicism bound the students together in a "warm and welcoming" environment that enabled them to transform the "hookup" script with no expectation of a relationship into a "hooking up for a relationship" script.

Finally, when there was a religiously diverse student body, so that the Catholic culture was not a socializing force and the institutional structures made Catholicism present but not "in your face," as on Somewhat Catholic campuses, then Catholicism had less of an impact on hooking up. It neither rejected nor transformed stereotypical hookup culture, leaving it to dominate students' expectations, even if it did not govern their actual behaviors. Yet these campuses also had great potential to reconfigure stereotypical hookup culture. Because students had already developed alternatives to hooking up, these colleges or universities could utilize their accompaniment Catholicism to enhance institutional structures—like clubs, academics, residence halls, and athletics—and change hookup culture on their campuses.

All of these different Catholic cultures suggested how hookup culture can be affected. These religious cultures can work against it, transform it, or have no direct impact at all. These cultures can provide reasons for rejecting hooking up, ways of bonding students together to guard against the risks of hooking up, or resources for students to use if they want to do so. These Catholic cultures suggest different ways hookup culture can be changed and alternatives can arise. They suggest opportunities for students to pursue relationships and in ways they desire. My hope is that, when I encounter those students looking for some practical advice about relationships, I will have something to tell them, and I will be able to empower them to forge alternatives that meet their needs and to transform the cultures of their campuses in ways that benefit themselves and others.

Methodology Appendix

The main goal of this study was to understand the religious and hookup cultures on Catholic campuses and explore if and how these two cultures affect each other. Previous work on the subject indicated a very tenuous relationship between the two, but the sample sizes involved were limited in both number and diversity of institutions. I began with a quantitative survey to elicit responses from numerous students and Catholic institutions. This quantitative survey suggested that students experienced three diverse Catholic cultures, three concomitant hookup cultures, and three differing dynamics of interaction. These results provided the foundation for the study as a whole and guided the subsequent qualitative study.

Building off of these initial results, I then deployed a qualitative survey at six schools from the previous survey, two representatives of each of the three types of Catholic cultures. I then interviewed a selection of the students who participated in this qualitative survey. The qualitative survey and the interviews were intended to gather student descriptions of their campuses and, thereby, complement the quantitative data.

The data from the quantitative survey, the qualitative survey, and the interviews were used in conjunction with each other as the best way to understand the interactions between the religious and hookup cultures on Catholic campuses.[1] This approach is known as a mixed method approach.[2] In using both qualitative and quantitative methods, a mixed method attempts to take advantage of the strengths of each, avoid their respective weaknesses, and arrive at an understanding of the data that is better than each in isolation. Quantitative data is easier to gather in large amounts, analyze using statistical methods, and, as such, guard against researchers' biases. Its weakness is that it often abstracts from particular contexts and people. Qualitative data provides a deeper understanding of participants and allows greater inclusions of their voices, but, because of the labor involved, it is often a small sample that limits its ability to be representative. My multistudy inquiry embeds the qualitative data in the quantitative analysis. My quantitative study helped me to discover different hookup cultures occurring at different Catholic campuses. The qualitative data could then be situated in these contexts and so provide a richer understanding of them grounded in student perspectives. Finally, I could check my interpretations of the qualitative data against the quantitative data to hedge against biases that can easily arise in research on "sex" and "Catholicism."

QUALITATIVE SURVEY CONSTRUCTION

For the 2012–2013 academic year, Saint Vincent College awarded me a research grant to construct a survey for this project. Part of this grant enabled me to hire a consultant, Dr. Mark Rivardo, a member of the Department of Psychological Science at Saint Vincent College, who has expertise in survey construction. He helped me develop a simple questionnaire that asked students about their perception of and participation in the Catholic culture and hookup culture on their campuses. The survey was to be quantitative and distributed via email to enable participation from a large number of students across several institutions.

I constructed the survey within Saint Vincent College's *Qualtrics* account. The online survey software provided the tools I needed to construct and deploy the survey: a library of questions and standard formats for questions, the ability to deploy surveys electronically via a link, a secure database to host responses to the survey, basic methods for analysis of data, and the option to export data into software capable of more advanced analysis.

The survey itself had four parts. Part one of the survey asked students about their religion. It approached the topic in three ways. First, the question asked students to identify their religious beliefs by choosing from a standard list of religions drawn from *Qualtrics*' library of questions. I added two options to this list: "Christian–Other (please specify)" and "Other (please specify)." Second, students who indicated that they were Christians were then asked to indicate on a Likert scale (a) how strongly they felt about certain Christian beliefs and then (b) how frequently they engaged in certain religious practices. While religious behavior, like frequency of worship attendance, is a better measure of religious commitment than beliefs, the beliefs and the behavior together appear to be better still.[3] Third, the survey asked all of the participants, Christians and non-Christians, to approximate how many of their friends shared their beliefs. It was an indirect measure of religious commitment by approximating the influence their beliefs, whatever they might be, on something as important and personal as friendships.[4]

Part two of the survey was constructed to investigate students' perceptions of the religious identity of their Catholic college or university. It took a twofold approach. First, the survey asked students to simply categorize the Catholic culture on their campus using one of four categories: Very Catholic Culture, Mostly Catholic Culture, Somewhat Catholic Culture, and Not Very Catholic Culture. Second, the survey asked participants questions about the frequency with which they encounter Catholicism in the classroom, in campus events, in residence halls, and among their peers.

Students indicated their experiences with these characteristics on a Likert scale ranging from "definitely true" to "definitely false."

I generated the latter questions about campuses' Catholic culture. Discussions of the Catholic culture on campuses have almost exclusively been philosophical or historical.[5] These works assumed or argued for certain characteristics as constitutive of Catholic identity. The only major study investigating characteristics of Catholic identity was Morey and Piderit's *Catholic Higher Education: A Culture in Crisis*.[6] While it did not provide quantitative data on Catholic identity as it was based on interviews of administrators, it further clarified which characteristics were assumed to impact Catholic identity.

Part three of the survey asked questions about hookup culture. This topic was approached in three ways. First, students were asked the degree to which they agreed with certain definitions of hooking up. These questions were intended to clarify students' operative understanding of hooking up as they answered questions about hookup culture. They responded to these definitions using a Likert scale. Second, students were asked about their perception of hookup culture on the campus. They were asked questions about, "in your opinion," how frequently people hooked up on their campus, how often these hookups involved intercourse, how often hooking up occurred between people who knew each other, and how often alcohol or drugs were involved. Students answered these questions using a Likert scale. Third, these perception questions were followed by two questions about their own participation in hookup culture: how many times did they hookup in the last year and, if they answered "one or more," how often these hookups involved intercourse. To answer both of these questions, students selected a number from a drop-down menu.

It should be noted that I did not ask specifics about the sexual actions of students, other than intercourse. This was because the nature of the study was to examine cultures, both Catholic and hookup, and to understand how students negotiated them. In other words, I was more interested in social forces and decision-making than students' specific sex acts. As a result of this approach, though, the generalness of the questions did not enable me to differentiate between heterosexual and homosexual activities on these campuses. Still, I wrote the questions trying not to presume heteronormativity.

Part four collected basic demographic information plus the year in school and the institutional affiliation. For demographic questions, I drew on the *Qualtrics* standard pool of questions based on U. S. Census demographic questions. For institutional affiliation, students chose from an alphabetical list of the Catholic colleges and universities in a drop-down menu. This was an attempt to eliminate variations in identifying institutions that would occur if entered manually (e.g., St. Patrick College, Saint Patrick College, St. Pats, St. Patrick's).

The rest of the survey's construction was for security and informed consent. The data were stored in *Qualtrics*' database and could be accessed only through my account. The survey itself was anonymous and required no information that could be used to individually identify students. Students were informed of this security in two ways. First, this security information was included on the first page of the survey as part of the informed consent page. Second, the information was included in the email soliciting participation for the survey. This email contained a link to the survey, so students ideally would have read the security information before they would have proceeded to the survey.

Informed consent was approached in a similar twofold manner. The email soliciting participation informed students that the survey was voluntary and could be stopped at any time without penalty. If students proceeded to the survey by clicking on the link in the email, the first page was an informed consent page. It described the nature of the survey, potential risks, privacy of the results, and the voluntary nature of the survey. To proceed, students had to click a "yes" or "no" button. If they clicked "yes," they would proceed with the survey. If they clicked "no," the survey would take them to the last page of the survey that thanked them for participating.

Once the survey was constructed, I used the rest of the Saint Vincent College grant to have the survey reviewed by two additional professors, one at Saint Vincent College and one at another institution. They suggested slight refinements to improve consistency in the way questions were asked and to include a "Don't Know" category in the Likert scales. The survey was revised to incorporate these suggestions. I then submitted the survey to the Institutional Review Board (IRB) at Saint Vincent College that approved the research. This process was completed in the fall of 2012.

DEPLOYMENT AND RESULTS

In the spring semester of 2013, I deployed the survey at several Catholic colleges and universities. I contacted people from thirty-five institutions asking if they would serve as onsite coordinators for the project. These individuals were typically chosen because they taught courses required of all students and, thus, would have a diverse representation of the student body at their institution. These people were provided with a copy of the survey, a project description, a copy of Saint Vincent College's IRB approval, and an email that they could use to solicit student participation. This email had a standard format that was to be adapted in three ways: the addition of a salutation, the addition of the onsite coordinator's name in a valediction, and an adaptation of the debriefing statement that added contact information for the particular institution's health and counseling services. I relied on onsite coordinators for two reasons. First, these individual would be able to acquire whatever permissions were required by their institutions to conduct the survey on their campus. Second, these onsite coordinators had direct contact with students through the classroom and, thus, would increase the chances of student participation.

The result of the process was participation by 1,099 students at twenty-six institutions. The survey completion rate was 89%. While the actual number of institutions chosen in the survey was twenty-nine, I discounted three entries for a total number of twenty-six. The three schools that I eliminated had the same characteristics: (1) they were not schools I had contacted, (2) their name in the drop-down menu appeared right before or after a school that did participate in the survey, and (3) they only had one entry where the school that participated had several. While I still used these students' data, I did not count these entries as additionally surveyed schools.

The institutions that participated varied in size of student population (table A1.1), Carnegie Classification (table A1.2), geographic region (table A1.3), and type of campus (table A1.4). The most obvious lacuna in the data is a sample of schools from the western region of the country. Although three schools were contacted from this region, none participated.

Table A1.1

Size of student population	%
< 4,000	65
4,000–9,000	8
> 9,000	27

N = 26.

Table A1.2

Carnegie classification	%
Baccalaureate colleges	35
Master's colleges and universities	35
Doctorate-granting universities	30

N = 26.

Table A1.3

Geographical location (U.S. Census categories)	%
Northeast	46
Midwest	26
South	15
West	0

N = 26.

Table A1.4

Type of campus	%
Rural	58
Urban	42

N = 26.

Although there are no quantitative measures of Catholic identity at Catholic colleges and universities, *First Things*, a publication of the Institute on Religion and Public Life, and the Cardinal Newman Society have composed lists of Catholic institutions of higher education to indicate if they have a strong Catholic identity.[7] Most of the approximately 250 Catholic colleges and universities do not appear on either of these lists. The Cardinal Newman Society's list is composed of only ten schools with strong Catholic identity, and *First Things* has two lists of ten, one for strong Catholic identity and one for weak Catholic identity. Both of these organizations would be considered "conservative" in Catholic circles. (There are no equivalent lists in "liberal" Catholic circles.) While these lists were not determinative for my selection of schools, I consulted them as a secondary way of ensuring that the Catholic colleges and universities I surveyed represented diversity with regard to their religious culture. Thus, three schools mentioned in these lists for strong Catholic identity participated in my survey, and two schools said to have weak Catholic identity participated in my survey.

The surveyed student population was also diverse. The academic classification was almost evenly distributed (table A2.1). With regard to race (table A2.2), the majority of the participants were white, with a distant second being Hispanic. Aggregate data about racial demographics at Catholic colleges and universities are difficult to obtain. One of the only studies addressing race is *Catholic Higher Education: An American Profile* from the Association of Catholic Colleges and Universities. Unfortunately, it was published in 1993, more than twenty years ago.[8] It indicated that 22% of full-time equivalents (FTEs) on Catholic campuses were minorities. This percentage reflected African Americans, Native Americans, Alaskan Natives, Asian Americans, Pacific Islanders, and Hispanic Americans combined. The report compared this percentage to the 20% minority population at independent institutions and 19% at four-year state schools.

Separate & Unequal, the study on race in higher education by Georgetown University's Center for Education and the Workforce, indicates higher rates of enrollment of African Americans and Hispanics at institution of higher education, but that these enrollments have been higher at community colleges and less selective institutions (36%) than at higher selective institutions (33%).[9] Unfortunately, this does not elucidate the state of Catholic colleges and universities as there is great variation in the level of selectivity among them. One can assume from these numbers, however,

Table A2.1

Academic classification	%
Freshman	21
Sophomore	25
Junior	23
Senior	31
Total	100

N = 1,057.

Table A2.2

Race	%
White/Caucasian	84
African American	3
Hispanic	6
Asian	4
Native American	1
Other	2

N = 1,058.

that the presence of minorities has grown on Catholic campuses. For my study, it implies that minorities are underrepresented. Further work should be done exploring these perspectives as the research on hookup culture suggests that racial minorities participate less frequently in hookup culture.[10]

The gender (table A2.3) was tilted toward females. This reflects the situation of Catholic colleges and universities however. As the Association of Catholic Colleges and Universities notes, "According to the National Center for Education Statistics' 2011 Digest of Education Statistics, during the 2010–11 academic year, 62.9% of students enrolled in Catholic universities and colleges were female; 37.1% were male. The ratio of males to females in Catholic colleges and universities is 1:1.7."[11]

The vast majority (89%) of students indicated that they were Catholic or Christian (table A2.4). The "other" categories also reflected a mostly Christian background. The higher number of Catholics and Christian is expected. The Higher Education Research Institute (HERI) survey, *The American Freshman*, indicated that approximately 60% of incoming freshmen at Catholic colleges and universities identified themselves as Catholic.[12] The higher number of Catholics in my study partly can be accounted for by the inclusion of Very Catholic campuses where 81% identify as

Table A2.3

Gender	%
Male	42
Female	58
Total	100

N = 1,052.

Table A2.4

Religion	%
Christian - Catholic	75
Christian - Protestant	8
Christian - Other (please specify)*	6
Jewish	0
Muslim	0
Buddhist	0
Hindu	0
Atheist	3
Agnostic	6
Other (please specify)**	2

N = 1,050.

*Entries for Christian: Other: 57% indicated denominations that were Protestant, 27% indicated nondenominational Christian, 13% indicated Orthodox, and 3% non-practicing.

**Entries for Other: 47% indicated no affiliations, 26% indicated some form of Protestant Christianity, 11% indicated spiritual, 11% indicated formerly Christian, and 5% indicated Orthodox.

Catholic. Even so, the numbers of self-identified Catholics and Christian in the study are probably overrepresented.

ANALYSIS

To analyze this quantitative data, I primarily used contingency tables.[13] Contingency tables are the most straightforward tool for analyzing the statistical significance of the relationship between variables. For example, one could use a contingency table to examine whether students' categorization of the Catholic culture of their college is correlated with their perception of the stringency of alcohol policies on campus. The null hypothesis is that the two variables are independent of one another, and this hypothesis can be tested using a chi-square test. I used a 95% confidence level throughout this study. Thus for p-values less than 0.05, I rejected the null hypothesis. For p-values greater than 0.05, I failed to reject the null. This methodology enables me to identify and test the significance of relationships between the variables measured in my quantitative survey.

In addition, I downloaded the data from *Qualtrics* into Excel. Working with a colleague familiar with statistics, Dr. Andrew Herr, Associate Professor of Economics at Saint Vincent College, I used this software to run several linear regressions, attempting to isolate the impact of independent variables on different dependent variables. The main result of these regressions was a discovery about student perceptions of their Catholic culture. After completing the quantitative survey, I compiled an extensive database of the twenty-six colleges where students participated, cataloguing information such as having a religious president (e.g., priest, sister, member of a religious congregation), having a service learning office, the number of required classes on Catholicism, the frequency of daily mass, the frequency of Sunday mass, the type of visitation rules in the dormitories, the alcohol policy in the dormitories, and the presence of coed or single-sex dorms. With students' "subjective" perceptions as the dependent variable and the institutional "objective" characteristics as independent variables, the linear regression yielded two main results: (1) institutional factors account for less than 25% of the variation in students' perceptions of their institutions, and (2) the most significant variables are those that students encounter on a daily basis (like residence hall policies and required courses on Catholicism). This analysis is part of chapter two of this project, and a more detailed explanation of the analysis is in the 2015 summer supplement of the *Journal of Catholic Higher Education* as "Does Catholic Identity Affect Students?" It was also partly funded by the Association of Catholic Colleges and Universities' Small Grant program.

QUALITATIVE SURVEY

The analysis of the data from the quantitative survey indicated three types of Catholic cultures, slightly different characteristics of each of these cultures, and different concomitant hookup cultures. Given these results, I constructed the qualitative survey to further explore these Catholic and hookup cultures. This survey was to allow students to use their own words and explanations for the cultures. The qualitative survey was more targeted than the quantitative survey. It used a representative sample of Catholic colleges and universities from the quantitative study to examine each of the three types of religious and hookup cultures. There were two schools that the majority of students had indicated had a Very Catholic Culture, two schools where students indicated a Mostly Catholic Culture, and two schools with a Somewhat Catholic Culture.

The qualitative survey was a series of open-ended questions asking students about their perceptions of the Catholic and hookup culture of their campus. Specifically, the survey asked students to describe their perceptions of (a) the Catholic culture on their campus, (b) hookup culture on their campus, and (c) relationships on their campus. I included demographic questions after these qualitative questions. At the end of this survey, I provided an option for students to enter an email address if they would be willing to be contacted directly for follow-up questions.

As before, I used *Qualtrics* for the creation and deployment of the survey. In the spring of 2014, the project was approved by Saint Vincent College's IRB, and then individuals at Catholic campuses were contacted to serve as onsite coordinators for the approval and distribution of the survey. I chose these onsite coordinators in two ways. First, I utilized ones from my previous study because they were familiar with the project and, as before, taught core classes that had a cross section of students. Second, I needed a representation of students from each of the three types of Catholic cultures. Thus, I contacted two previous onsite coordinators for each type of campus culture for a total of six contacts.

Of those contacted, all six participated. In total, the qualitative survey yielded 145 participants with a 77% completion rate. The participants of the qualitative survey reflected the participants of the qualitative survey. Year in school (table A3.1) was roughly the same. Race (table A3.2) was still predominately white. Gender (table A3.3) was weighted toward females. Religion (table A3.4) was predominately Christian. In addition, there were twenty-four participants from Very Catholic Culture campuses, seventy-four participants from Mostly Catholic Culture campuses, and forty-seven participants from Somewhat Catholic Culture campuses.

The qualitative survey ran through the spring semester of 2014. As these surveys were completed, I followed up with those who indicated that they would be willing to be interviewed. These interviews were also done in the spring of 2014. The opportunity to speak with students directly provided another means of understanding their perspectives. I constructed an interview protocol to guide the interviews. The protocol was based on the qualitative survey, but the interview allowed

Table A3.1

Academic classification	%
Freshman	18
Sophomore	30
Junior	27
Senior	25
Total	100

N = 142.

Table A3.2

Race	%
White/Caucasian	89
African American	4
Hispanic	4
Asian	4
Native American	0
Other	0

N = 112.

Table A3.3

Gender	%
Male	36
Female	64
Total	100

N = 112.

Table A3.4

Religion	%
Christian - Catholic	66
Christian - Protestant	13
Christian - Other (please specify)*	9
Jewish	0
Muslim	0
Buddhist	0
Hindu	2
Atheist	5
Agnostic	3
Other (please specify)**	3

N = 112.

* Entries for Christian: Other: 89% indicated denominations that were Protestant, 11% indicated nonpracticing Christian.

** Entries for Other: 66% indicated no affiliations, 33% indicated a mixture of different religions.

me to ask follow-up questions and pursue a deeper understanding of students' perceptions. I emailed everyone who, at the end of the qualitative survey, indicated that they would be willing to answer follow-up questions. When I began the interview, I informed them that I would protect their anonymity in the research and writing of the project by removing any identifying features and then, after explaining the nature of the interview, secured their verbal consent to participate.

Of the fifty-one who agree to follow-up questions and provided email addresses, twenty-two agreed to be interviewed by phone. Five were from Very Catholic Culture campuses, twelve were from Mostly Catholic Culture campuses, and five were from Somewhat Catholic Culture campuses. The gender was balanced, with eleven interviewees being female and eleven being male. There were seventeen Catholics, four Protestants, and one with no religious affiliation. Each interview lasted approximately forty-five minutes. The conversations were recorded and transcribed.

As presented in this text, the written comments of students from the qualitative survey and the spoken comments of those interviewed were changed only to preserve their anonymity and that of the institution to which they belonged. The modifications included replacing proper names with pronouns or synonyms, like changing references to residence halls or specific professors and, thus, did not alter the significance of the comments or interviews for this research. I only corrected minor typographical and grammatical errors in the written comments.

I analyzed the qualitative data for recurring themes in the culture—what I called frames and scripts. I began with no set categories for analyzing student comments. They emerged from my analysis of the material. I had a research assistant also read and categorize student comments. Differences in categorization were resolved through discussion, but these were minor because only the most prominent themes were utilized. As I was trying to discern widely accessible frames and scripts, only those that appeared clearly and frequently were relevant.

I guarded against biases in the analysis of the written comments in two ways. First, throughout the text I noted the percentages of comments that could be categorized under a specific frame or script so as to indicate that what was written was not just the perspective of a few outliers. Second, the qualitative comments were also contextualized by the quantitative analysis. Doing so linked student comments with what the statistics indicated was occurring on their campus.

CONCLUSION

The result of this project is a broadening of our understanding of religious and hookup cultures on the campuses of Catholic colleges and universities. It helps to clarify that there is diversity among the religious and hookup cultures. It also indicates that there are various ways that the two affect one another and various ways in which students navigate these cultures. While this project represented a step forward, more work needs to be done. At the basic level, more schools and more students should be surveyed. In addition, work gathering the perspectives of minorities and non-Christians on these campuses needs to be done. Hopefully, the results of this study provide a reliable foundation for subsequent work on hookup culture on the campuses of Catholic colleges and universities.

Notes

INTRODUCTION

1. Justin Garcia et al., "Sexual HookUp Culture: A Review," *Review of General Psychology* 16, no. 2 (2012): 161–162; Caroline Heldman and Lisa Wade, "Hook-Up Culture: Setting a New Research Agenda," *Sexual Research and Social Policy* 7, no. 4 (2010): 323–333.

2. Megan Manthos, Jesse Own, and Frank D. Fincham, "A New Perspective on Hooking Up Among College Students: Sexual Behavior as a Function of Distinct Groups," *Journal of Social and Personal Relationships* 31, no. 6 (2014): 815–829.

3. Garcia et al., "Sexual HookUp Culture," 167–168; Heldman and Wade, "Hook-Up Culture," 325.

4. Kathleen Bogle, *Hooking Up: Sex, Dating and Relationships on Campus* (New York: New York University Press, 2008).

5. Donna Freitas, *Sex and the Soul* (New York: Oxford University Press, 2008).

6. Amy Burdette et al., "Hooking Up at College: Does Religion Make a Difference?" *Journal for the Scientific Study of Religion* 48, no. 3 (2009): 535–551.

7. Heldman and Wade, "Hook-Up Culture," 328.

8. See Melanie M. Morey and John J. Piderit, *Catholic Higher Education: A Culture in Crisis* (New York: Oxford University Press, 2006).

9. Leslie Gordon Simons, Callie Harbin Burt, and F. Ryan Peterson, "The Effect of Religion on Risky Sexual Behavior Among College Students," *Deviant Behavior* 30 (2009): 467–483; Herbert W. Helm Jr. et al., "The Influence of a Conservative," 231–245; Sharon Scales Rostosky et al., "The Impact of Religiosity on Adolescent Sexual Behavior: A Review of the Evidence," *Journal of Adolescent Research* 19, no. 6 (2004): 677–697; Wade C. Rowatt and David P. Schmitt, "Associations Between Religious Orientation and Varieties of Sexual Experience," *Journal for the Scientific Study of Religion* 42, no. 3 (2003): 455–465; Alexander T. Vazsonyi

and Dusty D. Jenkins, "Religiosity, Self-Control, and Virginity Status in College Students from the 'Bible Belt': A Research Note," *Journal for the Scientific Study of Religion* 49, no. 3 (2010): 561–568.

10. See Mark Gray and Melissa Cidade, "Catholicism on Campus: Stability and Change in Catholic Student Faith by College Type," *Catholic Education: A Journal of Inquiry and Practice* 14, no. 2 (2010): 212–237; Michael E. McCullough and Brian L. B. Wiloughby, "Religion, Self-Regulation, and Self-Control: Associations, Explanations, and Implications," *Psychological Bulletin* 135, no. 1 (2009): 69–93; Helm Jr. et al., "The Influence of a Conservative Religion," 231–245; Leslie Gordon Simons, Callie Harbin Burt, and F. Ryan Peterson, "The Effect of Religion on Risky Sexual Behavior Among College Students," *Deviant Behavior* 30 (2009): 467–483; Tina M. Penhollow, Michael Young, and George Denny, "Impact of Personal and Organizational Religiosity on College Student Sexual Behavior," *American Journal of Health Studies* 27, no. 1 (2012): 13–21.

11. Marjorie Lindener Gunnoe and Kristin A. Moore, "Predictors of Religiosity Among Youth Aged 17–22: A Longitudinal Study of the National Survey of Children," *Journal of the Scientific Study of Religion* 41, no. 4 (2002): 613–622; Amy Adamczyk, "Socialization and Selection in the Link between Friends' Religiosity and the Transition to Sexual Intercourse," *Sociology of Religion* 70, no. 1 (2009): 5–27; Amy Adamczyk and Jacob Felson, "Friends' Religiosity and First Sex," *Social Science Research* 35 (2006): 924–947; Christian Smith, "Religious Participation and Network Closure among American Adolescents," *Journal for the Scientific Study of Religion* 42, no. 2 (2003): 259–267.

CHAPTER 1

1. Melissa A. Lewis et al., "Predictors of Hooking up Sexual Behaviors and Emotional Reactions Among U.S. College Students," *Archives of Sexual Behavior* 41 (2012): 1219.

2. Mark Regnerus and Jeremy Uecker, *Premarital Sex in America: How Young Americans Meet, Mate, and Think about Marrying* (New York: Oxford University Press, 2011), 105–106. I have cited this work by Mark Regnerus and Jeremy Uecker throughout this text as it is an extensive study that could not be excluded. My work does not focus on specific sexual activity or orientation, instead focusing on culture and students' agency. So Mark Regnerus' controversial essay "How Different Are the Adult Children of Parents Who Have Same-Sex Relationships? Findings from the New Family Structures Study," *Social Science Research* 41, no. 4 (2012): 752–770, does not intersect with my work and so is not used.

3. Kathleen Bogle, *Hooking Up: Sex, Dating and Relationships on Campus* (New York: New York University Press, 2008), 85. For similar numbers, see Elaine M. Eshbaugh and Gary Gute, "Hookups and Sexual Regret Among College Women," *The Journal of Social Psychology* 148, no. 1 (2008): 77–89.

4. For the first set of percentages, see Caroline Heldman and Lisa Wade, "Hook-Up Culture: Setting a New Research Agenda," *Sexual Research and Social Policy* 7, no. 4 (2010): 323–333. Heldman and Wade give the penal-vaginal intercourse rates as 38% and distinguish it from oral and anal intercourse. For the second review, see Justin Garcia et al., "Sexual HookUp Culture: A Review," *Review of General Psychology* 16, no. 2 (2012): 164. Throughout, I use the term "sex" to mean "sexual intercourse."

5. Megan Manthos, Jesse Own, and Frank D. Fincham, "A New Perspective on Hooking Up Among College Students: Sexual Behavior as a Function of Distinct Groups," *Journal of Social and Personal Relationships* 31, no. 6 (2014): 824.

6. Heldman and Wade, "Hook-Up Culture," 324; Regnerus and Uecker, *Premarital Sex in America*, 104. Also see Jess Owen et al, "'Hooking Up' Among College Students: Demographic and Psychosocial Correlates," *Archives of Sexual Behavior* 39 (2010): 653–663; Brian Sweeney, "Party Animals or Responsible Men: Social Class, Race, and Masculinity on Campus," *International Journal of Qualitative Studies in Education* 27, no. 6 (2014): 804–821; Lisa Wade and Caroline Heldman, "Hooking Up and Opting Out: Negotiating Sex in the First Year of College," in *Sex for Life: From Virginity to Viagra, How Sexuality Changes Throughout Our Lives,* eds. Laura M. Carpenter and John DeLamater (New York: New York University Press, 2012), 130.

7. N = 923.

8. Garcia et al., "Sexual HookUp Culture," 167–168.

9. Garcia et al., "Sexual HookUp Culture," 167–168.

10. Wade and Heldman, "Hook-Up Culture," 325. See also M. Lynne Cooper and Cheryl M. Shapiro, "Motivations for Sex and Risky Sexual Behavior Among Adolescents and Young Adults: A Functional Perspective," *Journal of Personality and Social Psychology* 73, no. 6 (1998): 1528–1558, and Emily J. Ozer, M. Margaret Dolcini, and Gary W. Harper, "Adolescents' Reasons for Having Sex: Gender Differences," *Journal of Adolescent Health* 33 (2003): 317–319.

11. Wade and Heldman, "Hooking Up and Opting Out," 140.

12. Marina Epstein et al., "'Anything from Making Out to Having Sex': Men's Negotiations of Hooking Up and Friends with Benefits Scripts," *Journal of Sex Research* 46 (2009): 415; See also Owen et al., "'Hooking Up' Among College Students," 660.

13. Epstein et al., "'Anything from Making Out to Having Sex,'" 419.

14. See Robyn L. Fielder and Michael P. Carey, "Prevalence and Characteristics of Sexual Hookups Among First-Semester Female College Students," *Journal of Sex & Marital Therapy* 36 (2010): 351, and Lewis et al., "Predictors of Hooking Up Sexual Behaviors," 1223.

15. N =960.

16. See Garcia et al., "Sexual HookUp Culture," 163; Epstein et al., "'Anything from Making Out to Having Sex,'" 419; Melissa A. Bisson and Timothy R. Levine,

"Negotiating a Friends with Benefits Relationship," *Archives of Sexual Behavior* 38 (2009): 66–73; Heldman and Wade, "Hookup Culture," 325, and Wade and Heldman, "Hooking Up and Opting Out," 136–137.

17. In her book, *The End of Sex: How Hookup Culture is Leaving a Generation Unhappy, Sexually Unfulfilled and Confused About Intimacy* (New York: Basic Books, 2013), 70–73, author Donna Freitas notes how not hooking up can often result in a kind of "social suicide."

18. See Bogle, *Hooking Up*, 67–71; Owen et al., "'Hooking Up' Among College Students," 653–663. Sweeney, "Party Animals or Responsible Men," 804–821; Robyn Fielder et al., "Predictors of Sexual Hookups: A Theory-Based, Prospective Study of First-Year College Women," *Archives of Sexual Behavior* 42 (2013): 1438.

19. This is not an atypical situation. See Mary Crawford and Danielle Popp, "Sexual Double Standards: A Review and Methodological Critique of Two Decades of Research," *The Journal of Sex Research* 40, no. 1 (2003): 13–26.

20. Lewis et al., "Predictors of Hooking up Sexual Behaviors," 1219–1229.

21. Elizabeth Auritt et al., "The Class of 2015 by the Numbers," *The Harvard Crimson*, May 28, 2015, http://features.thecrimson.com/2015/senior-survey/.

22. One of the most cited reasons for regret after hooking up was having gone against one's morals. See Sara B. Owsalt, Kenzie A. Cameron, and Jeffry J. Koob, "Sexual Regret in College Students," *Archives of Sexual Behavior* 34, no.6 (2005): 663–669.

23. Sweeney, "Party Animals or Responsible Men," 817

24. Sweeney, "Party Animals or Responsible Men," 818

25. Sweeney, "Party Animals or Responsible Men," 813.

26. Wade and Heldman, "Hooking Up and Opting Out," 130.

27. Center for Disease Control and Prevention, "Understanding Sexual Violence: Fact Sheet 2014," http://www.cdc.gov/violenceprevention/pdf/sv-factsheet.pdf.

28. See Arnold S. Kahn, "What College Women Do and Do Not Experience as Rape," *Psychology of Women Quarterly* 28 (2004): 9–15; Ruth Mann and Clive Hollin, "Sexual Offenders' Explanation for their offending," *Journal of Sexual Aggression* 13, no. 1 (March 2007): 3–9.

29. Antonia Abbey, "Alcohol-Related Sexual Assault: A Common Problem among College Students," *Journal of Studies on Alcohol, Supplement* 14 (2002): 118–119.

30. Abbey, "Alcohol-Related Sexual Assault," 118–119.

31. For a precise definition of frames, see "Frame of Reference, Definition 2," in Gary R. Vandenbos, ed., *APA Dictionary of Psychology* (Washington, DC: American Psychological Association, 2007), 388 (a frame is "a set of parameters defining either a particular mental schema or the wider cognitive structures by which an individual perceives and evaluates the world"). Frames were first posited by Amos Tversky (see Amos Tversky and Daniel Kahneman, "The Framing of Decisions and the Psychology of Choice," *Science* 211, no. 4481 (1981): 453–458; Amos Tversky and Richard Thaler, "Preference Reversals," *Journal of Economic Perspectives* 4, no. 3 (1990): 201–211 (republished as chapter 7 in Thaler's

Winner's Curse (New York: Princeton University Press, 1994)). For a precise definition of scripts, see "Script, Definition 2," in Vandenbos, *APA Dictionary of Psychology*, 820 (a script is "a cognitive schematic structure—a mental road map—containing the basic actions (and their temporal and causal relations) that comprise a complex action").

32. See Ann Swidler, *Talk of Love: How Culture Matters* (Chicago, IL: University of Chicago Press, 2003), 392; Svend Brinkmann, "Culture as Practices: A Pragmatist Conception," *Journal of Theoretical and Philosophical Psychology* 28 (2008): 192–210.

33. See chapter 2 of Swidler, *Talk of Love*; Gabriel Ignatow, "Theories of Embodied Knowledge: New Directions for Cultural and Cognitive Sociology?" *Journal for the Theory of Social Behavior* 37, no. 2 (2007): 115–135.

34. Epstein et al., "'Anything from Making Out to Having Sex,'" 414–424.

35. For discussions of these various scripts, see Swidler, *Talk of Love*, chap. 3; Naomi Quinn, "Culture and Contradiction: The Case of Americans Reasoning about Marriage," *Ethos* 24, no. 3 (1996): 391–425; Margaret Farley, *Just Love: A Framework for Christian Sexual Ethics* (New York: Continuum International Publishing Group, 2006).

36. Heldman and Wade, "Hook-Up Culture," 325.

37. See Matthew Hogben et al., "Legitimized Aggression and Sexual Coercion: Individual Differences in Cultural Spillover," *Aggressive Behavior* 27 (2001): 26–43; Laina Y. Bay-Cheng and Rebecca K. Eliseo-Arras, "The Making of Unwanted Sex: Gendered and Neoliberal Norms in College Women's Unwanted Sexual Experiences," *Journal of Sex Research* 45, no. 4 (2008): 386–397; Sarah R. Edwards and David L. Vogel, "Young Men's Likelihood Ratings to Be Sexually Aggressive as a Function of Norms and Perceived Sexual Interest," *Psychology of Men and Masculinity* 16, no. 1 (2015): 88–96.

38. For correlations between pornography and violence, especially as pornography supports beliefs in sexual aggression, see Martie P. Thompson and Deidra J. Morrison, "Prospective Predictors of Technology-Based Sexual Coercion by College Males," *Psychology of Violence* 3, no. 3 (2013): 233–246; Joetta L. Carr and Karen M. VanDuesen, "Risk Factors of Male Sexual Aggression on College Campuses," *Journal of Family Violence* 19, no. 5 (2004): 279–289; Kelly Cue Davis et al., "Men's Likelihood of Sexual Aggression: The Influence of Alcohol, Sexual Arousal, and Violent Pornography," *Aggressive Behavior* 32 (2006): 581–589.

39. Karen Lebacqz, "Love your Enemy: Sex, Power, and Christian Ethics," *Annual of the Society of Christian Ethics* 10, no. 1 (2006): 8.

40. See Pamela Paul, *Pornified: How Pornography Is Damaging Our Lives, Our Relationships, and Our Families* (New York: Times Book, 2005).

41. See Georgia T. Chao and Henry Moon, "The Cultural Mosaic: A Metatheory for Understanding the Complexity of Culture," *Journal of Applied Psychology* 90, no. 6 (2005): 1130–1132; Wan Ching et al., "Measuring Cultures through Intersubjective Cultural Norms: Implications for Predicting Relative

Identification With Two or More Cultures," *Journal of Cross-Cultural Psychology* 38, no. 2 (2007): 213–226; Baldwin Van Gorp, "The Constructionist Approach to Framing: Bringing Culture Back In," *Journal of Communication* 57 (2007): 63–64; Herbert C. Kelman, "Interests, Relationships, Identities: Three Central Issues for Individuals and Groups in Negotiating Their Social Environment," *Annual Review of Psychology* 57 (2006): 1–26; Rajiv N. Rimal and Kevin Real, "Understanding the Influence of Perceived Norms on Behaviors," *Communication Theory* 13, no. 2 (2003): 184–203; Rajiv N. Rimal, "Modeling the Relationship Between Descriptive Norms and Behaviors: A Test and Extension of the Theory of Normative Social Behavior," *Health Communication* 23 (2008): 105–106; Joanne R. Smith and Winnifred R. Louis, "Do as We Say *and* as We Do: The Interplay of Descriptive and Injunctive Group Norms in the Attitude-Behavior Relationship," *British Journal of Social Psychology* 47 (2008): 647–666; Carlos J. Torelli and Sharon Shavitt, "Culture and Concepts of Power," *Journal of Personality and Social Psychology* 99, no. 4 (2010): 703–723.

42. $N = 972$.

43. For why certain minorities feel comfortable and others do not based on their relationships to the perceived norms, see Kimberly Rios Morison and Dale T. Miller, "Distinguishing Between Silent and Vocal Minorities: Not All Deviants Feel Marginal," *Journal of Personality and Social Psychology* 94, no. 5 (2008): 871–882.

44. For an understanding of institutional structures, see Christian Smith, *What Is a Person?* (New York: Oxford University Press, 2010), 186, 317–329; Chi-Yue Chiu and Ying-Yi Hong, *Social Psychology of Culture* (New York: Psychology Press, 2006), 231–234.

45. Chao and Moon, "The Cultural Mosaic," 1136–1137. Markus Kemmelmeier and Ulrich Kühnen, "Culture as Process: the Dynamics of Cultural Stability and Change," *Social Psychology* 43, no. 4 (2012): 171–173.

46. George Sugai, Breda V. O'Keeffe, and Lindsay M. Fallon, "A Contextual Consideration of Culture and School Wide Positives Heavier Support," *Journal of Positive Behavior Interventions* 14, no. 4 (2012): 197–208.

47. In chapter 1 of *Social Psychology of Culture*, Chi-Yue Chiu and Ying-Yi Hong survey three different definitions of culture. They identify a material culture as the way people exchange goods, a social culture as the shared rules for behavior, and a subjective culture as the ideas that are shared by people. Based on this typology, my definition is mainly a subjective culture, though it draws on some of the institutional aspects typically associated with social culture. My attempt is not an exhaustive theory of culture but a definition that is sufficient for explaining the dynamics of hookup culture on Catholic campuses.

48. See Christian Smith, *Moral Believing Animals: Human Personhood and Culture* (New York: Oxford University Press, 2003), 26–33 and *What is a Person?*, 369–378.

CHAPTER 2

1. N = 977.

2. There is no commonly accepted list of characteristics defining Catholic identity, so, after a survey of the literature on Catholic identity, which is mostly philosophical or historical, I developed a list of information to gather from the institutions I surveyed. This list was not meant to be proscriptive but descriptive, attempting to gather what is commonly assumed as important for Catholic identity rather than advocating one set of characteristics or another. For some typical examples, see Stanley Hauerwas, *The State of the University: Academic Knowledges and the Knowledge of God* (Malden, MA: Blackwell Publishing, 2007); Kenneth Garcia, *Academic Freedom and the Telos of the Catholic University* (New York: Palgrave Macmillan, 2012); Alasdair MacIntyre, *God, Philosophy, Universities: A Selective History of the Catholic Philosophical Tradition* (Lanham, MD: Rowman & Littlefield, 2011); Mark Roach, *The Intellectual Appeal Of Catholicism and the Idea of a Catholic University* (Notre Dame, IN: University of Notre Dame Press, 2003); Melanie M. Morey and John J. Piderit, *Catholic Higher Education: A Culture in Crisis* (New York: Oxford University Press, 2006).

3. The original list also included a Catholic president, the existence of a campus ministry, the number of people staffing the campus ministry, the number of people staffing the office of service learning, the number of required classes on religion, the presence of a chapel, the percentage of faculty who were Catholic, and the percentage of the student body who were Catholic. But these variables were eliminated from the statistical analysis for several reasons. First, the "Catholic president" variable was eliminated because it would be redundant for institutions with a religious president. Moreover, twenty-four of the twenty-six schools had a Catholic president, so this variable would have limited value in explaining differences in students' perceptions. Second, the "campus ministry" variable was eliminated because every school surveyed had a campus ministry office. Thus, the presence of an office would have no value in explaining differences in student perceptions. Third, the data on the number of people staffing campus ministry offices and the number of people staffing offices of service learning were not used. The staffing levels of these offices indicated more the size of the institution than Catholic identity. Larger institutions had larger staffs than smaller institutions. Thus, this variable was not a good indicator for Catholic identity. Fourth, the percentage of faculty and percentage of students who were Catholic was eliminated. These numbers were rarely public, so the information was not available for most of the institutions. Thus, these percentages could not be used as a point of comparison. Finally, the "required courses in religion" variable was eliminated. Most institutions viewed classes in Catholicism as a subset of classes in religion. Thus, if required religion classes and required Catholic classes were both counted, classes in Catholicism would be counted twice. The elimination of required religion courses avoided this added weighting. Moreover, since the study was on Catholic culture, courses on Catholicism seemed the more appropriate variable. The general approach was

to be as inclusive as possible with the courses, so classes on topics within the Catholic Christian tradition (e.g., scripture, Christian history), courses on people or movements within Catholicism (e.g., Benedictine or Franciscan Heritage, Thomas Aquinas, Christian Mystics), and courses with Catholicism in the title (e.g., Catholic Social Thought, Basics of Catholic Belief) were all included. These decisions were made on a case-by-case basis, consulting course descriptions in cases of uncertainty. This process of elimination left the noted list.

4. Specifically, for the regression, student perceptions of the overall religious culture was the dependent variable, and the institutional characteristics were the independent variables. Based on the results of this initial regression, variables were systematically eliminated from the regression one by one. At each stage, the variable with the highest p-value was eliminated, and the regression was re-run with the remaining variables. At each step, the adjusted R squared of the regression was examined to see if it increased. If so, the variable was left out of the regression. If the adjusted R squared decreased when a variable was eliminated, then the variable was retained. Following the process, the following variables were removed in this order: (1) Sunday Mass, (2) Alcohol Policy, (3) Religious President, and (4) Service Learning. For a more detailed explanation of this process, see Jason King and Andrew Herr, "Does Catholic Identity Affect Students?" *Journal of Catholic Higher Education* 34 no. 2 (2015) 195–209.

5. Table 4 indicates the significant variables that emerged through the regressions. The R squared for this regression is 0.235, which indicates that this set of institutional characteristics explains 23.5% of the variance in students' perceptions of the religious culture of their institutions. The p-value for each remaining variable is close to 0, suggesting that each of the institutional characteristics in the final regression (Co-ed Dorms, Visitation Policy, Daily Mass frequency, and Required Catholic Courses) significantly impacts student perception of religious culture. Furthermore, the coefficient of each of these variables is positive, indicating that the direction of the impact of each institutional characteristic is what we would expect: as institutional characteristic becomes "more Catholic," students perceive the institution to be "more Catholic."

6. Both Christian Smith et al. in *Young Catholic America: Emerging Adults In, Out of, and Gone from the Church* (New York: Oxford University Press, 2014), 126–154, and Amy Burdette et al., in "'Hooking Up' at College: Does Religion Make a Difference?" *Journal for the Scientific Study of Religion* 48, no. 3 (2009): 537, note the need for attending to religious affiliation by using more variables than just self-identification. I address these variables in subsequent chapters discussing specific Catholic cultures (chapters 4, 7, and 10).

7. This correlation did not hold for non-Catholics and their friends. Whereas the correlation between students' characterization of their friendship networks as Catholic or not and the campus culture had a p-value of 0.00, the correlation between non-Catholic friends and the campus culture was not statistically significant, with a

p-value of 0.85. To be clear, this does not mean that non-Catholic students do not shape a campus's Catholic culture. They can and do shape it in other ways. It is just that their faith and their network of friends with the same faith do not indicate whether these students feel the campus is Very, Mostly or Somewhat Catholic.

8. P-value = 0.00 for Catholics and p-value = 0.01 for non-Catholics.

CHAPTER 3

1. N = 221.
2. N = 24.
3. N = 237.
4. Saint Augustine, *Confessions* (New York: Penguin Books, 1961), 1; Dorothy Day, *The Long Loneliness* (New York: HarperCollins: 1997), 286.
5. N = 24.
6. See Acts 9 for an account of Paul's conversion. See Bernard Lonergan, *Method in Theology*, chapter 10 (Toronto: University of Toronto Press, 1972) for his account of conversion. See Flannery O'Connor's *The Complete Stories* (New York: Farrar, Straus and Giroux, 1971) for her stories and *Mystery and Manners: Occasional Prose* (New York: Farrar, Straus and Giroux, 1969) for her reflections on conversions in these stories.
7. Christian Smith et al., *Young Catholic America: Emerging Adults In, Out of, and Gone from the Church* (New York: Oxford University Press, 2014), 51.
8. This conclusion is echoed in other studies. See Mark Gray and Melissa Cidade, "Catholicism on Campus: Stability and Change in Catholic Student Faith by College Type," *Catholic Education: A Journal of Inquiry and Practice* 14, no. 2 (2010): 212–237; Paul Perl and Mark Gray, "Catholic Schooling and Disaffiliation from Catholicism," *Journal for the Scientific Study of Religion* 46, no. 2 (2007): 269–280; Jeremy Uecker, Mark Regnerus, and Margaret Vaaler, "Losing my Religion: The Social Sources of Religious Decline in Early Adulthood," *Social Forces* 85, no. 4 (2007): 1667–1692.
9. This oppositional script also fits with a countercultural view of Catholicism in the United States that spans the early days of Catholicism as an immigrant community to more recent tensions between Catholicism and the state. See Kenneth Garcia, *Academic Freedom and the Telos of the Catholic University* (New York: Palgrave Macmillan, 2012); Philip Gleason, *Contending with Modernity: Catholic Higher Education in the United States* (New York: Oxford University Press, 1995); Joseph A. Komonchak, "Modernity and the Construction of Roman Catholicism," *Cristianismo nella storia* 18 (1997): 353–385.

CHAPTER 4

1. N = 24.
2. See chapter 2 for this argument.

3. The Angelus is a traditional Catholic prayer typically recited at six in the morning, noon, and six in the evening and in conjunction with the ringing of bells. See "Angelus," *New Catholic Encyclopedia*, 2nd ed., vol. 1 (Detroit, MI: Gale, 2003), 427–428.

4. For a standard explanation of these types of freedom, see Dana Dillon and David McCarthy, "Natural Law, Law, and Freedom," in *Gathered for the Journey: Moral Theology in Catholic Perspective*, eds. David Matzko McCarthy and M. Therese Lysaught (Grand Rapids, MI: William B. Eerdmans Publishing Company, 2007), 168–172.

5. In chapter 2, I used similar charts to indicate the correlation between these factors and student perceptions of the overall culture. The percentages in this chart differ because it is not divided by perception but by campus where the majority of students identified it as Very, Mostly, or Somewhat Catholic.

6. Christian Smith, "Religious Participation and Network Closure among American Adolescents," *Journal for the Scientific Study of Religion* 42, no. 2 (2003): 259–267. For similar conclusions on the effects of friends with a shared faith, see Marjorie Lindner Gunnoe and Kristin A. Moore, "Predictors of Religiosity Among Youth Aged 17–22: A Longitudinal Study of the National Survey of Children," *Journal of the Scientific Study of Religion* 41, no. 4 (2002): 613–622; Amy Adamczyk, "Socialization and Selection in the Link between Friends' Religiosity and the Transition to Sexual Intercourse," *Sociology of Religion* 70, no. 1 (2009): 5–27; Amy Adamczyk and Jacob Felson, "Friends' Religiosity and First Sex," *Social Science Research* 35 (2006): 924–947.

7. William Portier, "Here Come the Evangelical Catholics," *Communio: International Catholic Review* 31 (2004): 35–66.

8. Portier, "Here Come the Evangelical Catholics," 55.

9. Portier, "Here Come the Evangelical Catholics," 65.

10. Portier, "Here Come the Evangelical Catholics," 44–45.

11. See Sharon Rostosky et al., "The Impact of Religiosity on Adolescent Sexual Behavior: A Review of the Evidence," *Journal of Adolescent Research* 19, no. 6 (2004): 677–697; Tina Penhollow, Michael Young, and George Denny, "Impact of Personal and Organizational Religiosity on College Student Sexual Behavior," *American Journal of Health Studies* 27, no. 1 (2012): 13–22; Leslie Simons, Callie Burt, F. Ryan Peterson, "The Effects of Religion on Risky Sexual Behavior Among College Students," *Deviant Behavior* 30 (2009): 467–483.

12. Simons, Burt, and Peterson, "The Effect of Religion on Risky Sexual Behavior Among College Students," 467–483; Herbert W. HelmJr. et al., "The Influence of a Conservative Religion on Premarital Sexual Behavior of University Students," *North American Journal of Psychology* 11, no. 2 (2009): 231–245; Rostosky, Wilcox, Wright, and Randall, "The Impact of Religiosity on Adolescent Sexual Behavior," 677–697; Wade C. Rowatt and David P. Schmitt, "Associations Between Religious Orientation and Varieties of Sexual Experience," *Journal for the Scientific Study of Religion* 42, no. 3

(2003): 455–465; Alexander T. Vazsonyi and Dusty D. Jenkins, "Religiosity, Self-Control, and Virginity Status in College Students from the 'Bible Belt': A Research Note," *Journal for the Scientific Study of Religion* 49, no. 3 (2010): 561–568.

CHAPTER 5

1. Paul Eastwick and Lucy Hunt, "Relational Mate Value: Consensus and Uniqueness in Romantic Evaluations," *Journal of Personality and Social Psychology*, 106, no. 5 (May 2014): 728–751.
2. Eastwick and Hunt, "Relational Mate Value," 728.
3. Eastwick and Hunt, "Relational Mate Value," 745.
4. See Donna Freitas and Jason King, "Sex, Time, and Meaning: A Theology of Dating." *Horizons* 30 (2003): 25–40.
5. N = 24.
6. Association of Catholic Colleges and Universities, "FAQs: Catholic Higher Education," http://www.accunet.org/i4a/pages/index.cfm?pageid=3797#CatholicStudents.
7. Christian Smith et al., *Young Catholic America: Emerging Adults In, Out of, and Gone from the Church* (New York: Oxford University Press, 2014). His perspective of emerging Catholics reflects the broader trajectory of decline in religious participating by millennials. See David Kinnaman, *You Lost Me: Why Young Christians are Leaving Church . . . and Rethinking Faith* (Grand Rapids, MI: Baker Books, 2011) and the Institute for the Study of Society Issues, "More Americans Have No Religious Preference: Key Findings from the 2012 General Social Survey," March 2013, http://issi.berkeley.edu/sites/default/files/shared/docs/Hout%20et%20al_No%20Relig%20Pref%202012_Release%20Mar%202013.pdf.
8. Smith, *Young Catholic America*, 91.
9. Smith, *Young Catholic America*, 110.
10. Smith, *Young Catholic America*, 51.
11. The Cardinal Newman Society, "The Newman Guide to Choosing a Catholic College," http://www.cardinalnewmansociety.org/TheNewmanGuide/RecommendedColleges.aspx
12. For this list of publicly available data collected, see chapter 2.
13. See Caroline Heldman and Lisa Wade, "Hook-Up Culture: Setting a New Research Agenda," *Sexual Research and Social Policy* 7, no. 4 (2010): 325; Megan E. Patrick et al., "Measurement of Motivations for and Against Sexual Behavior," *Assessment* 18, no. 4 (2011): 506.
14. Melissa A. Lewis et al., "Predictors of Hooking up Sexual Behaviors and Emotional Reactions Among U. S. College Students," *Archives of Sexual Behavior* 41 (2012): 1227; Sara B. Oswalt, "Beyond Risk: Examining College Students' Sexual Decision Making," *American Journal of Sexuality Education* 5 (2010): 230–231.

15. Elaine M. Eshbaugh and Gary Gute, "Hookups and Sexual Regret Among College Women," *The Journal of Social Psychology* 148, no. 1 (2008): 83.

16. This kind of marginalization was not something that was mentioned directly by students on Very Catholic campuses. It is the implication of those in the qualitative survey who voice dissatisfaction with their campuses for being too accommodating and for not being "Catholic to the core" as one student wrote. It is also an extension of the socializing dynamics of cultures. Finally, there is also some evidence that Catholic campuses can be exclusionary when it comes to differences in religion. See Nicholas Bowman and Jenny Small, "Do College Students Who Identify with a Privileged Religion Experience Greater Spiritual Development? Exploring Individual and Institutional Dynamics," *Research in Higher Education* 51 (2010): 595–614.

17. Derek V. Price, "Learning Communities and Student Success in Postsecondary Education: A Background Paper," December 2005, http://www.mdrc.org/publications/418/full.pdf; Nancy S. Shapiro and Jodi H. Levine, *Creating Learning Communities: A Practical Guide to Winning Support, Organizing for Change, and Implementing Programs* (San Francisco, CA: Jossey-Bass, 1999).

18. Price, "Learning Communities."

19. Aaron M. Brower and Karen Kurotsuchi Inkelas, "Living-Learning: One High Impact Education Practice," *Liberal Education* 96, no. 2 (Spring 2010): 39.

20. Martha L. A. Stassen, "Student Outcomes: The Impact of Varying Living-Learning Community Models," *Research in Higher Education* 44, no. 5 (2003): 582–584. See also Kathe Taylor, *Learning Community Research and Assessment: What we Know Now* (Washington, DC: National Learning Communities Project Monograph Series, 2003); Vincent Tinto, "Learning Better Together: The Impact of Learning Communities on Student Success," *Promoting Student Success in College*, (Syracuse, NY: Higher Education Monograph Series, 2003), 1–8.

21. Price, "Learning Communities," 1.

22. Loyola University Chicago, "Residence Life: Currents LCs," http://www.luc.edu/learningcommunity/currentlcs/.

23. Marquette University, "Social Justice Living-Learning Community," http://www.marquette.edu/orl/res/specialty/dorothyday.shtml.

24. Duquesne University, "Learning Communities," http://www.duq.edu/academics/schools/liberal-arts/for-undergraduate-students/learning-communities.

25. See Stassen, "Student Outcomes," 608.

CHAPTER 6

1. Jason King, "A Theology of Dating for a Culture of Abuse," in *Leaving and Coming Home: New Wineskins for Catholic Sexual Ethics*, ed. David Cloutier (Eugene, OR: Cascade Books, 2010).

2. $N = 74$.

3. N = 571.

4. Craig Hill and Leslie Preston, "Individual Differences in the Experience of Sexual Motivation: Theory and Measurement of Dispositional Sexual Motives," *Journal of Sex Research* 33 (1996): 27–45; Cindy M. Meston and David M. Buss, "Why Humans Have Sex," *Archives of Sexual Behavior* 36 (2007): 477–507; Sara B. Oswalt, "Beyond Risk: Examining College Students' Sexual Decision Making," *American Journal of Sexuality Education* 5 (2010): 217–239; Megan E. Patrick, Jennifer L. Maggs, M. Lynne Cooper, and Christine M. Lee, "Measurements of Motivations for and Against Sexual Behavior," *Assessment* 18, no. 4 (2011): 502–516.

5. Herbert W. Helm, Jr., Duane C. McBride, David Knox, and Marty Zusman, "The Influence of a Conservative Religion on Premarital Sexual Behavior of University Students," *North American Journal of Psychology* 11, no. 2 (2009): 231–245.

6. Lisa Wade and Caroline Heldman, "Hooking Up and Opting Out—Negotiating Sex in the First Year of College," in *Sex for Life: From Virginity to Viagra, How Sexuality Changes Throughout Our Lives*, eds. Laura M. Carpenter and John DeLamater (New York: New York University Press, 2012); Elaine M. Eshbaugh and Gary Gute, "Hookups and Sexual Regret Among College Women," *The Journal of Social Psychology* 148, no. 1 (2008): 77–89; Conor Kelly, "Sexism in Practice: Feminist Ethics Evaluating the Hookup Culture," *Journal of Feminist Studies in Religion* 28, no. 2 (2012): 27–48; Kari-Shane Davis Zimmerman, "In Control? The Hookup Culture and the Practice of Relationships," in *Leaving and Coming Home: New Wineskins for Catholic Sexual Ethics*, ed. David Cloutier (Eugene, OR: Cascade Books, 2010).

7. Justin Garcia et al., "Sexual HookUp Culture: A Review," *Review of General Psychology* 16, no. 2 (2012): 168–169; see Robyn L. Fielder and Michael P. Carey, "Prevalence and Characteristics of Sexual Hookups Among First-Semester Female College Students," *Journal of Sex & Marital Therapy* 36 (2010): 352; Melissa A. Lewis et al., "Predictors of Hooking up Sexual Behaviors and Emotional Reactions Among U. S. College Students," *Archives of Sexual Behavior* 41 (2012): 1220–1221. Caroline Heldman and Lisa Wade, "Hook-Up Culture: Setting a New Research Agenda," *Sexual Research and Social Policy* 7, no. 4 (2010): 328; Antonia Abbey, "Alcohol-Related Sexual Assault: A Common Problem among College Students," *Journal of Studies on Alcohol Supplement* 14 (2002): 118–128.

8. Kate Taylor, "Sex on Campus: She Can Play That Game, Too," *New York Times*, ST1, July 14, 2013.

9. See Andy Soon Leong Tan, "Through the Drinking Glass: An Analysis of the Cultural Meanings of College Drinking," *Journal of Youth Studies* 15, no. 1 (2012): 132, for the various ways alcohol is used in social situations, especially those where sex is a possibility.

10. N = 599.

11. N = 74.

12. See Ann Swidler, "Settled and Unsettled Lives," *Talk of Love: How Culture Matters* (Chicago, IL: University of Chicago Press, 2003).

13. Donna Freitas, "Why We Get Boys Wrong: The Emotional Glass Ceiling," *The End of Sex: How Hookup Culture is Leaving a Generation Unhappy, Sexually Unfulfilled, and Confused about Intimacy* (New York: Basic Books, 2013).

14. Freitas, *The End of Sex*, 114–115.

CHAPTER 7

1. N = 74.

2. N = 23.

3. N = 422; N = 291.

4. N = 43.

5. N = 31.

6. The term *communio* represents a school of thought whose origins are often attributed to the 1985 Extraordinary meeting of the Synod of Bishops that celebrated the twentieth year anniversary of the closing of the council and used *communio* as an interpretive framework for the ecclesiology of the Second Vatican Council. By claiming that the Catholic culture of Mostly Catholic campuses is a *communio* Catholicism, I am not claiming that this culture is an intentional or systematic implementations of this school of thought. Instead, I am using *communio* in a more general sense that emphasizes the priority of relationships. It is an understanding closest to the ecclesiology of Elizabeth Johnson in *She Who Is: The Mystery of God in Feminist Theological Discourse* (New York: Crossroad, 1996) and *Friends of God and Prophets: A Feminist Theological Reading of the Communion of Saints* (New York: Continuum, 1999). For a discussion of how Johnson fits in with *communio* ecclesiology and the other versions of *communio* ecclesiology, see Dennis Doyle, *Communion Ecclesiology: Vision and Versions* (New York: Orbis Books, 2000).

7. The basic view is found in *Lumen Gentium* (The Dogmatic Constitution on the Church), but is expanded to include non-Catholics Christians in *Unitatis redintegratio* (Decree on Ecumenism), non-Christians in *Nostra Aetate* (Declaration on the Relation of the Church and Non-Christian Religions), and those in heaven *Sacrosanctum concilium* (the Constitution on the Sacred Liturgy). These documents can be found in Austin Flannery, ed., *Vatican Council II: The Conciliar and Post Conciliar Documents* (New York: Costello Publishing Company, Inc., 1992).

8. N = 63.

9. See table 7.1, "Contraception is wrong," "the pope can speak infallibly on faith and morals," and "the Magisterium is a teaching authority." While the last two might not seem linked to the church's sexual teachings, some of the central arguments supporting the church's sexual teaching are about issues of authority. See Charles Curran and Richard McCormick, eds., *Readings in Moral Theology No. 6: Dissent* (New York: Paulist Press, 1987).

CHAPTER 8

1. For example, see Nancy Jo Sales, "Tinder and the Dawn of the 'Dating Apocalypse,'" *Vanity Fair* (September 2015), and Alex Williams, "The End of Courtship?" *New York Times*, January 13, 2013, ST1.

2. N = 74.

3. N = 74.

4. For the studies on texting and relationships, see Sarah Coyne et al., "'I luv u:)!': A Descriptive Study of the Media Use of Individuals in Romantic Relationships," *Family Relations* 60 (2011): 150–162; Jeffery Hall, and Nancy Baym, "Calling and Texting (Too Much): Mobile Maintenance Expectations, (Over) Dependence, Entrapment, and Friendship Satisfaction," *New Media & Society* 14 (2012): 316–331; Aimee Miller-Ott, Lynne Kelly, and Robert Duran, "The Effects of Cell Phone Usage Rules on Satisfaction in Romantic Relationships," *Communication Quarterly* 60, no. 1 (2012): 17–34.

5. Jesse Fox and Katie M. Warber, "Romantic Relationship Development in the Age of Facebook: An Exploratory Study of Emerging Adults' Perceptions, Motives, and Behaviors," *Cyberpsychology, Behavior, and Social Networking* 16, no. 1 (2013): 3–7. Fox and Warber do note that there is some discrepancy in the value men and women place on the status of FBO, with women placing more importance on it than men. Still, it is noted as one of the key relationship markers.

6. For a description of the program, see "Healthy Relationships Initiative," http://www.stvincent.edu/Student_Life/Healthy_Relationships/Healthy_ Relationships/. It was originally presented by Bob Baum and Mary Collins as "Healthy Relationships: Remembering Romance" at the 2011 National Conference of Association of Student Affairs at Catholic Colleges and Universities in Boston. For the press release on the Association of Student Affairs at Catholic Colleges and Universities award, see "ASACCU Announces Mission Integration Winners," http://www.asaccu.org/index.php/in-the-news/ 136-asaccu-announces-mission-integration-winners.

CHAPTER 9

1. N = 47.

2. N = 136.

3. See Megan Barriger and Carlos Vélez-Blasini, "Descriptive and Injunctive Social Norm Overestimation in Hooking Up and Their Role as Predictors of Hook-Up Activity in a College Student Sample," *Journal of Sex Research* 50, no. 1 (2013): 84–89; Matthew Martens et al., "Differences Between Actual and Perceived Student Norms: An Examination of Alcohol Use, Drug Use, and Sexual Behavior," *Journal of American College Health* 54, no. 5 (2006): 295–300.

4. N = 136.

5. N = 47.

6. Justin Garcia et al., "Sexual HookUp Culture: A Review," *Review of General Psychology* 16, no. 2 (2012): 167–168.

7. Garcia et al., "Sexual HookUp Culture," 167–168.

8. Lisa Wade and Caroline Heldman, "Hooking Up and Opting Out: Negotiating Sex in the First Year of College," in *Sex for Life: From Virginity to Viagra, How Sexuality Changes Throughout Our Lives*, eds. Laura M. Carpenter and John DeLamater (New York: New York University Press, 2012), 140.

9. Sara Oswalt, Kenzie Cameron, and Jeffrey Koob, "Sexual Regret in College Students," *Archives of Sexual Behavior* 34, no. 6 (2005): 663–669; Megan Patrick, Jennifer Maggs, M. Lynne Cooper, and Christine Lee, "Measurement of Motivation For and Against Sexual Behavior," *Assessment* 18, no. 4 (2011): 502–516; Elaine M. Eshbaugh and Gary Gute, "Hookups and Sexual Regret Among College Women," *The Journal of Social Psychology* 148, no. 1 (2008): 77–89.

10. Mark Regnerus and Jeremy Uecker, *Premarital Sex in America: How Young Americans Meet, Mate, and Think about Marrying* (New York: Oxford University Press, 2011), 102.

11. For people tending not to speak out against the established norms, see Kimberly Rios Morrison and Dale Miller, "Distinguishing Between Silent and Vocal Minorities: Not All Deviants Feel Marginal," *Journal of Personality and Social Psychology* 94, no. 5 (2008): 871–882.

CHAPTER 10

1. N = 47.

2. N = 47.

3. These examples are taken from actual policies of the participating Catholic colleges and universities.

4. N = 47.

5. See Christian Smith et al., *Young Catholic America: Emerging Adults In, Out of, and Gone from the Church* (New York: Oxford University Press, 2014).

6. For a longer explanation of the forces driving Catholic institutions down this road, see Jason King, "After *Ex Corde Ecclesiae*," *Journal of Moral Theology* 4, no. 2 (2015): 167–191.

7. Matthew Garrett, "The Identity of American Catholic Higher Education: A Historical Overview," *Catholic Education: A Journal of Inquiry and Practice* 10, no. 2 (2006): 235–236.

8. See Kenneth Garcia, *Academic Freedom and the Telos of the Catholic University* (New York: Palgrave Macmillan, 2012), 119.

9. Garrett, "The Identity of American Catholic Higher Education," 236.

10. Susan Poulson and Loretta Higgins, "Gender, Coeducation, and the Transformation of Catholic Identity in American Catholic Higher Education," *Catholic Historical Review* 89, no. 3 (2003): 501.

11. Poulson and Higgins, "Gender, Coeducation, and the Transformation of Catholic Identity," 501.

12. See Thomas Reese, "Francis' Ecclesiology Rooted in the Emmaus Story," *National Catholic Reporter*, August 16–29, 2013, http://ncronline.org/news/spirituality/pope-francis-ecclesiology-rooted-emmaus-story.

CONCLUSION

1. This is typical. See Paul Eastwick and Lucy Hunt, "Relational Mate Value: Consensus and Uniqueness in Romantic Evaluations," *Journal of Personality and Social Psychology* 106, no. 5 (2014): 728–751.

2. For the ability of institutions to affect change by engaging these aspects of students' campus lives, see Lori E. Varlotta, "Teaching Students How to Talk About, Think About, and Do Community," *NASPA Journal* 45, no. 3 (2008): 329; David Cheng, "Students' Sense of Campus Community: What It Means, and What to Do About It," *NASPA Journal* 41, no. 2 (Winter 2004): 216–234; Larry Braskamp, Lois Calian Trautvetter, and Kelly Ward, "Putting Students First: Promoting Lives of Purpose and Meaning," *About Campus* 13, no. 1 (March–April 2008): 26–32.

3. Walter May, "The History of Student Governance in Higher Education," *The College Student Affairs Journal* 28, no. 2 (2010): 207–220.

4. John D. Foubert and Lauren U. Granger, "Effects of Involvement in Clubs and Organizations on the Psychosocial Development of First-Year and Senior College Students," *NASPA Journal* 43, no. 1 (2006): 166–182.

5. John P. Dugan, "Students' Involvement in Group Experiences and Connections to Leadership Development," *New Directions for Institutional Research, Assessment Supplement* (2011): 17–32. He gives an overview of types of clubs and accounts for the different kinds of contributions that they make to student involvement in the culture.

6. See Cheng, "Students' Sense of Campus Community," 229, for the importance of residence halls to the students' sense of belonging.

7. See Sandra M. Estanek, "The Association for Student Affairs at Catholic Colleges and Universities 1996–2009: Building a Community of Practice," *Journal of Catholic Higher Education* 33, no. 2 (2014): 187–205.

8. Frank Shushok Jr. et al., "A Tale of Three Campuses: Unearthing Theories of Residential Life That Shape the Student Learning Experience," *About Campus* 16, no. 3 (2011): 13–21.

9. May, "The History of Student Governance in Higher Education," 214.

10. J. Cherie Strachan, "Using the Classroom to Cultivate Student Support for Participation in Campus Life: The Call for Civic Education Interventions," *Journal of Political Science Education* 4 (2008): 21–41.

11. Dean Yin and Simon Lei, "Impacts of Campus Involvement on Hospitality Student Achievement and Satisfaction," *Education* 128, no. 2 (2007): 282–293.

12. Like most cultures, there can be a problematic side to the socializing aspect. Student groups can become stratified based on class, with the lower classes being excluded from groups and their benefits. See Jenny Stuber, "Class, Culture, and Participation in the Collegiate Extra-Curriculum," *Sociological Forum* 24, no. 4 (December 2009): 877–900.

13. Amy Frykholm, "Courage to Date," *The Christian Century*, January 12, 2012, http://www.christiancentury.org/article/2012-01/courage-date.

14. For an overview of Kerry Cronin's assignment, see Donna Freitas, *The End of Sex* (New York: Basic Books, 2013), 168–176.

15. Ken Bain, *What the Best College Teachers Do* (Cambridge, MA: Harvard University Press, 2004), 38–39.

16. Yin, "Impacts of Campus Involvement," 290.

17. James Brenner and Kathleen Swanik, "High-Risk Drinking Characteristics in Collegiate Athletes," *Journal of American College Health* 56, no. 3 (2007): 267–272. Katherine P. Theall et al., "Social Capital in the College Setting: The Impact of Participation in Campus Activities on Drinking and Alcohol-Related Harms," *Journal of American College Health* 58, no. 1 (2009): 15–23.

18. See Todd Crosset, Jeffrey Benedict, and Mark McDonald, "Male Student-Athletes Reported for Sexual Assault: A Survey of Campus Police Departments and Judicial Affairs Offices," *Journal of Sports and Social Issues* 19, no. 2 (1995): 126–140; Anders Sønderlund et al., "The Association between Sports Participation, Alcohol Use and Aggression and Violence: A Systematic Review," *Journal of Science and Medicine in Sports* 17, no. 1 (2013): 2–7.

19. See Jesse A. Steinfeldt and Matthew Clint Steinfeldt, "Profile of Masculine Norms and Help-Seeking Stigma in College Football," *Sport, Exercise, and Performance Psychology* 1, no. 1 (2012) 58–71; Jason Ford, "Alcohol Use among College Students: A Comparison of Athletes and Nonathletes," *Substance Use & Misuse* 42 (2007): 1367–1377; Gregory S. Wilson, Mary E. Pritchard, and Jamie Schaffer, "Athletic Status and Drinking Behavior in College Students: The Influence of Gender and Coping Styles," *Journal of American College Health* 52, no. 6 (2004): 269–273.

20. Emilie Buchwalkd, Pamela Fletcher, and Martha Roth, *Transforming Rape Culture* (Minneapolis, MN: Milkweed Editions, 1993); bell hooks, *Talking Back: Thinking Feminist, Thinking Black* (Boston, MA: South End Press, 1989).

21. For a fuller description of these policies and additional ones of importance, see American Association of University Professors, "Campus Sexual Assault: Suggested Policies and Procedures," November 2012, http://www.aaup.org/report/campus-sexual-assault-suggested-policies-and-procedures.

22. For the importance of these elements in sexual assault prevention, especially in athletics, see H. Wesley Perkins, "Social Norms and the Prevention of Alcohol Misuse in Collegiate Contexts," *Journal of Studies on Alcohol Supplement* 14 (2002): 164–172; Theall et al., "Social Capital in the College Setting," 15–23;

David S. Lee et al., "Sexual Violence Prevention," *The Prevention Researcher* 14, no. 2 (2007): 15–20.

23. See Pope Francis, *Evangelii Gaudium*, 171, November 24, 2013, http://w2.vatican. va/content/francesco/en/apost_exhortations/documents/papa-francesco_ esortazione-ap_20131124_evangelii-gaudium.html.

METHODOLOGY APPENDIX

1. For the use of a mixed method approach for analyzing culture, see Adam Cohen, "Many Forms of Culture," *American Psychologist* 64, no. 3 (2009): 201.

2. D. T. Campbell and D. W. Fisks, "Convergent and Discriminant Validation by the Multitrait-Multimethod Matrix," *Psychological Bulletin* 56 (1959): 81–105, is often viewed as the first categorization of the practice of mixed method research. The mixed method approach—referred to at times as multi-trait research, methodological triangulation, combined or hybrid methods—rose to more prominence in the late 1980s and acquired wide acceptability with the National Institutes of Health's Office of Behavioral and Social Sciences Research 1999 publication of guidelines for mixed methods research. For overviews of this methodology, see R. Burke Johnson, Anthony Onwuegbuzie, and Lisa Turner, "Toward a Definition of Mixed Methods Research," *Journal of Mixed Methods Research* 1, no. 2 (2007): 112–133, and John Creswell, *Research Design: Qualitative, Quantitative, and Mixed Methods Approaches*, 4th ed. (New York: Sage Publications, 2014).

3. Duane Alwin et al., "Measuring Religious Identities in Surveys," *Public Opinion Quarterly* 70, no. 4 (2006): 530–564.

4. Christian Smith noted friends as a measure for religious commitment in his *Soul Searching: The Religious and Spiritual Lives of American Teenagers* (New York: Oxford University Press, 2005), 57–58.

5. For some typical examples, see Anne Clifford, "Identity and Vision at Catholic Colleges and Universities," *Horizons* 35, no. 2 (2008): 356–362; Stanley Hauerwas, *The State of the University: Academic Knowledges and the Knowledge of God* (Malden, MA: Blackwell Publishing, 2007); Kenneth Garcia, *Academic Freedom and the Telos of the Catholic University* (New York: Palgrave Macmillan, 2012); Matthew Garrett, "The Identity of American Catholic Higher Education: A Historical Overview," *Catholic Education: A Journal of Inquiry and Practice* 10, no. 2 (2006): 230–231; Alasdair MacIntyre, *God, Philosophy, Universities: A Selective History of the Catholic Philosophical Tradition* (Lanham, MD: Rowman & Littlefield, 2011).

6. Melanie M. Morey and John J. Piderit, *Catholic Higher Education: A Culture in Crisis* (New York: Oxford University Press, 2006).

7. "College Rankings," *First Things*, November 2010, http://www.firstthings.com/ article/2010/11/college-rankings; "The Newman Guide to Choosing a Catholic College," *The Cardinal Newman Society*, http://www.cardinalnewmansociety.org/ TheNewmanGuide/RecommendedColleges.aspx.

8. Frances Freeman, *Catholic Higher Education: An American Profile* (Association of Catholic Colleges and Universities, 1993).

9. Anthony Carnevale and Jeff Strohl, "Separate & Unequal," *Center for Education and the Workforce*, July 31, 2013, https://cew.georgetown.edu/separateandunequal.

10. See Kathleen Bogle, *Hooking Up: Sex, Dating, and Relationships on Campus* (New York: New York University Press, 2008), 67–68.

11. Association of Catholic Colleges and Universities, "FAQs: Catholic Higher Education," http://www.accunet.org/i4a/pages/index.cfm?pageid=3797#Enrolled.

12. See Association of Catholic Colleges and Universities, "FAQs: Catholic Higher Education," http://www.accunet.org/i4a/pages/index.cfm?pageid=3797#CatholicStudents.

13. *Qualtrics* refers to contingency tables as "cross-tabulations."

Bibliography

Abbey, Antonia. "Alcohol-Related Sexual Assault: A Common Problem among College Students." *Journal of Studies on Alcohol, Supplement* 14 (2002): 118–128.

Adamczyk, Amy. "Socialization and Selection in the Link between Friends' Religiosity and the Transition to Sexual Intercourse." *Sociology of Religion* 70, no. 1 (2009): 5–27.

Adamczyk, Amy and Jacob Felson. "Friends' Religiosity and First Sex." *Social Science Research* 35 (2006): 924–947.

Alwin, Duane, Jacob Felson, Edward Walker, and Paula Tufis. "Measuring Religious Identities in Surveys." *Public Opinion Quarterly* 70, no. 4 (2006): 530–564.

American Association of University Professors. "Campus Sexual Assault: Suggested Policies and Procedures." November 2012. http://www.aaup.org/report/campus-sexual-assault-suggested-policies-and-procedures.

Association of Catholic Colleges and Universities. "FAQs: Catholic Higher Education." http://www.accunet.org/i4a/pages/index.cfm?pageid=3797#CatholicStudents.

Saint Augustine. *Confessions.* New York: Penguin Books, 1961.

Auritt, Elizabeth, Libby Coleman, Nicholas Fandos, Jacob Feldman, Mikita Kansra, Jared Lucky, and Samuel Weinstock. "The Class of 2015 by the Numbers." *The Harvard Crimson,* May 28, 2015. http://features.thecrimson.com/2015/senior-survey/.

Bain, Ken. *What the Best College Teachers Do.* Cambridge, MA: Harvard University Press, 2004.

Barriger, Megan and Carlos Vélez-Blasini. "Descriptive and Injunctive Social Norm Overestimation in Hooking Up and Their Role as Predictors of Hook-Up Activity in a College Student Sample." *Journal of Sex Research* 50, no. 1 (2013): 84–94.

Bay-Cheng, Laina Y. and Rebecca K. Eliseo-Arras. "The Making of Unwanted Sex: Gendered and Neoliberal Norms in College Women's Unwanted Sexual Experiences." *Journal of Sex Research* 45, no. 4 (2008): 386–397.

Bisson, Melissa A. and Timothy R. Levine. "Negotiating a Friends with Benefits Relationship." *Archives of Sexual Behavior* 38 (2009): 66–73.

Bogle, Kathleen. *Hooking Up: Sex, Dating and Relationships on Campus.* New York: New York University Press, 2008.

Bowman, Nicholas and Jenny Small. "Do College Students Who Identify with a Privileged Religion Experience Greater Spiritual Development? Exploring Individual and Institutional Dynamics." *Research in Higher Education* 51 (2010): 595–614.

Braskamp, Larry, Lois Calian Trautvetter, and Kelly Ward. "Putting Students First: Promoting Lives of Purpose and Meaning." *About Campus* 13, no. 1 (March–April 2008): 26–32.

Brenner, James and Kathleen Swanik. "High-Risk Drinking Characteristics in Collegiate Athletes." *Journal of American College Health* 56, no. 3 (2007): 267–272.

Brinkmann, Svend. "Culture as Practices: A Pragmatist Conception." *Journal of Theoretical and Philosophical Psychology* 28 (2008): 192–210.

Brower, Aaron M. and Karen Kurotsuchi Inkelas. "Living-Learning: One High Impact Education Practice." *Liberal Education* 96, no. 2 (Spring 2010): 36–43.

Buchwalkd, Emilie, Pamela Fletcher, and Martha Roth. *Transforming Rape Culture.* Minneapolis, MN: Milkweed Editions, 1993.

Burdette, Amy, Christopher Ellison, Terrence Hill, and Norval Glenn. "'Hooking Up' at College: Does Religion Make a Difference?" *Journal for the Scientific Study of Religion* 48, no. 3 (2009): 535–551.

Campbell, D. T. and D. W. Fisks. "Convergent and Discriminant Validation by the Multitrait-Multimethod Matrix." *Psychological Bulletin* 56 (1959): 81–105.

The Cardinal Newman Society. "The Newman Guide to Choosing a Catholic College." http://www.cardinalnewmansociety.org/TheNewmanGuide/Recommended Colleges.aspx.

Carnevale, Anthony and Jeff Strohl. "Separate & Unequal." *Center for Education and the Workforce,* July 31, 2013. https://cew.georgetown.edu/separateandunequal.

Carr, Joetta L. and Karen M. VanDuesen. "Risk Factors of Male Sexual Aggression on College Campuses." *Journal of Family Violence* 19, no. 5 (2004): 279–289.

Center for Disease Control and Prevention. "Understanding Sexual Violence: Fact Sheet 2014." http://www.cdc.gov/violenceprevention/pdf/sv-factsheet.pdf.

Chao, Georgia T. and Henry Moon. "The Cultural Mosaic: A Metatheory for Understanding the Complexity of Culture." *Journal of Applied Psychology* 90, no. 6 (2005): 1128–1140.

Cheng, David. "Students' Sense of Campus Community: What It Means, and What to Do About It." *NASPA Journal* 41, no. 2 (Winter 2004): 216–234.

Ching, Wan, Chi-Yue Chiu, Siqing Peng, and Kim-Pong Tam. "Measuring Cultures through Intersubjective Cultural Norms: Implications for Predicting Relative Identification with Two or More Cultures." *Journal of Cross-Cultural Psychology* 38, no. 2 (2007): 213–226.

Chiu, Chi-Yue and Ying-Yi Hong. *Social Psychology of Culture*. New York: Psychology Press, 2006.

Clifford, Anne. "Identity and Vision at Catholic Colleges and Universities." *Horizons* 35, no. 2 (2008): 356–362.

Cohen, Adam. "Many Forms of Culture." *American Psychologist* 64, no. 3 (2009): 194–204.

Collins, Mary and Bob Baum. "Healthy Relationships: Remembering Romance." Presentation at the National Conference of the Association of Student Affairs at Catholic Colleges and Universities, Boston, MA, 2011.

Cooper, M. Lynne and Cheryl M. Shapiro. "Motivations for Sex and Risky Sexual Behavior Among Adolescents and Young Adults: A Functional Perspective." *Journal of Personality and Social Psychology* 73, no. 6 (1998): 1528–1558.

Coyne, Sarah, Laura Stockdale, Dean Busby, Bethany Iverson, and David Grant. "'I luv u:)!': A Descriptive Study of the Media Use of Individuals in Romantic Relationships." *Family Relations* 60 (2011): 150–162.

Crawford, Mary and Danielle Popp, "Sexual Double Standards: A Review and Methodological Critique of Two Decades of Research," *The Journal of Sex Research* 40, no. 1 (2003): 13–26.

Creswell, John. *Research Design: Qualitative, Quantitative, and Mixed Methods Approaches*. 4th ed. New York: Sage Publications, 2014.

Crosset, Todd, Jeffrey Benedict, and Mark McDonald. "Male Student-Athletes Reported for Sexual Assault: A Survey of Campus Police Departments and Judicial Affairs Offices." *Journal of Sports and Social Issues* 19, no. 2 (1995): 126–140.

Curran, Charles and Richard McCormick, eds. *Readings in Moral Theology No. 6: Dissent*. New York: Paulist Press, 1987.

Davis, Kelly Cue, Jeanette Norris, William H. George, Joel Martell, and Julia Heiman. "Men's Likelihood of Sexual Aggression: The Influence of Alcohol, Sexual Arousal, and Violent Pornography." *Aggressive Behavior* 32 (2006): 581–589.

Day, Dorothy. *The Long Loneliness*. New York: HarperCollins, 1997.

Dillon, Dana and David McCarthy. "Natural Law, Law, and Freedom." In *Gathered for the Journey: Moral Theology in Catholic Perspective*, edited by David Matzko McCarthy and M. Therese Lysaught, 153–176. Grand Rapids, MI: William B. Eerdmans Publishing Company, 2007.

Doyle, Dennis. *Communion Ecclesiology: Vision and Versions*. New York: Orbis Books, 2000.

Dugan, John P. "Students' Involvement in Group Experiences and Connections to Leadership Development." *New Directions for Institutional Research* Supplement 1 (2011): 17–32.

Eastwick, Paul and Lucy Hunt. "Relational Mate Value: Consensus and Uniqueness in Romantic Evaluations." *Journal of Personality and Social Psychology* 106, no. 5 (May 2014): 728–751.

Edwards, Sarah R. and David L. Vogel. "Young Men's Likelihood Ratings to Be Sexually Aggressive as a Function of Norms and Perceived Sexual Interest." *Psychology of Men and Masculinity* 16, no. 1 (2015): 88–96.

Epstein, Marina, Jerel P. Calzo, Andrew Smiler, and L. Monique Ward. "'Anything from Making Out to Having Sex': Men's Negotiations of Hooking Up and Friends with Benefits Scripts." *Journal of Sex Research* 46 (2009): 414–424.

Eshbaugh, Elaine M. and Gary Gute. "Hookups and Sexual Regret Among College Women." *The Journal of Social Psychology* 148, no. 1 (2008): 77–89.

Estanek, Sandra M. "The Association for Student Affairs at Catholic Colleges and Universities 1996–2009: Building a Community of Practice." *Journal of Catholic Higher Education* 33, no. 2 (2014): 187–205.

Farley, Margaret. *Just Love: A Framework for Christian Sexual Ethics*. New York: Continuum International Publishing Group, 2006.

Fielder, Robyn L. and Michael P. Carey. "Prevalence and Characteristics of Sexual Hookups Among First-Semester Female College Students." *Journal of Sex & Marital Therapy* 36 (2010): 346–359.

Fielder, Robyn L., Jennifer L. Walsh, Kate B. Carey, and Michael P. Carey. "Predictors of Sexual Hookups: A Theory-Based, Prospective Study of First-Year College Women." *Archives of Sexual Behavior* 42 (2013): 1425–1441.

First Things. "College Rankings." November 2010. http://www.firstthings.com/article/2010/11/college-rankings.

Flannery, Austin, ed. *Vatican Council II: The Conciliar and Post Conciliar Documents*. New York: Costello Publishing Company, Inc., 1992.

Ford, Jason. "Alcohol Use among College Students: A Comparison of Athletes and Nonathletes." *Substance Use & Misuse* 42 (2007): 1367–1377.

Foubert, John D. and Lauren U. Granger. "Effects of Involvement in Clubs and Organizations on the Psychosocial Development of First-Year and Senior College Students." *NASPA Journal* 43, no. 1 (2006): 166–182.

Fox, Jesse and Katie M. Warber. "Romantic Relationship Development in the Age of Facebook: An Exploratory Study of Emerging Adults' Perceptions, Motives, and Behaviors." *Cyberpsychology, Behavior, and Social Networking* 16, no. 1 (2013): 3–7.

Pope Francis. *Evangelii Gaudium*. Vatican City: Libreria Editrice Vaticana, 2013. http://w2.vatican.va/content/francesco/en/apost_exhortations/documents/papa-francesco_esortazione-ap_20131124_evangelii-gaudium.html.

Freitas, Donna. *The End of Sex: How Hookup Culture is Leaving a Generation Unhappy, Sexually Unfulfilled and Confused About Intimacy*. New York: Basic Books, 2013.

———. *Sex and the Soul: Juggling Sexuality, Spirituality, Romance, and Religion on America's College Campuses*. New York: Oxford University Press, 2008.

Freitas, Donna and Jason King. "Sex, Time, and Meaning: A Theology of Dating." *Horizons* 30 (2003): 25–40.

Freeman, Frances. *Catholic Higher Education: An American Profile*. Association of Catholic Colleges and Universities, 1993.

Frykholm, Amy. "Courage to Date." *The Christian Century*, January 12, 2012. http://www.christiancentury.org/article/2012-01/courage-date.

Garcia, Justin, Chris Reiber, Sean G. Massey, and Ann M. Merriwether. "Sexual HookUp Culture: A Review." *Review of General Psychology* 16, no. 2 (2012): 161–176.

Garcia, Kenneth. *Academic Freedom and the Telos of the Catholic University.* New York: Palgrave Macmillan, 2012.

Garrett, Matthew. "The Identity of American Catholic Higher Education: A Historical Overview." *Catholic Education: A Journal of Inquiry and Practice* 10, no. 2 (2006): 229–247.

Gleason, Philip. *Contending with Modernity: Catholic Higher Education in the United States.* New York: Oxford University Press, 1995.

Gray, Mark and Melissa Cidade. "Catholicism on Campus: Stability and Change in Catholic Student Faith by College Type." *Catholic Education: A Journal of Inquiry and Practice* 14, no. 2 (2010): 212–237.

Gunnoe, Marjorie Lindener and Kristin A. Moore. "Predictors of Religiosity Among Youth Aged 17–22: A Longitudinal Study of the National Survey of Children." *Journal of the Scientific Study of Religion* 41, no. 4 (2002): 613–622.

Hall, Jeffery, and Nancy Baym. "Calling and Texting (Too Much): Mobile Maintenance Expectations, (Over) Dependence, Entrapment, and Friendship Satisfaction." *New Media & Society* 14 (2012): 316–331.

Hauerwas, Stanley. *The State of the University: Academic Knowledges and the Knowledge of God.* Malden, MA: Blackwell Publishing, 2007.

Heldman, Caroline and Lisa Wade. "Hook-Up Culture: Setting a New Research Agenda." *Sexual Research and Social Policy* 7, no. 4 (2010): 323–333.

Helm Jr., Herbert W., Duane C. McBride, David Knox, and Marty Zusman. "The Influence of a Conservative Religion on Premarital Sexual Behavior of University Students." *North American Journal of Psychology* 11, no. 2 (2009): 231–245.

Hill, Craig and Leslie Preston. "Individual Differences in the Experience of Sexual Motivation: Theory and Measurement of Dispositional Sexual Motives." *Journal of Sex Research* 33 (1996): 27–45.

Hogben, Matthew, Donn Byrne, Merle E. Hamburger, and Julie Osland. "Legitimized Aggression and Sexual Coercion: Individual Differences in Cultural Spillover." *Aggressive Behavior* 27 (2001): 26–43.

hooks, bell. *Talking Back: Thinking Feminist, Thinking Black.* Boston, MA: South End Press, 1989.

Ignatow, Gabriel. "Theories of Embodied Knowledge: New Directions for Cultural and Cognitive Sociology?" *Journal for the Theory of Social Behavior* 37, no. 2 (2007): 115–135.

Institute for the Study of Society Issues. "More Americans Have No Religious Preference: Key Findings from the 2012 General Social Survey." March 2013. http://issi.berkeley.edu/sites/default/files/shared/docs/Hout%20et%20al_No%20Relig%20Pref%202012_Release%20Mar%202013.pdf.

Johnson, Elizabeth. *Friends of God and Prophets: A Feminist Theological Reading Of The Communion Of Saints.* New York: Continuum, 1998.

Johnson, Elizabeth. *She Who Is: The Mystery of God in Feminist Theological Discourse.* New York: Crossroad, 1996.

Johnson, R. Burke, Anthony Onwuegbuzie, and Lisa Turner. "Toward a Definition of Mixed Methods Research." *Journal of Mixed Methods Research* 1, no. 2 (2007): 112–133.

Kahn, Arnold S. "What College Women Do and Do Not Experience as Rape." *Psychology of Women Quarterly* 28 (2004): 9–15.

Kelly, Conor. "Sexism in Practice: Feminist Ethics Evaluating the Hookup Culture." *Journal of Feminist Studies in Religion* 28, no. 2 (2012): 27–48.

Kelman, Herbert C. "Interests, Relationships, Identities: Three Central Issues for Individuals and Groups in Negotiating Their Social Environment." *Annual Review of Psychology* 57 (2006): 1–26.

Kemmelmeier, Markus and Ulrich Kühnen. "Culture as Process: the Dynamics of Cultural Stability and Change." *Social Psychology* 43, no. 4 (2012): 171–173.

King, Jason. "After *Ex Corde Ecclesiae.*" *Journal of Moral Theology* 4, no. 2 (2015): 167–191.

———. "A Theology of Dating for a Culture of Abuse." In *Leaving and Coming Home: New Wineskins for Catholic Sexual Ethics,* edited by David Cloutier. Eugene, OR: Cascade Books, 2010.

King, Jason and Andy Herr, "Does Catholic Identity Affect Students?" *Journal of Catholic Higher Education* 34, no. 2 (2015) 195–209.

Kinnaman, David. *You Lost Me: Why Young Christians are Leaving Church . . . and Rethinking Faith.* Grand Rapids, MI: Baker Books, 2011.

Komonchak, Joseph. "Modernity and the Construction of Roman Catholicism." *Cristianismo nella storia* 18 (1997): 353–385.

Lebacqz, Karen. "Love your Enemy: Sex, Power, and Christian Ethics," *Annual of the Society of Christian Ethics* 10, no. 1 (2006): 3–23.

Lee, David S., Lydia Guy, Brad Petty, Chad Keoni Sniffen, and Stacy Alamo Mison. "Sexual Violence Prevention." *The Prevention Researcher* 14, no. 2 (2007): 15–20.

Lewis, Melissa A., Hollie Granato, Jessica A. Blayney, Ty W. Lostutter, Jason R. Kilmer. "Predictors of Hooking up Sexual Behaviors and Emotional Reactions Among U.S. College Students." *Archives of Sexual Behavior* 41 (2012): 1219–1229.

Lonergan, Bernard, *Insight.* Toronto: University of Toronto Press, 1997.

———. *Method in Theology.* Toronto: University of Toronto Press, 1972.

MacIntyre, Alasdair. *God, Philosophy, Universities: A Selective History of the Catholic Philosophical Tradition.* Lanham, MD: Rowman & Littlefield, 2011.

Mann, Ruth and Clive Hollin. "Sexual Offenders' Explanation for their Offending." *Journal of Sexual Aggression* 13, no. 1 (March 2007): 3–9.

Manthos, Megan, Jesse Own, and Frank D. Fincham. "A New Perspective on Hooking Up Among College Students: Sexual Behavior as a Function of Distinct Groups." *Journal of Social and Personal Relationships* 31, no. 6 (2014): 815–829.

Martens, Matthew, Jennifer Page, Emily Mowry, Krista Damann, Kari Taylor, and M. Dolores Cimini. "Differences Between Actual and Perceived Student Norms: An Examination of Alcohol Use, Drug Use, and Sexual Behavior." *Journal of American College Health* 54, no. 5 (2006): 295–300.

May, Walter. "The History of Student Governance in Higher Education." *The College Student Affairs Journal* 28, no. 2 (2010): 207–220.

McCullough, Michael E. and Brian L. B. Wiloughby. "Religion, Self-Regulation, and Self-Control: Associations, Explanations, and Implications." *Psychological Bulletin* 135, no. 1 (2009): 69–93.

Meston, Cindy M. and David M. Buss. "Why Humans Have Sex." *Archives of Sexual Behavior* 36 (2007): 477–507.

Miller-Ott, Aimee, Lynne Kelly, and Robert Duran. "The Effects of Cell Phone Usage Rules on Satisfaction in Romantic Relationships." *Communication Quarterly* 60, no. 1 (2012): 17–34.

Morey Melanie M. and John J. Piderit. *Catholic Higher Education: A Culture in Crisis*. New York: Oxford University Press, 2006.

Morrison, Kimberly Rios and Dale T. Miller. "Distinguishing Between Silent and Vocal Minorities: Not All Deviants Feel Marginal." *Journal of Personality and Social Psychology* 94, no. 5 (2008): 871–882.

O'Connor, Flannery. *The Complete Stories*. New York: Farrar, Straus and Giroux, 1971.

———. *Mystery and Manners: Occasional Prose*. New York: Farrar, Straus and Giroux, 1969.

Oswalt, Sara B. "Beyond Risk: Examining College Students' Sexual Decision Making." *American Journal of Sexuality Education* 5 (2010): 217–239.

Oswalt, Sara B., Kenzie A. Cameron, and Jeffry J. Koob. "Sexual Regret in College Students." *Archives of Sexual Behavior* 34, no.6 (2005): 663–669.

Owen, Jess, Galena Rhoades, Scott Stanley, and Frank Fincham. "'Hooking Up' Among College Students: Demographic and Psychosocial Correlates." *Archives of Sexual Behavior* 39 (2010): 653–663.

Ozer, Emily J., M. Margaret Dolcini, and Gary W. Harper. "Adolescents' Reasons for Having Sex: Gender Differences." *Journal of Adolescent Health* 33 (2003): 317–319.

Patrick, Megan E., Jennifer L. Maggs, M. Lynne Cooper, and Christine M. Lee. "Measurements of Motivations for and Against Sexual Behavior." *Assessment* 18, no. 4 (2011): 502–516.

Paul, Pamela. *Pornified: How Pornography Is Damaging Our Lives, Our Relationships, and Our Families*. New York: Times Book, 2005.

Penhollow, Tina, Michael Young, and George Denny. "Impact of Personal and Organizational Religiosity on College Student Sexual Behavior." *American Journal of Health Studies* 27, no. 1 (2012): 13–22.

Perkins, H. Wesley. "Social Norms and the Prevention of Alcohol Misuse in Collegiate Contexts." *Journal of Studies on Alcohol Supplement* 14 (2002): 164–172.

Perl, Paul and Mark Gray. "Catholic Schooling and Disaffiliation from Catholicism." *Journal for the Scientific Study of Religion* 46, no. 2 (2007): 269–280.

Portier, William. "Here Come the Evangelical Catholics." *Communio: International Catholic Review* 31 (2004): 35–66.

Poulson, Susan and Loretta Higgins. "Gender, Coeducation, and the Transformation of Catholic Identity in American Catholic Higher Education." *Catholic Historical Review* 89, no. 3 (2003): 489–510.

Price, Derek V. "Learning Communities and Student Success in Postsecondary Education: A Background Paper." December 2005. http://www.mdrc.org/publications/418/full.pdf.

Quinn, Naomi. "Culture and Contradiction: The Case of Americans Reasoning about Marriage." *Ethos* 24, no. 3 (1996): 391–425.

Reese, Thomas. "Francis' Ecclesiology Rooted in the Emmaus Story." *National Catholic Reporter*, August 16–29, 2013. http://ncronline.org/news/spirituality/pope-francis-ecclesiology-rooted-emmaus-story.

Regnerus, Mark and Jeremy Uecker. *Premarital Sex in America: How Young Americans Meet, Mate, and Think about Marrying.* New York: Oxford University Press, 2011.

Rimal, Rajiv N. "Modeling the Relationship Between Descriptive Norms and Behaviors: A Test and Extension of the Theory of Normative Social Behavior." *Health Communication* 23 (2008): 103–116.

Rimal, Rajiv N. and Kevin Real. "Understanding the Influence of Perceived Norms on Behaviors." *Communication Theory* 13, no. 2 (2003): 184–203.

Roach, Mark. *The Intellectual Appeal Of Catholicism and the Idea of a Catholic University.* Notre Dame, IN: University of Notre Dame Press, 2003.

Rostosky, Sharon Scales, Brian L. Wilcox, Margaret Laurie Corner Wright, and Brandy A. Randall. "The Impact of Religiosity on Adolescent Sexual Behavior: A Review of the Evidence." *Journal of Adolescent Research* 19, no. 6 (2004): 677–697.

Rowatt, Wade C. and David P. Schmitt. "Associations Between Religious Orientation and Varieties of Sexual Experience." *Journal for the Scientific Study of Religion* 42, no. 3 (2003): 455–465.

Sales, Nancy Jo. "Tinder and the Dawn of the 'Dating Apocalypse.'" *Vanity Fair.* September 2015. http://www.vanityfair.com/culture/2015/08/tinder-hook-up-culture-end-of-dating.

Shapiro, Nancy S. and Jodi H. Levine. *Creating Learning Communities: A Practical Guide to Winning Support, Organizing for Change, and Implementing Programs.* San Francisco, CA: Jossey-Bass, 1999.

ShushokJr., Frank, T. Laine Scales, Rishi Sriram, and Vera Kidd. "A Tale of Three Campuses: Unearthing Theories of Residential Life That Shape the Student Learning Experience." *About Campus* 16, no. 3 (2011): 13–21.

Simons, Leslie Gordon, Callie Harbin Burt, and F. Ryan Peterson. "The Effect of Religion on Risky Sexual Behavior Among College Students." *Deviant Behavior* 30 (2009): 467–483.

Smith, Christian. *What Is a Person?* New York: Oxford University Press, 2010.

———. *Soul Searching: The Religious and Spiritual Lives of American Teenagers.* New York: Oxford University Press, 2005.

———. *Moral Believing Animals: Human Personhood and Culture.* New York: Oxford University Press, 2003.

———. "Religious Participation and Network Closure among American Adolescents." *Journal for the Scientific Study of Religion* 42, no. 2 (2003): 259–267.

Smith, Christian, Kyle Longest, Jonathan Hill, and Kari Christofferson. *Young Catholic America: Emerging Adults In, Out of, and Gone from the Church.* New York: Oxford University Press, 2014.

Smith, Joanne R. and Winnifred R. Louis. "Do as We Say *and* as We Do: The Interplay of Descriptive and Injunctive Group Norms in the Attitude-Behavior Relationship." *British Journal of Social Psychology* 47 (2008): 647–666.

Sønderlund, Anders, Kerry O'Brien, Peter Kremer, Bosco Rowland, Florentine De Groot, Petra Staiger, Lucy Zinkiewicz, and Peter Miller. "The Association between Sports Participation, Alcohol Use and Aggression and Violence: A Systematic Review." *Journal of Science and Medicine in Sports* 17, no. 1 (2013): 2–7.

Stassen, Martha L. A. "Student Outcomes: The Impact of Varying Living-Learning Community Models." *Research in Higher Education* 44, no. 5 (2003): 581–613.

Steinfeldt, Jesse A. and Matthew Clint Steinfeldt. "Profile of Masculine Norms and Help-Seeking Stigma in College Football." *Sport, Exercise, and Performance Psychology* 1, no. 1 (2012): 58–71.

Strachan, J. Cherie. "Using the Classroom to Cultivate Student Support for Participation in Campus Life: The Call for Civic Education Interventions." *Journal of Political Science Education* 4 (2008): 21–41.

Stuber, Jenny. "Class, Culture, and Participation in the Collegiate Extra-Curriculum." *Sociological Forum* 24, no. 4 (December 2009): 877–900.

Sugai, George, Breda V. O'Keeffe, and Lindsay M. Fallon. "A Contextual Consideration of Culture and School Wide Positives Heavier Support." *Journal of Positive Behavior Interventions* 14, no. 4 (2012): 197–208.

Sweeney, Brian. "Party Animals or Responsible Men: Social Class, Race, and Masculinity on Campus." *International Journal of Qualitative Studies in Education* 27, no. 6 (2014): 804–821

Swidler, Ann. *Talk of Love: How Culture Matters.* Chicago, IL: University of Chicago Press, 2003.

Tan, Andy Soon Leong. "Through the Drinking Glass: An Analysis of the Cultural Meanings of College Drinking." *Journal of Youth Studies* 15, no. 1 (2012): 119–142.

Taylor, Kate. "Sex on Campus: She Can Play That Game, Too." *New York Times*, ST1, July 14, 2013.

Taylor, Kathe. *Learning Community Research and Assessment: What we Know Now.* Washington, DC: National Learning Communities Project Monograph Series, 2003.

Bibliography

Thaler, Richard. *Winner's Curse*. Princeton, NJ: Princeton University Press, 1994.

Theall, Katherine P., William DeJong, Richard Scribner, Karen Mason, Shari Kessel Schneider, and Neal Simonsen. "Social Capital in the College Setting: The Impact of Participation in Campus Activities on Drinking and Alcohol-Related Harms." *Journal of American College Health* 58, no. 1 (2009): 15–23.

Thompson, Martie P. and Deidra J. Morrison. "Prospective Predictors of Technology-Based Sexual Coercion by College Males." *Psychology of Violence* 3, no. 3 (2013): 233–246.

Tinto, Vincent. "Learning Better Together: The Impact of Learning Communities on Student Success." *Promoting Student Success in College*. Syracuse, NY: Higher Education Monograph Series, 2003.

Torelli, Carlos J. and Sharon Shavitt. "Culture and Concepts of Power." *Journal of Personality and Social Psychology* 99, no. 4 (2010): 703–723.

Tversky, Amos and Daniel Kahneman. "The Framing of Decisions and the Psychology of Choice." *Science* 211, no. 4481 (1981): 453–458.

Tversky, Amos and Richard Thaler. "Preference Reversals." *Journal of Economic Perspectives* 4, no. 3 (1990): 201–211.

Uecker, Jeremy, Mark Regnerus, and Margaret L. Vaaler. "Losing my Religion: The Social Sources of Religious Decline in Early Adulthood." *Social Forces* 85, no. 4 (2007): 1667–1692.

Van Gorp, Baldwin. "The Constructionist Approach to Framing: Bringing Culture Back In." *Journal of Communication* 57 (2007): 60–78.

Vandenbos, Gary R., ed. *APA Dictionary of Psychology*. Washington, DC: American Psychological Association, 2007.

Varlotta, Lori E. "Teaching Students How to Talk About, Think About, and Do Community." *NASPA Journal* 45, no. 3 (2008): 327–349.

Vazsonyi, Alexander T. and Dusty D. Jenkins. "Religiosity, Self-Control, and Virginity Status in College Students from the 'Bible Belt': A Research Note." *Journal for the Scientific Study of Religion* 49, no. 3 (2010): 561–568.

Wade, Lisa and Caroline Heldman. "Hooking Up and Opting Out: Negotiating Sex in the First Year of College." In *Sex for Life: From Virginity to Viagra, How Sexuality Changes Throughout Our Lives*, edited by Laura M. Carpenter and John DeLamater, 128–145. New York: New York University Press, 2012.

Williams, Alex. "The End of Courtship?" *New York Times*. January 13, 2013, ST1.

Wilson, Gregory S., Mary E. Pritchard, and Jamie Schaffer. "Athletic Status and Drinking Behavior in College Students: The Influence of Gender and Coping Styles." *Journal of American College Health* 52, no. 6 (2004): 269–273.

Yin, Dean Yin and Simon Lei. "Impacts of Campus Involvement on Hospitality Student Achievement and Satisfaction." *Education* 128, no. 2 (2007) 282–293.

Zimmerman, Kari-Shane Davis. "In Control? The Hookup Culture and the Practice of Relationships." In *Leaving and Coming Home: New Wineskins for Catholic Sexual Ethics*, edited by David Cloutier. Eugene, OR: Cascade Books, 2010.

Index

Tables are indicated by *t*, and figures are indicated by *f*.